# HAVING IT ALL IN THE BELLE EPOQUE

# HAVING IT ALL IN THE BELLE EPOQUE

How French
Women's Magazines
Invented the
Modern Woman

Rachel Mesch

Stanford University Press • Stanford, California

Stanford University Press
Stanford, California

©2013 by the Board of Trustees of the Leland Stanford Junior University. All rights reserved.

No part of this book may be reproduced or transmitted in any form or by any means, electronic or mechanical, including photocopying and recording, or in any information storage or retrieval system without the prior written permission of Stanford University Press.

Printed in the United States of America on acid-free, archival-quality paper

Library of Congress Cataloging-in-Publication Data

Mesch, Rachel, author.

  Having it all in the Belle Epoque : how French women's magazines invented the modern woman / Rachel Mesch.
    pages cm
  Includes bibliographical references and index.
  ISBN 978-0-8047-8424-5 (cloth : alk. paper)
  1. Women's periodicals, French--France--History--20th century. 2. French literature--Women authors--History and criticism. 3. Feminist literature--France--History and criticism. 4. Feminism--France--History--20th century. 5. Femininity in literature. 6. Women in literature. 7. Femininity in art. 8. Women in art. I. Title.
  PN5184.W6M47 2013
  054'.1082--dc23                                                2013013863
  ISBN 978-0-8047-8713-0 (electronic)

Typeset by Bruce Lundquist in 11/15 Bell MT

In memory of my mother,
Caryl Mesch,

and for my daughters,
Abby and Eliza

# CONTENTS

Acknowledgments   *ix*

Introduction: *Femina*, *La Vie Heureuse* and the Invention of the *Femme Moderne*   *1*

**PART I**   **READERS AND WRITERS**

*Chapter 1*   *Chères lectrices*: Cinderella Powder, Poet Queens and the Woman Reader   *33*

*Chapter 2*   Beyond the Bluestocking: Images of Work-Life Balance in the Belle Epoque   *55*

*Chapter 3*   The "Oriental" Authoress: Myriam Harry and Lucie Delarue-Mardrus   *85*

*Chapter 4*   The Writer Writes Back   *107*

**PART II**   **TEXTS AND CONTEXTS**

*Chapter 5*   A New Man for the New Woman? Belle Epoque Literary Feminism and the French Marriage Plot   *123*

*Chapter 6*   Jean Lorrain's Women's Magazine: Emma Bovary Meets Celebrity Culture   *144*

*Chapter 7*   A Belle Epoque Media Storm: Marcelle Tinayre and the Legion of Honor   *155*

Conclusion: Imagining the *Académicienne*   *173*

| | |
|---|---:|
| Notes | *197* |
| Selected Bibliography | *225* |
| Index | *233* |

# ACKNOWLEDGMENTS

It was, in a sense, love at first sight. From the moment I first laid eyes on *Femina* and *La Vie Heureuse,* spooling through microfilm in a dark annex at the French national library, I knew that I had to find a way to build a project around them. While researching my first book on French women writers, I had already spent many an hour in these somber research chambers, just above the faint din of the reading rooms where scholars stretched from table to table in what seemed, from my isolated space, like beautiful camaraderie, thumbing through actual books (while, because of the nature of the paper used, nearly everything between 1870 and 1914 could only be accessed through microfilm). If I were going to begin this solitary process again, I should at least have an object of study as gorgeous and tantalizing as these magazines.

As it turned out, there was plenty of paper to be thumbed through, and plenty of camaraderie to be had in what has been not nearly as monastic a venture as the first time around. I have been greatly aided along the way by the collections in the Bibliothèque historique de la Ville de Paris, the Bibliothèque Marguerite Durand, and the Institut Mémoires de l'édition contemporaine, not to mention PriceMinister, TDMpresse, eBay, and the wonderful old magazine shop La Galcante, on the rue de l'arbre sec in Paris.

I would first like to acknowledge Yeshiva University, which has funded this project through the office of Provost Morton Lowengrub. The book also received two generous grants from the Kenneth Chelst Faculty Book Fund, which supported research in France and publication costs associated with the book. Deans Barry Eichler, Fred Sugarman and Raji Viswanathan have been steadfast supporters and I am grateful for their eternal collegiality and friendship. Jess Olson and Jeffrey Freedman read drafts of an article that would be the seed for this book, and helped steer my entry into the field of cultural history. Paula Geyh read early chapters and offered valuable insights and general encouragement at every step. Adam Zachary Newton and Joanne Jacobson offered helpful comments on my book proposal and have been valued mentors since I arrived at Yeshiva. If it weren't for Nora Nachumi's invitation to speak in her Advanced Women Studies seminar, I might never have discovered the link between Marcelle Tinayre and Tina Fey (see note 53 in Chapter 2). The open doors of Steven Fine, Shalom Holtz, Aaron Koller, David Lavinsky, Ronnie Perelis, Liesl Schwabe, Gillian Steinberg and Ria Van Ryn have in general made the workplace the opposite of lonely. Debra Kaplan fundamentally understands what this book has meant to me, intellectually and personally; at so many times, that shared understanding has made all the difference. Johanna Lane and Silke Aisenbrey, as colleagues, feminist soul sisters and cherished friends, have been integral to this work in ways that I won't even bother to attempt to squeeze into this space.

This project has fundamentally transformed my experience of research, transcending my literary training to force me to think about literary production, communities, feminist history and cultural artifacts in wholly different ways. I am especially grateful to colleagues in disciplines beyond my own who have offered their expertise, as well as those with specialized knowledge that helped inform my analysis. Historian Karen Offen generously read parts of the manuscript and offered her deep knowledge of the multiple feminisms of this time period with detailed, incisive comments. Lenard Berlanstein's early generosity and humble support was crucial to moving this project forward. Ruth Iskin has been an incredible resource with her vast knowledge of late nineteenth-century art and consumer culture. Marni Kessler has taught me a great deal through her own work about the analysis of nineteenth-century visual culture; I thank her for reading chapters and responding generously with references and insights.

Closer to my disciplinary home, I am grateful to Margot Irvine, who works on overlapping subject matter, for all of her generous sharing along the way: research discoveries including rare archival finds; deep insights and careful readings of articles and chapters; her own works-in-progress; and tips for charming hotels in Paris. Susan Hiner provided detailed, thoughtful comments that have surely enhanced the quality of this work. Elizabeth Emery, who knows so much about photojournalism, allowed me to read her brilliant chapters in proof form, which instantly became crucial points of reference for my own analysis. She offered careful readings, helpful research tips and cheerful, prompt answers to my multiple follow-up questions. She and Mike Garval, fellow collector/researchers, shared their insights into the perils and pleasures of amassing materials through the Internet. Masha Belenky has been an unwavering source of support since our graduate schools days. Our idyllic shared research trip in the fall of 2010 propelled this project forward through a congenial mix of *cafés crèmes*, croissants and the warm halls of the Bibliothèque historique de la Ville de Paris. I am immensely grateful for her friendship as well as for her insightful readings of huge portions of the manuscript.

A book is always the result of many voices and conversations pushing it forward. I am grateful for an early conversation with Lisa Gordis, who picked up on my enthusiasm and urged me to build a new project around the object and questions that were visibly exciting to me. Cathy Nesci has been an enthusiastic supporter and helped arrange an MLA session crucial to the development of this work. Joanna Stalnaker and Vincent Debaene offered invaluable advice and camaraderie as we sought publishers for our works-in-progress. Many pleasurable chats with Andrew Counter, Nigel Harkness, Elisabeth Ladenson, Bettina Lerner, Jann Mattlock, Gerald Prince, Maurie Samuels and Nick White at conferences and cafés around the globe have helped guide me forward.

There have been numerous tasks associated with the production of this book that fall slightly beyond what a PhD in French literature prepares one for. I want to thank my research assistant Daniel Winchester for cataloging hundreds of images of *Femina* and *La Vie Heureuse* from my research as well as for coming to my rescue in the preparation of the bibliography. Phone Dumas graciously helped with the herculean task of preparing my images. Katy Adair tracked down materials for me in Paris when I could not get there myself. Clément Oudart generously gave of his own research time to bravely tackle microfilm at the Bibliothèque nationale in the eleventh hour. Matthew Udkovich made an "emergency" trip to La Galcante to retrieve a magazine and always faithfully scoured the *bouquinistes* for errant *Femina*s in my absence.

At Stanford University Press, I am lucky to have found an editor with a PhD in French literature herself. I am indebted to Emily-Jane Cohen for her deep understanding of this book and its potential appeal. Emma Harper has been an absolute delight to work with, and I thank Xenia Lisanevich and Mariana Raykov for their copyediting expertise.

Conversations with friends near and far have energized this work in various essential ways. Thanks go to Natalie Blitt, Claire Goldstein, Idana Goldberg, Tamar Gordon, Jessica Hirsch, Stephanie Ives, Tova Mirvis, Judith Rosenbaum, Rachel Jacoby Rosenfield, Adam Segal, Jessica Seessel, Rona Sheramy and Jessica Yood. Thanks also to Emily Bazelon and Allison Benedikt of Slate.com for helping me to participate more broadly in the cultural conversation around work-life balance.

Working mothers everywhere will appreciate the fundamental challenge of trying to write a book about "having it all" while attempting to do just that. This book could not have been completed without the expert care and competence of Daniela Maria Baldo. Sylvia and Norman Fisher have always provided much more than just childcare; the time my children spend with them is full of joyful nurturing and constant learning and discovery. The need to sustain myself through intellectual query is surely inherited from my father, Barry Mesch, a professor himself, who has delighted in every step of this book's progress. Thanks to my sister for her calming presence and for her sisterhood, in the fullest meaning of that term.

My husband, Eric Fisher, very much a "new man" himself, has been a constant and comforting reminder that the struggle to have it all is no longer just a woman's problem. His unwavering partnership, shared feminist values, patience and kindness have made these pages possible.

I dedicate this work to the memory of my mother, who found her own very satisfying way to have it all, and would have gotten a real kick out of this French feminism with a twist. I also dedicate this book to my daughters, Abby and Eliza, who, I hope, will one day forgive me for the countless hours I spent with "my magazines." I can only wish that by the time they are old enough to truly understand, feminist history will have no need to still be repeating itself. As for my sweet Sammy, the next book will have to be for you.

# HAVING IT ALL IN THE BELLE EPOQUE

# INTRODUCTION
## Femina, La Vie Heureuse *and the Invention of the* Femme Moderne

IN the inaugural issue of the wildly successful women's photographic magazine *La Vie Heureuse*, the beloved countess and critically acclaimed poet Anna de Noailles is pictured in her beautifully appointed living room with her young son delicately set upon her lap (Fig. I.1). This image faces a slightly larger photograph of the countess in profile, her billowing skirt cradling not her baby this time, but her most recent book. Noailles' graceful presence in this five-page photo spread diffused brewing tensions between feminism and femininity in the Belle Epoque through the precisely measured equilibrium of books and babies. Indeed, rather than books becoming substitutes for babies, and thus—as contemporary fears dictated—leading to infertility, depopulation and inevitably (or so the logic went) the collapse of French society, books and babies appeared side by side throughout, as the magazine consistently depicted women authors as devoted mothers.[1] Just like its rival publication *Femina*, *La Vie Heureuse* celebrated achieving women in dazzling feature stories sandwiched between elaborate fashion plates and advertisements for beauty creams, corsets and high-end furniture. Regardless of the nature of their achievements—not just as writers, but as lawyers, doctors, actresses, explorers or athletes—their femininity remained fully and vividly intact.

This book argues that *Femina* and *La Vie Heureuse*, launched within a year of each other in 1901 and 1902, introduced a significant and often overlooked image of modern French femininity, in deliberately stark contrast to stereotypes of the feminist activist and the New Woman—the two figures that have been most closely associated with Belle Epoque challenges to gender norms. Thanks to their savvy exploitation of

UN TAPIS presque blanc, les murs tendus d'une soie bleu pâle ; point d'encombrement, mais des choses précieuses ; un voile d'un très beau point de Milan posé sur la chaise longue. Rien que des choses anciennes, assemblées et choisies, et qui dans cette clarté vivent de l'air le plus nouveau. Le meuble fut d'abord modern style. Mais Madame de Noailles ne put vivre dans l'élancement disparate de tant de formes aiguës. Elle revint aux bergères et aux chaises à médaillons. Dans un vase, des branches de pied-d'alouette, fleur de la vieille France.

## Une Femme Poète Appréciée par une Femme de Lettres

Cl. Otto.

### LA COMTESSE MATHIEU DE NOAILLES

*IL Y A quelques années circulaient sous le manteau des pièces de vers, qu'on lisait pour ainsi dire en confidence, l'esprit charmé de leur ligne flexible et droite, et étonné d'apprendre qu'ils étaient composés par une jeune fille.*

*Mademoiselle Bibesco, devenue Madame la comtesse Mathieu de Noailles, a donné par la suite au public deux volumes de ces vers : l'un s'appelle le Cœur Innombrable, et le second, tout récent, l'Ombre des Jours.*

*Qu'une femme, en notre temps, ait été touchée du rayon charmant ; qu'avec une grâce naturelle, les mots choisis et les rythmes répètent son émotion devant la vie universelle ; c'en est assez pour que cette Revue lui donne cette place.*

IL y a quelque chose de nouveau qui pénètre les œuvres de femmes. Les hommes ne s'en doutent pas encore. Ils ne sentent pas combien nos œuvres sont moins souvent timides, artificielles ou vaines. Le devons-nous déjà à l'obligation plus générale de travailler autrement, nous aussi, que pour des distractions oisives ?... Je ne sais trop, mais il est un fait indéniable, c'est que dans tous les arts s'affirment peu à peu des natures féminines personnelles, sculpteurs, peintres et poètes.

Comme je reposais sur mes genoux le beau

(8)

**Figure I.1** Feature story on Anna de Noailles in the first issue of *La Vie Heureuse* (October 1902).

# UNE FEMME POÈTE

PORTRAIT DE LA COMTESSE DE NOAILLES, par la Baronne A. de Rothschild.

livre de Mme de Noailles, la mémoire enchantée et le cœur pressé, à mon tour, des battements de ce *Cœur innombrable*, je songeais combien une pareille œuvre eût été impossible en France il y a cent ans. Il y eut bien le génie fiévreux de Mme Desbordes-Valmore, mais ses plaintes bondissantes et désaccordées ne tenaient presque plus de l'art ; elles n'avaient rien de cette maturité dans la jeunesse et de cette sensation savoureuse qui marquent le talent qu'avec joie je salue ici.

Je voudrais pouvoir reprendre page à page ces poèmes et vous les transcrire tout au long de mon émotion et de leur beauté.

Je n'ai rien à révéler, du reste. L'admiration pour les poèmes de Mme de Noailles s'est répandue. Il convient seulement à une femme de toucher de plus près une œuvre de femme, de montrer en quoi ce livre est très nouveau pour nous.

Remarquez : les œuvres les meilleures, lorsqu'elles sont vraiment d'une femme, lorsqu'elles ne s'efforcent pas d'imiter la carrure virile, sont prolixes, cursives. Elles sont flexibles, fines et penchées — ou débordantes ; elles n'ont pas de contours stricts ni pleins. Celle-ci, de féminité absolue, tout au contraire, on la sent, ferme, charnue et nette comme un fruit.

Chaque poème nous donne cette sensation du fruit, et chaque strophe, et chaque vers. L'épithète la plus fréquente est peut-être « lourd » ; elle dit le poids écrasant de l'été, la chaleur ardente de la terre, le poids de l'ombre mûre et de l'amour. Et l'on voit la petite main qui *presse* les choses comme les choses pressent le cœur.

Aussi est-il frappant de saisir la suite harmonique des mots qui concourent à cette impression. Harmonie nombreuse et pleine, riche et coulante.

Nature au cœur profond, sur qui les cieux reposent,
Nul n'aura comme moi si chaudement aimé
La lumière du jour et la douceur des choses,
L'eau luisante et la terre où la vie a germé.

Ou encore :

La nature comme une abeille
Est lourde de nuit et d'odeur,
Le vent se berce dans les fleurs,
Et tout l'été luisant sommeille.

C'est donc à travers une incessante com-

photographic technologies, their embrace of new artistic currents and literary trends and their exquisite presentation of famous women, these magazines became the arena through which a powerful model of French femininity emerged—one that has exerted a lasting, if rarely recognized, influence on French expression.

Often referred to simply as the *femme moderne*, the feminine role model promoted in *Femina* and *La Vie Heureuse* was a bundle of decidedly new contradictions, as she embraced a newfound sense of equality without completely abandoning traditional gender roles. For many in this generation of newly educated women—the product of the reforms of the 1880s that guaranteed secondary schooling for girls—the most crucial challenge was that of reconciling traditional family structures with an independence of mind and spirit their mothers had never dreamed of.[2] In the pages of *Femina* and *La Vie Heureuse*, this fantasy became a beautiful reality: the *femme moderne* offered an inspiring image of "having it all" in the Belle Epoque—devoted husband, fulfilling family, beautiful home, and, if not a satisfying vocation, at least some sort of outlet for self-expression, all while maintaining her impeccable appearance.

This new ideal embodied the hopes and dreams as well as the most pressing internal conflicts of large numbers of French women during what was a period of profound social and cultural change. Indeed, the contradictory stance of the *femme moderne* as both progressive in her pursuit of equality and conservative in her embrace of conventional gender differences reflected the essential ambivalence of the Belle Epoque itself, caught as it was between a postrevolutionary past in which gender roles were sharply divided and a rapidly modernizing future in which many of those long-held divisions were quickly falling away. This book proposes a new way, then, to consider the oft-posed question of whether there was a Belle Epoque for women.[3] The richly coded pages of *Femina* and *La Vie Heureuse* offer an ideal vantage point from which to examine this moment of society in transition: poised to accept women in more powerful, visible roles than ever before, but not always certain as to how to imagine them inhabiting those roles.

The editors of both *Femina* and *La Vie Heureuse*—led by Pierre Lafitte and Caroline de Broutelles respectively—were firmly ensconced in what was known as the literary *Tout Paris*: a world of elite, highly intellectual, largely conservative-leaning writers, many of whom were published in a wide array of magazines and newspapers. This was the world of popular writers and journalists like Jules Clarétie, Paul Hervieu, Marcel Prévost and Paul Adam, and that of celebrity literary couples: the Rostands, the Catulle Mendèses, the Daudets, the Dieulafoys.[4] *Femina* and *La Vie Heureuse* were, in a sense, offshoots of the vibrant literary salons that so many of these figures attended, often together.[5] In his memoirs, writer J.-H. Rosny described the Maison Pierre Lafitte as "the most scintillating" publishing house, hosting dinners where one could see "the most brilliant literary stars" at the same table, from the poet Countess Anna de Noailles to the best-selling writer and media darling Marcelle Tinayre to the eccentric Lucie Delarue-Mardrus.[6] Similarly, articles in *La Vie Heureuse* about the parties surrounding its annual literary prize proudly described the attendance of the "elite *Tout Paris* of arts, letters and the *monde*."[7]

But these magazines were also products of the democratizing forces of fin-de-siècle mass culture: even as they often presented an aristocratic universe within their pages, they were, at least in theory, available to all.[8] While readers were largely based in Paris, they extended to the provinces and represented a variety of socioeconomic backgrounds. We might describe the space created by *Femina* and *La Vie Heureuse*, then, as a fusion of the exclusiveness of the salon with the openness of the department store, displaying for an aspiring public the amenities of the upper classes.[9] The luxuries associated with this milieu, however, were not limited to high-end goods. Quite remarkably, *Femina* and *La Vie Heureuse* made available and desirable for a broad female readership the creative, intellectual endeavors of the *monde littéraire*; they encouraged readers not only to dress and shop like the social elite, but to be reflective and literary themselves in myriad ways that we will explore in the pages that follow.

Acceptance within the Belle Epoque literary world required a tacit disavowal of turn-of-the-century feminist movements, lumped together in the collective consciousness as a direct threat to "traditional" French values. *Femina* and *La Vie Heureuse* consistently rejected the feminist label for that reason. "This magazine is not about 'feminism' or 'social emancipation,'" the editors of *Femina* insisted in their introductory mission statement. "We'll leave to others the work of masculinizing women and robbing them of their delightful charm."[10] This harsh stereotyping, hardly reflective of turn-of-the-century feminism's diverse causes and supporters, allowed the editors to invent a "straw feminist," as it were, from which to draw a vivid distinction with their own work.[11] And yet, I am arguing, it would be a mistake not to recognize the import of these magazines in the context of a more capacious feminist history.[12] In what follows, I use the term *Belle Epoque literary feminism* (whose precise contours I elaborate on below) to designate *Femina* and *La Vie Heureuse*'s stance as one occupied with expanding women's roles even as they carefully avoided explicit political engagement. Despite their own initial resistance to the label, this book recognizes as feminist, then, the energetic efforts of these magazines and their surrounding web of fictional texts to help Belle Epoque women imagine themselves comfortably inhabiting modern roles.

Belle Epoque literary feminism was defined in large part by the unique discursive space that it fostered—the network of readers and writers that connected *Femina* and *La Vie Heureuse* and the novels associated with them, stemming from the enclosed world of the literary *Tout Paris* to a wide web of readers who would respond to their surveys and contests by the thousands.[13] In presenting this new space, I would like to recognize its place as part of the new media of the twentieth century, through which lines between public and private were increasingly elided.[14] As we shall see, the magazines were quite innovative for their time, with their reliance on photography, their cultivation of celebrity culture (often in the service of certain ideological positions), and their willingness to envision new modern heroines and ideals that might lead their readers to see themselves differently. While we may be familiar with the mimetic pressures of celebrity culture—which continue to function in much the same way to this day—we have not yet considered the particular way that early celebrity and mass culture in France shaped a new model of womanhood, one that not only soldered the association between consumerism and femininity, but also encouraged women to develop their own critical and creative voices.[15]

Recently Lenard Berlanstein and Colette Cosnier have debated the feminism of *Femina*, with Berlanstein linking its progressive strategies to that of Marguerite Durand's *La Fronde*—the publication most visibly associated with Belle Epoque feminism—and Cosnier rejecting the feminist label for a magazine edited largely by men.[16] It is certainly worth noting that *Femina*'s publisher and most of its editors were men; that many of the most frequent collaborators at both magazines were as well; and that so many women writers' presence in their pages was secured by their link to an already famous husband.[17] In these ways the magazines were fundamentally different from the all-woman run *La Fronde*.[18] Notwithstanding *Femina*'s patriarchal structures, however, the most visible success of Belle Epoque literary feminism pertained to women writers—figures caricatured throughout the nineteenth century among the very same elite as haggard, man-hating *bas bleus*, or *bluestockings*. In the 1840s, cartoonist Honoré Daumier's Les bas bleus series for *Le Charivari* had infamously ridiculed such women while betraying the profound anxiety they elicited as a potential threat to bourgeois domestic norms. Women who wrote were, in Daumier's eyes, terrible wives and even worse mothers (Fig. I.2). In image after image, women writers were depicted as abandoning or sabotaging their traditional roles; worse yet, their husbands were left emasculated, forced into the roles their wives had evacuated. Long after Daumier, the *bas bleu* continued to be a reviled figure throughout the century, her threats vilified in writer Barbey d'Aurevilly's treatise by the same name, not to mention countless other cartoons, satires and literary and journalistic asides.[19]

The Belle Epoque woman writer, on the other hand, emerges in *Femina* and *La Vie Heureuse* as the gorgeous conjugation of new equalities with traditional values, and thus a key example of the *femme moderne*. While largely absent from French literary histories, these magazines were credited during their time with facilitating an astonishing growth in the numbers of women writers, opening the way for women writers to be elected to the Société de gens de lettres and to regularly earn the Legion of Honor, facilitating women's creation of their own literary prize (which would become the Prix Femina), and contributing to the overall sense that women were on the cusp of being admitted to the Académie française (even if this would not in fact happen for several more decades).

Moreover, this study adds to previous scholarship a full exploration of the medium itself, which, I am arguing, was crucial to the magazines' feminist expression. If *La Fronde* was often referred to as *Le Temps* in skirts, this was in part because it had the same format as mainstream dailies, with headlined columns over several text-filled pages. The alternative model of femininity that *Femina* and *La Vie Heureuse* proposed,

**Figure I.2** *Honoré Daumier*, "Les bas bleus." (*Le Charivari*, February 26, 1844). The caption reads: "The mother is in the heat of composition; the baby is in the bathwater." Courtesy of the Bibliothèque nationale de France.

on the other hand, was profoundly visual, and the magazines' wide variety of images and photographic innovations contributed to the sense of the dynamic possibilities they offered within, always, a hyper-feminized context. Thus, the story that I am presenting is as much about the history of French women as it is about the history of mass culture and the media in France; the *femme moderne* was as important for the freedoms that she openly embraced as for the kinds of journalistic innovations that allowed her to be celebrated. Belle Epoque literary feminism was primarily a work of imagination: of examining, exploring and most fundamentally, fantasizing about what the fully realized modern woman could be—and this, importantly, was done by both men and women. In its imaginative work, it was truly separate from the contemporary feminist movement, deliberately steering away from their serious political and social work, which was grounded in a searing and not entirely pleasant social reality.[20] Often, as we shall see, the images depicted in *Femina* and *La Vie Heureuse* did not even reflect upper bourgeois or aristocratic reality—few women, comparatively, were doctors or lawyers, the balance of work and family was not effortless, equal partnership in marriage was not embraced in every household. Moreover, the ideals shared in these magazines were often misunderstood beyond the context of their devoted readerships. For legions of Belle Epoque women, on the other hand, the magazines represented a vibrant universe, an alternative reality in which certain kinds of feminist fantasies were normalized, made both accessible and desirable. *Femina* and *La Vie Heureuse* thus gently moved women forward by vividly displaying before them a compelling future in which their success was a given.

## *Succès Oblige*

The first issue of *Femina* in February of 1901 proudly described its mission in a full-page statement. This illustrated review would be for women, "in text and image," what *L'Illustration* and *La Vie au grand air*, two of publisher Pierre Lafitte's previously successful ventures, were for news and sports.[21] The enterprising Lafitte, just under thirty years old, developed this venture with some of the most popular and talented journalists of the time: among others, Paul Adam and René Maizeroy; Marcel L'Heureux, who would be his editor-in-chief; Daniel Lesueur (pseudonym of Jeanne Lapauze), the first woman writer to receive the Legion of Honor; Maurice Leblanc, who would go on to write the Arsène Lupin series first published in Lafitte's *Je sais tout*; and Henri Barbusse, who would win the Prix Goncourt for his harrowing tale of war, *Le Feu*, in 1916.[22] The idea, inspired by publications from across the channel, was to launch a women's magazine that would be both family-oriented and high-class, run by men "who love them and admire them."[23] In the opening address, a friendly, welcoming editorial voice claimed that France had no real women's magazine, and that *Femina* would fill that void, and not a moment to soon. Without mentioning his competitors by name, Lafitte decried the limited nature of existing fashion magazines, noting "there's more to offer women than what is currently offered under the guise of 'Fashion,' 'Society' and 'Family.'" In this, Lafitte was politely taking down Caroline de Broutelles' *La Mode Pratique* (launched by Hachette in 1891), whose subtitle was *"Journal de la famille."* This successful women's magazine was filled with fashion plates, clothing patterns and tips on accessories and recipes. *Femina* shared *La Mode Pratique*'s large illustrated format (a little over thirteen inches in height) as well as its feminized fonts and *gravures de mode*. But to this homogenized and rather dreary mix Lafitte added the dynamic visual displays and chatty style of his sports magazine *La Vie au grand air*, which always featured dozens of photographs of the most successful and most unusual athletes (bodybuilders, runners, circus performers, race car drivers).[24] He threw in the kinds of celebrity interviews and feature stories that dominated *L'Illustration*, while diverting the focus to famous women and couples.[25] He added to that mix the novels in feuilleton and poems by famous authors, extensive book reviews, and commentaries that were central to so many well-established publications. In other words, Lafitte borrowed all the most pleasing features of the burgeoning mass press around him, offering new and improved versions of elements most likely to interest women readers. He bound these disparate parts together with a gorgeous layout ("a dazzling orgy of colors, plates, pen and ink on glossy paper")[26] and a clear, consistent editorial voice that spoke directly to *Femina*'s female reader, guiding her towards what she was meant to appreciate in its pages. Recognizing that "woman's domain is vast and magnificent,"[27] this editorial voice promised its *chères lectrices*—dear (female) readers—everything from theatre to art, literature, cooking, music, hairstyles, fashion, jewelry, interior design, animals and flowers, and writings by the most famous women writers of the day. It was a kind of variety never previously seen under one French masthead.

*FEMINA*, all caps and in quotes, in a savvy and persistent branding effort that prevailed in every issue, thus reclaimed the linguistic roots of femininity, promising something that was both all woman and thoroughly modern. This precise and original balance between tradition and modernity was both what defined *Femina* and what situated it in an ambivalent feminist space. Some of *Femina*'s internal tensions were apparent from the first issue. The cover of the magazine featured a model photographed by the Reutlingers, in an elegant gown, a bow wrapped under her chin, locking a heart-shaped flowered hat in place

(Fig. I.3). The bouquet of peonies she holds in her arms obscures her actual hands, blurring the boundary between woman and flower. This lovely ultra-feminine figure would become *Femina*'s icon—her detached head would later find a place in the upper corner of the magazine's bimonthly covers. An inner frontispiece featured a photograph of a demure Empress of Russia. Inside, one finds articles on Queen Wilhelmine (in a section on "The Royal Court") and Prince Roland Bonaparte's residence ("The Great Salons of Paris"), all matched with sumptuous photographs of lavish interiors. There were also articles: "The Century of Children," "The Fashion of Tomorrow"; the opera star Mademoiselle Bréval; a song with music and lyrics written especially for the magazine; a section on jewelry and crafts, and beauty for self and home—all of which reflect an elegant, upper-bourgeois milieu, accessible to anyone for fifty centimes

**Figure I.3** Cover of the first issue of *Femina* (February 1, 1901).

per issue.[28] Amidst this list of traditional feminine features, one also finds a few elements that signal change and give a sense of the direction that *Femina* would take within months of its launch: the article on Queen Wilhelmine is signed by Madame Alphonse Daudet, wife of the famous decadent novelist and published author herself; the magazine included the first episode of a novella by Daniel Lesueur, who would become a key representative of the magazine and a member of its prize committees; the interior cover advertised an exercise contraption that promised to put an end to "anemic young women," offering them "strength, appetite, color, agility, flexibility, grace and nimbleness" (Fig. I.4).

Finally, and perhaps most significantly, the last article in the magazine, under the rubric "Sportswomen," considered the question of women and driving. Illustrating the article's title, a line drawing by Maurice de

**Figure I.4** Advertisement for the Sandow exercise machine. *Femina* (February 1, 1901).

Thoren pictures Artemis, Greek goddess of the hunt. Bow and arrow poised, her hair flows behind her in the whiplash lines of art nouveau graphics, as hunting dogs and bunnies scurry past.[29] In a large photograph in the middle of the page, an elegant woman, hat firmly in place, calmly drives a car, accompanied by what appear to be her smiling son and daughter (Fig. I.5). Can a woman drive, asks the title? She most certainly can, the article responds, but through its own particular idiom, which captures both the audacity and the conservatism of the publication: "the modern woman is no longer chained to the hearth, or rather, the hearth has widened."[30] Reinforcing the iconography of the piece, the article declares woman's freedom within the context of her traditional role, just as the woman in the photograph is accompanied by her children. This is hardly, then, the frightening independence of the *femme nouvelle*, or New Woman, so often pictured alone on her bicycle, a vehicle rumored to cause both self-pleasuring and infertility.[31] Rather, the car is figured as a family-friendly expansion of the woman's traditional private sphere, while at the same time announcing a new kind of mother: stronger, more visible and a challenge to the traditional circumscription of that separate sphere. The strength and power suggested by this alliance of woman and vehicle is alluded to in the graphics surrounding the title. Artemis, after all, is a highly aggressive figure whose connection to Greek mythology mitigates her threat; her graphic evocation here inscribes her perfectly within Belle Epoque aesthetics. But while the title seems to suggest that driving is considered a modern sport, the article ultimately reveals something far less audacious. The photograph pictured is that of the family of Georges Richard, an automobile engineer who had worked to design a family-friendly vehicle, so that "the safe and economical comfortable family car has replaced the dubious sports car." Indeed, it would be only a slight exaggeration to say that this piece ostensibly devoted to the vehicles of "Sportswomen" turns out to be about an early model of the minivan.

This one article captures much of the zeitgeist of the magazine, the spirit that would lead it to have 130,000 subscribers by its third year.[32] The magazine's zeitgeist was defined—at least on the surface—by a rather untortured ambivalence, one that masked its own contradictions at every turn. Explicitly eschewing the overtly political, *Femina* embraced a discourse of aspiration and achievement. Women, it seemed to

# SPORTSWOMEN

### Une femme peut-elle conduire une automobile?

C'est une chose avérée et bien humaine d'ailleurs qu'il n'y a pour ainsi dire point pour l'homme de plaisir complet s'il n'est partagé. Et je doute que jamais la bicyclette ou l'automobile eussent eu leur succès, si la femme n'avait pu prendre part aux joies qu'elles nous donnent, aux échappées dont elles sont l'occasion et le prétexte. D'ailleurs bicyclette et automobile ne sont-elles pas, dans l'esprit de leurs partisans enthousiastes, destinées à remplacer ce bon vieux cheval, et le cheval n'est-il pas l'occasion pour la femme d'un de ces sports délicieux, fait de confiance et de danger, et auquel, sans nul doute, les femmes eussent difficilement renoncé, tout renoncement étant déjà presque une abdication.

La femme moderne n'est d'ailleurs plus enchaînée au foyer, ou plutôt le foyer s'est élargi, j'allais presque dire qu'il s'est multiplié, à Paris, à la campagne, à la mer, aux eaux. Nous avons trouvé charmant de relier ces foyers divers par la route; pourquoi veut-on que les femmes qui ont, à coup sûr, plus que nous encore, l'esprit d'indépendance et de liberté, ne se prennent point, elles aussi, de passion (et la passion est toute féminine) pour cette bicyclette ou cette automobile grâce auxquelles, un moment, on peut goûter dans sa plénitude l'illusion de se croire seul et seul maître, de l'espace et du pays qu'on traverse sans s'y arrêter. De même que, jadis, au temps où tout le monde allait à cheval, il s'était peu à peu créé une race spéciale pour la femme, les haquenées, sur lesquelles une femme pouvait presque égaler sans fatigue l'étape des cavaliers, de même il se crée dans l'automobile une race spéciale de véhicules à la fois simples, coquets, élégants, faciles à diriger, allant une vitesse moyenne, faisant en un mot de ce qui était autrefois une fatigue et une lutte de l'homme contre son appareil, une simple partie de plaisir. En résumé, un moteur galant est trop bien élevé pour jamais faire à une femme l'impolitesse de la laisser en panne, une voiture trop aimable pour jamais la verser; ce sont là des plaisanteries de bon goût avec un homme, complètement déplacées avec une femme, et que dans la société l'on ne se permet point.

J'en causais l'autre jour avec l'un de nos constructeurs qui ont le plus orienté l'automobile dans cette voie de progrès et de vulgarisation qui la met à la portée de tous. M. Georges Richard, car c'est de lui qu'il s'agit, y fut d'autant plus naturellement et d'autant plus facilement amené que sa charmante femme adore l'automobile et adore y conduire ses bébés. En faisant une automobile pour sa femme et pour ses enfants, M. Georges Richard nous donne tout d'emblée la voiture qui convient à merveille à toutes les femmes et à tous les enfants.

C'est un peu dans l'automobile la race des poneys et des ponettes qui ont fait la joie de toutes les femmes et de tous les bébés. Notez d'ailleurs que pour être aussi douce et plus facile à conduire que n'importe quel poney, ces voitures, dans lesquelles M⁽ᵐᵉ⁾ Georges Richard conduit elle-même sa petite famille, ont les jambes un peu plus longues et le trot un peu plus vif. Ce que c'est, du reste, que s'intéresser pour soi-même à quelque chose, et comme on le perfectionne plus vite quand on le fait aussi pour soi!

L'année dernière, elles trottaient tout juste à 25 kilomètres à l'heure, ce qui est déjà gentil, et je connais pas de chevaux qui en fassent autant. Cette année elles galopent sans plus de danger à 40 kilomètres à l'heure et grimpent toutes les côtes deux fois plus vite qu'elles ne le faisaient auparavant.

Simples, exemptes de toutes ces complications, charmantes peut-être pour le constructeur, mais bien désagréables pour une femme, surtout lorsqu'elle doit batailler avec elles sur la route, et que vous ne tenez point à lire votre femme d'un mécanicien, d'une facilité de direction telle qu'en moins d'une heure la femme du plus nerveux et douée de la plus charmante maladresse apprend à les conduire sans peur et sans danger, — ce sont bien les véhicules rêvés pour toutes celles qui cherchent dans l'automobile un simple plaisir personnel et non l'occasion de se faire remarquer.

Il est un dernier point sur lequel il n'est peut-être pas inutile non plus d'insister: c'est la question économique. Madame veut bien promener les enfants, mais il ne faut pas que la question dépense vienne entraver ces beaux projets. Or, elle l'a entendu dire, une automobile, ça coûte cher, et surtout cela dépense beaucoup.

Je me permettrai encore de signaler l'intéressante solution que M. Richard a su donner à cette question; je le ferai d'autant plus volontiers que c'est une vieille idée à moi d'essayer de rendre l'automobile peu coûteuse.

Or, dans un concours de dépense et de consommation que nous instituâmes en novembre dernier, M. Georges Richard enleva les deux premiers prix; nous ne fit voir deux voitures réellement merveilleuses. L'une à deux places, dans la course de Paris à Meulan, soit 70 kilomètres, a dépensé 1 fr. 45 d'essence, soit 2 centimes par kilomètre, 1 centime par personne. Quel sera le mari assez cruel pour vous refuser cela? Voulez-vous emmener vos enfants et leur faire faire 70 kilomètres, respirer le bon air? Prenez une voiture à 4 places. Elle a dépensé 2 fr. 20, soit 3 centimes par kilomètre. C'est moins cher et autrement agréable que la classique voiture aux chèvres.

On le voit, le goût a vaincu là aussi la mode et, de même qu'à l'écuyère automobile a succédé l'amazone automobile, de même à la voiture de sport douteux a succédé la confortable voiture de famille sûre et peu coûteuse.

On peut donc dire qu'aujourd'hui la femme peut faire de l'automobile. Le goût est né et le véhicule est fait.

GEORGES PRADE.

M⁽ᵐᵉ⁾ GEORGES RICHARD ET SES ENFANTS EN AUTOMOBILE.

Le prochain Numéro de FEMINA paraîtra le 15 Février.

**Figure I.5** "Can a Woman Drive an Automobile?" *Femina* (February 1, 1901).

announce on page after page, yes you can—but not only that—you already are! Women's progress was not about making demands, but about performance and possibility, about the simple facts of modern femininity, evidenced by an array of photographs that repeatedly demonstrated the new things that women were, in fact, doing. While the first issues deliberately seemed to steer clear of controversial issues (this final article on driving comes the closest to pushing the envelope), or simply those of substance, by the end of 1902, one finds articles on women lawyers, doctors, athletes and explorers. Ironically, this may have been a result of a staff overhaul that replaced many of the original female staffers associated with preexisting women's magazines with more daring young male journalists.[33] By 1903 divorce and marriage reform were discussed regularly; by 1906, articles on suffrage begin to appear. If *Femina*'s formula was developed by market-savvy men, women quickly responded and became integral voices in that formula; soon after the early overhaul, the male-dominated editorial staff was joined by regular women contributors, from journalists to famous women writers, whose efforts helped shape the magazine's message. *Femina*'s success, if measured by its own accounts, was stunning, comparable to those of the most influential mainstream periodicals of the day.[34] Within months, it seemed, one could find it everywhere: "on the *guéridons* of aristocrats, the dressing tables of actresses, the tablecloths of housewives, rolled up in the shopping baskets of *midinettes*, and hidden in the desktops of schoolgirls."[35] By 1907, Lafitte's success was such that he could move *Femina*'s offices to a *hôtel particulier* on the Champs Elysées. Every aspect of this new "maison des magazines" reflected Lafitte's desire to be at the forefront of the modern. Equipped with telephones, elevator and modern heating, the building housed a photo studio (where for no small sum one could be photographed much like the celebrities within his magazine), a theater and a ballroom.[36] According to the magazine's own reports, the opening reception for this new establishment was host to five thousand guests, a veritable who's who of *Tout Paris*.[37]

One early sign of *Femina*'s success was the launch of its rival, the monthly *La Vie Heureuse*, in October 1902, by the equally enterprising publisher Hachette under the direction of Caroline de Broutelles, the general editor of *La Mode Pratique*.[38] In contrast to *Femina*, then, *La Vie*

*Heureuse* was run by a woman. Both the similarity of *La Vie Heureuse* to *Femina* and the subtle distinctions with which it invented itself tell us a good deal about what *Femina* had already become.[39] Above a neoclassic still life, the cover of this "Revue Féminine Universelle Illustrée" listed its topics as "The Home and the World"; "Sports and Games"; "Our Favorite Animals"; "Fields and Gardens"; "News"; and "Arts and Ideas" (Fig. I.6). Over the masthead reads the simple inscription: "Women represent half of humanity." On the front page, the magazine addressed itself to "all women," in recognition that women had recently acquired "a societal role and social influence never before seen."[40] *La Vie Heureuse* reiterated *Femina*'s promise to deliver "through text and image" the infinite spectacle of modern femininity. Their aesthetics were so similar as to be interchangeable, the majority of famous contributors appeared

**Figure I.6** Cover of the first issue of *La Vie Heureuse* (October 1902).

in both magazines and their prices were identical; but *La Vie Heureuse*, at least at its outset, appealed directly to a more serious audience. (This might explain why the editors of *Femina* felt the need to fill a full page of their December 15, 1903 edition with headshots of their contributors, declaring in bold that "*Femina* is the most literary of all illustrated magazines.")[41] In their opening issue, the editors of *La Vie Heureuse* invoked women as members of a new generation, taking on new roles, increasingly outside of the home. The "infinite spectacle" of femininity in 1902 would include "supreme elegance," first and foremost. But the list continued in some unconventional ways that seemed to allow for multiple incarnations of modern femininity: "exciting sports, endless amusements, lives of intelligence, courage, goodwill and devotion; productive careers, acts of generosity, women of beauty and talent, acts of heroism and strength, images and stories about women of exceptional lives." Indeed, recognizing that women have different interests, *La Vie Heureuse* promised that their magazine would be devoted to "universal life [ . . . ] in a dynamic, attractive and varied manner," and therefore "speak to all." Like *Femina*, *La Vie Heureuse* appears to have taken off rapidly. Although its first three issues were approximately 8 x 11 inches, its first Christmas issue contained a flyer announcing a new larger format, under the title "succès oblige." Beginning in January of 1903, it became the same 13 x 11 inch size as *Femina*.

## La Femme Moderne

Two years before the first issue of *Femina* hit the stands, the protagonist of Camille Pert's 1899 novel *Leur égale* (*Their Equal*) dreamt of developing her own photographic magazine devoted to a growing mass of women "who reflect, who think, who seek to teach others." Of this future magazine, Pert wrote, "Women will only subscribe to it or buy it for the pictures on the cover, or the fashion inlays . . . the tips on shopping, the theater, exhibits and department stores . . ." Attracted and entertained by these features, "they'll eat up all the articles on philosophy and social issues thrown into the mix!" (281).[42] The name of this magazine: *La Femme Moderne*. For Pert's heroine Thérèse, the existence of a new kind of woman was simply a fact, a product of the changing society in which she lived. This progress was described as an effect of women not actively resisting the currents pushing them forward, rather than a deliberate, combative effort to break down barriers. When one of Thérèse's colleagues tries to categorize her reflections as feminist, she responds in frustration: "I don't know exactly what you mean by this term . . . there are so many trends, so many different flags being waved! All of our efforts will aim to make women better able to wear the mantle that, by the force of events, has been slid upon her shoulders" (141). Thérèse rejects the feminist label because she does not see herself as an activist; she has no interest in being "the champion of ridiculous demands" (echoing, again, a caricatured sense of fin-de-siècle feminism). Rather, she simply is what she is: "man's true equal," in her ambition, in the pleasure she takes in her work, and in her thirst for knowledge. Her very existence is its own argument; her competence proof of what women can be, without, importantly and explicitly, being any less feminine because of it. "And why should she be less of a woman, for having a head full of serious ideas instead of troublesome nonsense?" (145) she asks herself.

The struggles of Pert's compelling heroine challenge prevailing narratives of resistance to gender norms in the Belle Epoque. Both contemporary scholars and writers of the time have written extensively about the New Woman, or *femme nouvelle*, an Anglo-Saxon import who burst on the scene in the 1890s.[43] Based on an accumulation of stereotypes circulated through the mass press, the *femme nouvelle* was "reified in the French imagination" as mannish and severe, sporting pants and spectacles, smoking cigarettes, riding bicycles, and unabashedly entering male-dominated professional realms.[44] During the same time period, French feminism was forcefully emerging while still struggling to define itself. As historian Karen Offen has demonstrated, in the 1890s and early 1900s, feminists took up a wide variety of causes in France, including the rights of women workers, poor women and prostitutes; infant mortality; changes to the French civil code; and, eventually, suffrage. The far-reaching concerns of the movement and its multiple incarnations are reflected in the multiple ways in which feminists self-identified: as "familial feminists," "Christian feminists," "socialist feminists" and "radical feminists," to name a few. Six feminist congresses took place between 1892 and 1913; numerous feminist periodicals appeared, and discussion of "the woman question" proliferated in wide-ranging publications.[45]

While recent scholarship has worked to distinguish between New Women and feminists, these figures were often conflated in the Belle Epoque imagination.[46] If they were to be differentiated, it was as two sides of the same coin. The fact that many feminists hinged their demands for equal rights to their dutiful fulfillment of domestic roles was lost on much of the public. Caricatures of these modern women in the popular press often portrayed both figures as mannish, aggressive creatures refusing traditional feminine roles, suggesting that women must choose between the conventional, domestic feminine self and the feminist overhaul of traditional gender roles. This choice was most often depicted as a violent rupture to the social order, an undermining of social structures and a refusal of conventional feminine norms. An 1896 cartoon from the satirical Republican newspaper *Le Grelot* entitled "Revendications féminines" (Women's Demands) demonstrated the shared tropes of this threat as well as its debt to Daumier: the woman pictured, in pantaloons, smoking a cigarette and holding her bicycle—all forms of visual shorthand for the New Woman—is off to a feminist congress, while her incredulous yet wasted husband is left inhabiting the traditional role of wife, to tend to feeding children and washing dishes (Fig. I.7).[47] Just as in many of Daumier's own caricatures, the threat of women's public roles was visited directly upon the hapless male partner, and, by implication, on marriage (read: French society) itself.

In reality, however, there was no single way for Belle Epoque women to enter the public domains that were rapidly opening up for them, and these two labels masked a far more complex picture of the evolving women of this generation.[48] *Femina* and *La Vie Heureuse* were both quick to distance themselves from any association with the organized feminist movement, and the term *femme nouvelle* is rarely found in their pages.[49] There are numerous examples both in the magazines and in novels like Pert's in which women explicitly reject these identifications while expressing their desire to embrace modern roles.[50] In light of this, one of the aims of this book is to flesh out the figure promoted by *Femina* and *La Vie Heureuse* as an alternate means of expressing resistance to gender norms during the Belle Epoque. For Thérèse, the *femme moderne* was explicitly articulated as a work in progress, an evolving news story that the magazine's task was to pursue. The precise contours of that figure were conventionally feminine, yet strategically ill-defined ("very

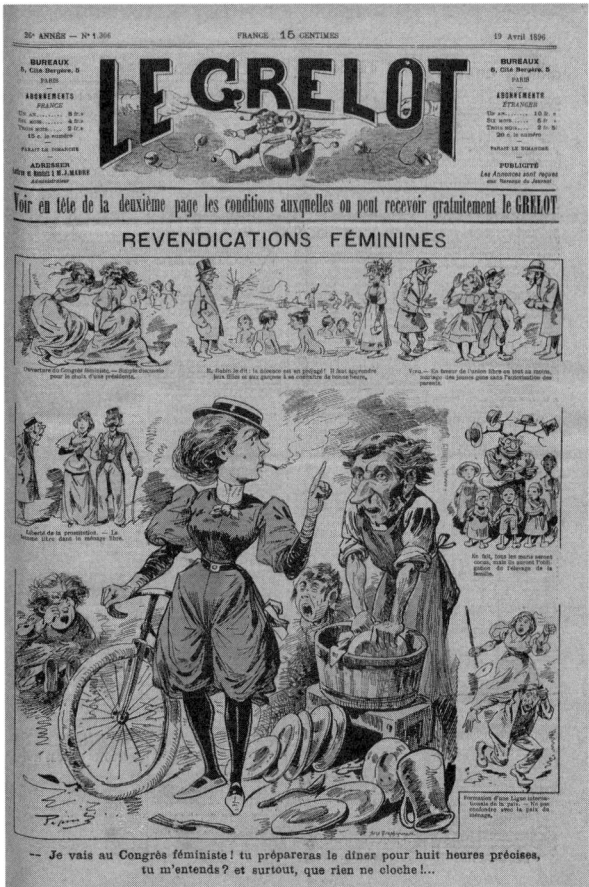

**Figure I.7** "Women's Demands." *Le Grelot* (April 19, 1896). The caption reads: "I am going to the feminist congress! Make dinner for 8:00 sharp, do you hear me? And nothing gets messed up!" Courtesy of Universitätbiblothek Heidelberg.

eclectic, very omnibus"), her ideas nonthreatening, open to conversation. Pert's novel, as well as a series on "la femme moderne" that appeared in the *Revue Encyclopédique* in 1896, suggest that this more nuanced terminology predated the magazines.[51] The *femme moderne* offered a flexible mode of identification that unsettled the categories of feminist and New Woman, while pointing to a resistance to these politicizing labels shared by many women of this generation, even as they sought to update their roles. In September 1910, Marie-Anne Bovet offered a definition in *La Vie Heureuse* that comes close to summarizing the competing energies of this figure, who sought to balance conventional feminine roles with new kinds of power: "Good feminism is one that doesn't destroy the make up of the family, one that, in making professionals out of those who have the need or desire, allows the wife, the mother, the housewife, the *mondaine* even, to continue to exist; it's a feminism that virilizes—which is a strength—without masculinizing, which would be disgraceful."[52]

Pert's literary fantasy is of course just that, but as such it takes us into what both *Femina* and *La Vie Heureuse* might have symbolized for so many, while shining light on the symbiotic, mutually sustaining relationship between these magazines and women's fiction. The publication Thérèse could only dream about in 1899 was a thriving reality within a few years, and her own heroine's sober, solitary ending stands in stark contrast to the happy endings of the novels we will explore in Chapter 5. These happy endings and brighter outlook, I will suggest, were very much enabled by the edifying vision of modern femininity and the community of female readers and writers fostered by *Femina* and *La Vie Heureuse*. Even as she distanced herself from feminist activism, then, the *femme moderne* nonetheless delineated an important new space for feminist discussion.

The human-interest stories that filled both magazines' pages can be read as sustained metaphors for the positive images of modern femininity that the magazines aimed to promote, and thus a kind of extended advertisement for this Belle Epoque modern woman. A September 1, 1903 article in *Femina* entitled "An Excursion to the Mer de Glace" offers but one example. The first of several articles about female explorers and mountain climbers, this article takes up the hyper-feminized epistolary form, addressed to "My dear Simonne," and signed "Yvonne." The challenging excursion described in this letter is one where a towering mountain is compared to a gigantic sugar loaf and later Santa Claus. Yvonne's trek involves an adorable "conversation with a goat" and a brief encounter with danger followed by arrival at "a cute little chalet." In the photographs, "real alpinistes" (in the feminine) are pictured contemplating their next move, while *Femina*'s own alpinistes "powder their noses before entering the chalet." The true danger, the author assures, will be left to some "intrepid English women," thus marking a cultural distinction between French women's new roles and those hailing from the land of the New Woman.[53] The article, then, sets out rather explicitly many of the contradictions and jumbled messaging of the women's press as it imagined women reaching, as it were, new heights. Written explicitly by a man under a female pseudonym (the editorial practice was to reveal the true author—in this case André Chaignon, one of Lafitte's close associates—under the heading "pour copie conforme"—for a certified copy), the article brings into relief the gendered role-playing involved in this messaging, as a male editor took on a female voice in order to perform this updated femininity. While *Femina* was a magazine *for* women, it was not always written *by* women (although as time went on, this increasingly became the case). Troubling as it might now seem, this role-playing was part of a wider strategy of encouraging women's achievement by modeling for them roles they might not yet comfortably assume on their own.

Perhaps most importantly, the article on women climbers brings out the particular idiom of the women's press, in its savvy exploitation of the synergistic effects of text and image. In the language of *Femina*, the relationship between the literal and the metaphoric was always suggestively and powerfully intertwined. French women, suggested the article above, you can climb mountains, as long as you recognize your feminine limits. Nearly every page of *Femina* and *La Vie Heureuse* helped flesh out this thoroughly modern figure, and the message of success was insistently disseminated through image after image, article after article. To be a modern woman, these articles declared, as much through the writing itself as through the accompanying photographs, was to climb mountains and explore new realms, all the while looking beautiful and carefree. Over a very short period of time, these images gained in audacity, with *Femina* edging out *La Vie Heureuse* in terms of visual potency and photographic innovation. Each new example literalized the possibility for readers: the fact that there *were* female mountain climbers made the fantasy of climbing mountains—real and metaphorical—all the more compelling. Indeed, the literal realities conveyed through the magazines steadily insinuated metaphorical possibilities of future, or more personalized, feminine success. In this sense any symbolic difference was effaced between the woman worker repairing a skyscraper (Fig. I.8),[54] the courageous rock climber (in a clearly doctored image, Fig. I.9), the tennis star (Fig. I.10), the bowler (Fig. I.11), the young lawyer (Fig. I.12), the impossibly elegant woman writer (Fig. I.13), the lovely mother (Fig. I.14), the legions of princess brides, the dozens of devoted *associées*—the term used to describe wives who helped their husbands professionally—or the simple *lectrice* entering poetry contests while tending to her family; they were all metonyms of *Femina* and *La Vie Heureuse*'s modern femininity, mirror images of a feminine achievement that had once seemed nearly impossible but was now placed, at least figuratively, within reach.

**Figure I.8** "Feminism on a High Scale." Cover of *Femina* (September 15, 1910).

**Figure I.9** "An Intrepid Alpinist," on the cover of *Femina* (August 15, 1908).

**Figure I.10** Tennis player Madame Fenwick on the cover of *Femina* (July 15, 1908).

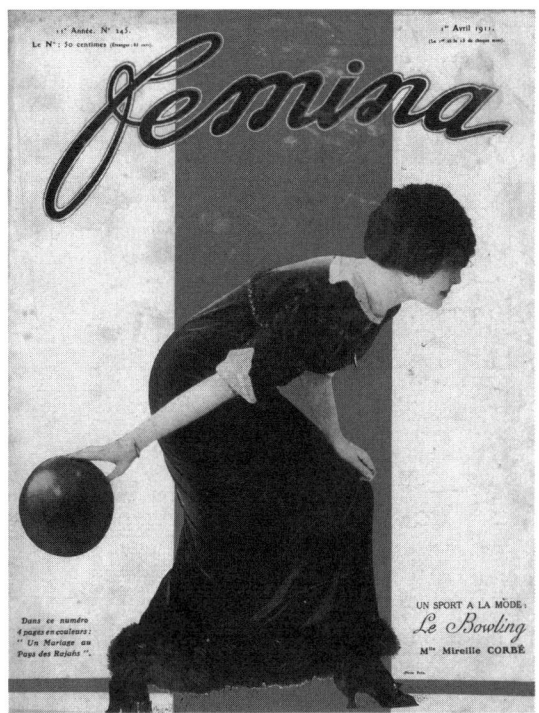

**Figure I.11** "Un sport à la mode: Le bowling." Cover of *Femina* (April 1, 1911).

**Figure I.12** "The Débuts of Women Lawyers." *La Vie Heureuse* (September 1905).

**Figure I.13** Poet and novelist Countess Anna de Noailles, frontispiece to *La Vie Heureuse* (February 1905).

**Figure I.14** Cover of *La Vie Heureuse* by art nouveau illustrator A. E. Marty (June 15, 1913).

## Having It All in the Belle Epoque

I have divided the book into two parts: "Readers and Writers" and "Texts and Contexts." The first half examines the ways that Belle Epoque literary feminism constructed, in text and image, a shared fantasy of modern femininity. This fantasy was promoted in large part through an intimate relationship with the magazines' readers (explored in Chapter 1), who were encouraged to identify with what they found displayed before them. The next two chapters situate *Femina* and *La Vie Heureuse* in the context of Belle Epoque visual and mass culture and the history of photography. These chapters explore the dazzling iconography of the woman writer within the pages of both magazines, where she is figured in ways that seek to wholly expurgate the legacy of the dowdy *bas bleu* of the previous century, while tacitly promoting the ideals of the *femme moderne*. Finally, Chapter 4 explores women writers' own relationship to their public image as a way to gain insight into their own relationship to the feminist strategies deployed by the magazines.

The second half of the book moves beyond the borders of the magazines themselves in order to explore their reception and influence. In Chapter 5, I explore the interactive, almost symbiotic relationship between *Femina* and *La Vie Heureuse* and popular women's fiction. The novels that were reviewed and discussed in the magazines functioned as a kind of laboratory for the *femme moderne*, grappling rather explicitly with the complexities of issues that the glossies introduced but could not engage in the same way. The final two chapters then test the impact of the magazines beyond their exclusive female readership, where much of the work of the magazines was largely misunderstood. I explore this disconnect through both fiction and history: through Jean Lorrain's parodic send-up of the women's press, and then through a real-life media scandal surrounding beloved author Marcelle Tinayre. Finally, by way of conclusion, I examine the renewed discussions surrounding the possibility of letting women into the Académie française that took place in 1909 and 1910. These discussions, as well as *Femina*'s elegant way of sidestepping them, illustrate the surprisingly imaginative mechanisms of the magazine's own alternative reality.

The difference in emphasis between French and American feminism is often noted, in particular with respect to the privileging of traditional forms of femininity within the French tradition.[55] The chapters that follow offer important historical context for this emphasis, as they provide evidence of early efforts to strike a balance between preserving conventionally feminine roles and achieving feminist goals. Recognizing the nature of these efforts, I contend, forces us to reevaluate traditional narratives of Belle Epoque gender history in a variety of disciplines—visual, literary and historical—leading ultimately to a sharper understanding of this period and the profound changes it ushered in. At the same time, addressing the overlooked significance of the Belle Epoque modern woman is crucial to understanding the path that French feminism took in the twentieth century and beyond. The questions raised in this book are thus both historical and timely, as they offer a new context through which to consider continuing debates about whether women can be both "feminine" and "feminist." Indeed, the women figured in the Belle Epoque women's press sought a balance that remains the holy grail of achieving women to this day, on both sides of the Atlantic.

Ultimately, as I will demonstrate in the pages that follow, *Femina* and *La Vie Heureuse* worked to prove again and again that traditional femininity and new, public female roles were not an either-or choice but rather, identities that needed to be integrated, family and femininity intact.[56] The possibility of such integration was something that the prevailing categories of New Woman and feminist seemed to flatly deny: to embrace modern female roles was associated necessarily with the rejection of conventional ones. In the magazines, on the other hand, the issue was not whether to be feminist or not, but rather an unexplored struggle surrounding *how* to be feminist without using that term, that is, how to embrace women's equality, and how to be modern *and* a woman. As reticent as these magazines were to be political, then, they do also need to be recognized as an effort to expand Belle Epoque feminism's parameters so that it did not force women to choose between femininity and equality. To the extent that she rejected the image of the shabby suffragette or audacious *femme à bicyclette*, what, precisely, should the modern woman look like, these magazines asked, in all earnestness? How should the working woman decorate her home? Where should she buy her clothes? It would be a mistake not to recognize the serious import of these questions.[57] In the context of the magazines' struggle to reconcile competing values, they were part of a concerted effort to carve out an alternative female identity, both modern and traditional.

More crucially, they helped women to *imagine* themselves living a reality that was not yet fully in place.

The story that I present in the pages that follow covers a narrow yet rich and significant slice of history. For the most part, it is limited to the first ten years of these magazines' existence, from 1901 to 1911, a period characterized by *Femina* and *La Vie Heureuse*'s energetic efforts to define a new feminine ideal. Lafitte's bold entrepreneurial spirit, which pushed him towards risk-taking new projects, finally caught up with him after his 1910 launch of *Excelsior*. The first photographic daily newspaper, and thus a major event in the history of the press, *Excelsior* was not financially successful. *Femina* and *La Vie Heureuse* merged in late 1916 after Hachette rescued Lafitte from bankruptcy; the reimagined magazine struggled to find its voice anew following the war.[58] In her important article on fin-de-siècle French feminist movements, historian Florence Rochefort has asked: "Did the inventiveness of French feminism during the Belle Epoque bear fruit?" Her answer to the question was decidedly measured, noting that "from a purely legislative point of view, the progress achieved did not measure up to feminist hopes."[59] I am not sure, however, that this is the best question to ask of Belle Epoque feminism. This book will be concerned, instead, with something much more difficult to gauge: a shift in the way of thinking about feminine possibilities, and in the way French women were encouraged to imagine themselves and their potential. This book is about the significance of that imaginative work, which moved women forward by offering them an airbrushed view of their present, thus raising the bar in terms of what they expected of themselves.

Flipping through the pages of contemporary women's magazines in nearly any Western country, it is hard not to recognize, for better and for worse, the influence of the idealized *femme moderne* celebrated by *Femina* and *La Vie Heureuse* as a model of female achievement. We continue to be fascinated by many of the things that secured the attention of so many Belle Epoque readers, and women's professional success is still often circumscribed by their willingness to occupy roles in ways that are sensitive to gender norms and social constraints. How can a woman be both an actress/writer/journalist/athlete *and* a mother? we still want to know. What should a female politician wear to a debate, or on the floor of the Assemblée nationale?[60] Is it possible to have a satisfying marriage and achieve success in a demanding career? By offering important historical context for these contemporary conversations, this book reminds us that the challenges of educated women are hardly new, and reveals that choices that might appear retrograde or antifeminist with the hindsight of a century were once lived as important steps towards change.

# PART I
# READERS AND WRITERS

## CHAPTER 1
# CHÈRES LECTRICES
*Cinderella Powder, Poet Queens and the Woman Reader*

IN the back pages of *Femina*'s first issues, full-page advertisements described the wonders of the beauty-enhancing Cinderella powder and soap (Fig. 1.1).[1] Drawing on the fairy tale heroine, one advertisement claimed that Cinderella's dramatic transformation was not unfamiliar to many women: "All creatures of beauty and seduction have a double life." Furthermore, the ad insisted that Cinderella was very much alive in Belle Epoque France—as witnessed by several recent performances and publications—and was poised to pass on her secrets to "all women, her sisters, so that they could be, like her, sure to please."[2]

This advertisement performs, I would suggest, the work of *Femina* and *La Vie Heureuse* themselves: they both served as a kind of Cinderella powder, introducing women to new worlds that fascinated because of their exclusiveness and inaccessibility, while at the same time allowing women to identify with the realm of the elite and to view their own existences as refracted through its beautifying, edifying lens. Cinderella powder promised to transport women to a realm of fantasy in the context of their daily lives. At the same time, as the advertisement suggested, Cinderella was no longer an exclusive sort of figure. All readers were capable of—and entitled to—her upscale existence; it was simply a matter of learning her secrets. Cinderella thus symbolized at once an aristocratic elegance inscribed in a longstanding and revered courtly tradition, and the democratization of that elegance, available now to all, regardless of birth.

Both *La Vie Heureuse* and *Femina* were in this sense perfect vehicles for the democratization of luxury that Emile Zola had identified decades before in his novel about the department store, whose drama grew di-

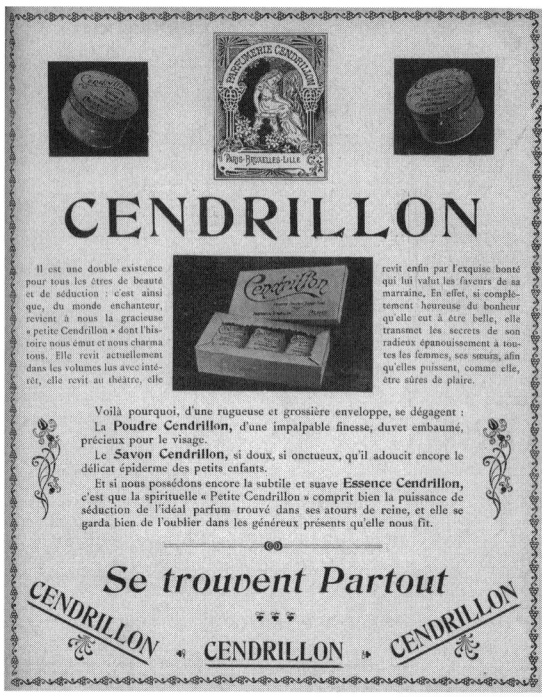

**Figure 1.1** Advertisement for Cinderella powder and soap, *Femina* (March 15, 1902).

rectly out of women's newly available purchasing power.[3] The magazines were filled with articles on real-life royals, alongside advertisements for fashion and furs; study these women's lavish interiors and then run to the furniture shop advertised a few pages later and buy that same lamp. This was, at least, the initial way in which those whose privileged destinies were meant only to cast a little warm light on a mundane existence very quickly became models to emulate. Yet while the Cinderella advertisement focused on beauty and seduction, both magazines were soon coupling their affirmation of conventional feminine norms with an insistence on women's capacity for other kinds of stunning transformations, as they featured them in an array of compelling new roles. Indeed, both publications energetically invited readers to not just admire these new models of female achievement but to imitate them; the democratization of luxury so clearly celebrated in these magazines at the outset became, over time, tightly linked to what I am calling a democratization of female intellect, as the magazines insistently encouraged their readers to become thinkers and writers themselves.[4] This chapter explores the process through which *Femina* and *La Vie Heureuse* constructed a new kind of reflective woman reader, who was seen not just as a consumer of goods, but of culture and literature. Part of Belle Epoque literary feminism's most important work—and its appeal—was to make its devoted *lectrices* into veritable *collaboratrices*, an outcome that, by both magazines' own admission, was both welcome and unexpected.

## Becoming a Princess

The first issue of *La Vie Heureuse* explicitly formulated a proposed relationship between its readers and the select, elite women who would be featured in its pages. In the mission statement included in their inaugural issue, the editors wrote:

> There are female destinies so brilliant that the world seems to look at them with admiration. Their luminous reputations, their large estates and their radiant youth make these marvelous Women dazzle. But isn't it good for other hardworking women to occasionally catch a glimpse, as if in a dream, of the lives of queens and princesses, of Women who are the most refined expression of the elite of all species? In this heaven filled with fortune and splendor shouldn't the less fortunate get to see the care, worries and obligations that compensate for the privileges with which these ones had the fortune to be born?[5]

This justification for readers' anticipated fascination with famous women conforms to certain traditional theories of fame through which celebrities were viewed as models of an ideal existence that offered a respite from the banality of the fan's own necessarily more mundane reality.[6] Inscribed explicitly in an aristocratic model, the elite women to be featured in the magazine were deemed worthy of attention simply because of their birth. The ideal of happiness embodied by these special "Women" would appear in *La Vie Heureuse*, "in its true state," promised the editors, as they offered readers comfort from—while inevitably reminding them of—their lesser lot. Those lucky enough to catch a glimpse of these bright lights could thus "return more satisfied to the modest calm of their own condition."

And yet, even with this insistence on traditional class structures, the editors clearly suggested a shift towards a more democratic paradigm: while these exceptional women were born into their superior role, realizing their grace required work. By opening a window onto the "care, worries and obligations" required of them, the magazine also ensured a lessening of the gulf between humble readers and *destinées brillantes*—between "women" and "Women," as it were. In appealing to an aristocratic model, *La Vie Heureuse* addressed a conservative readership eager to hinge modern femininity to familiar French ideals. Yet the fact of putting these women, their homes, children and intimate thoughts on display through a captivating layout of images and text was actually a key step in making these famous women more accessible, collapsing the distance between admired and admirer.

In fact, the women of *La Vie Heureuse* were compelling at once because of their exceptionalness, and because of the ordinariness and familiarity of their domestic preoccupations. The magazine's repeated depiction of female royals tending to their children provides a perfect example of this dynamic. The June 15, 1910 frontispiece featured a startling photograph of the queen of England giving her young son a piggyback ride (Fig. 1.2). Similarly, a September 1907 story, "Young Royal Mothers," showed several queens and princesses holding their children. On the one hand, the text of this particular story details the somewhat exotic rituals that follow a royal birth, like the firing of one hundred canons. On the other hand, what the accompanying iconography demonstrates in a series of images of mothers cradling children, and what the article ultimately concludes, is that royal motherhood is no different from that of the rest of society: "Outside of political realms, queens are nothing more than young women watching tenderly over their precious, frail offspring [...] under their sparkling crowns, they laugh with their babies like the most modest of their subjects." *La Vie Heureuse*'s success thus offers perfect evidence for Lenard Berlanstein's and Vanessa Schwartz's claims that celebrity "united rather than divided the upper classes and the masses" by the late nineteenth century in France, and that spectatorship—in this case, through an endless array of photographs—"had the power to convert potentially antagonistic classes into a culturally unified crowd."[7] Readers of this story, mothers everywhere, were asked to see the royals they admired as fundamentally no different from themselves.

Rather than "return more satisfied to the modest calm of their own condition," then, everything about *La Vie Heureuse* seemed to encourage women to see a better version of themselves in the ever-expanding smorgasbord of models of modern femininity. Bit by bit, it seems, the

**Figure 1.2** The queen of England (*left*) giving a piggyback ride to her son, the duke of Cornwall; her mother-in-law, Queen Alexandra (*right*), holding her oldest daughter. Frontispiece to *La Vie Heureuse* (June 15, 1910).

stars whose privileged destinies were meant only to cast a little warm light on a mundane existence easily became paragons of achievement, if not models to emulate. The very women celebrated within the pages of both magazines immediately invited this slippage. *La Vie Heureuse* seemed at first to suggest that the women it would feature had gained their distinction by birth. The first issue contained an article, just a few pages after the mission statement cited above, on the acclaimed poet Countess Anna de Noailles, seemingly confirming this fact. And yet, her presence in the magazine was assured as much by her literary prowess as by her aristocratic lineage, which turned out to be the main focus of the article, in which her poetry was quoted and extensively commented upon. In fact, within the first months of the magazine's existence, the distinction between women born into glory and those who had earned it by talent quickly dissolved: distinguished women writers and artists were regularly depicted as celebrities in the magazine, alongside queens and princesses. In feature after feature, these women's children were pictured, their home decor and sartorial choices examined and glorified. They had become veritable celebrities, a status defined in part by the blurring of the line between their public accomplishments and private lives.[8]

## "Chères lectrices"

Like *La Vie Heureuse*'s, *Femina*'s aristocratic valences were mitigated by its repeated efforts to draw the reader closer, collapsing social boundaries between reader and editor, between the aristocratic world that it glorified and the lives of the readers it sought to enhance. This is apparent from its very first issue of February 1901, even as it featured the Empress of Russia on its cover, Queen Wilhelmine in its first article, replete with images of her in royal garb and pictures of her estate, and lavish photographs of Prince Roland Bonaparte's home (Fig. 1.3). To be a woman was, *Femina* explicitly argued, in itself a very special privilege, a kind of nobility really, and that is why the magazine would devote itself to offering "an exact idea of everything that takes place in her charming kingdom."[9]

*Femina* cultivated its readers as a community, referring to them consistently and throughout each issue directly as "chères lectrices" (dear readers, in the feminine), if not "charmantes lectrices" (charming readers). The directness of this second person address encouraged readers to see themselves as fully part of, indeed implicated in, a conversation, rather than simply observers. It transformed the editorial voice into the semblance of an actual person on the other end. The repetition of the refrain also suggested a single person where there were many, bridging the gulf between reader and writer(s). In the regular column she began in 1908, writer Lucie Delarue-Mardrus encouraged readers to think of her as an "attentive and trustworthy friend," and that was indeed the overall persona of *Femina*'s editorial voice. In addition, the repeated invocation of the magazine's plurality of female readers served as a reminder to each individual that she was not alone, but rather part of a shared community of women that was separate, distinct and special.[10] In her history of mass culture in fin-de-siècle France,

Chères lectrices    39

L'HOTEL DU PRINCE ROLAND BONAPARTE. — Le grand Salon.

**Figure 1.3** Prince Roland Bonaparte's salon, from the first issue of *Femina* (February 1, 1901).

Vanessa Schwartz argues that at the end of the nineteenth century "the apprehension of urban experience and modern life through visual re-presentation was a means of forming a new kind of crowd" and that these "re-presentations" had the effect of effacing class and gender "in their conceit that diverse consumers should, could and would have similar access to them."[11] The women's press offered a similar experience in its effacement of class lines, while maintaining a deliberately gendered point of view that only further contributed to the illusion of exclusiveness, in the special kingdom of women.

The recurring second-person address also had the effect of fleshing out the alternative universe of the magazine. Not only were readers invited to see celebrated actresses and writers as alternate images of themselves, but they could also see better versions of themselves through their *consœurs*, their fellow *lectrices*, who shared many qualities with their favorite celebrities. In April 1908, the novelist Marcel Prévost, a frequent contributor to *Femina*, accepted Pierre Lafitte's invitation to offer a monthly *chronique* in which he would "converse with the *Femina* reader."[12] (This was, incidentally, described as *Femina*'s effort to associate itself more with literature and art.) Doing precisely what he promised, Prévost began his first chat with a meditation on the term "lectrice de *Femina*" in which he offered those readers myriad tantalizing images of modern femininity from which to self-identify:

> [I thought of] the French society woman or wealthy foreigner who thumbs through the magazine while stretched out on a 10,000 Franc chaise longue, amid her priceless trinkets . . . the elegant Parisian woman, well-off, cultured, for whom the magazine is both a document and a distraction . . . the clever bourgeoise, who with her precise budget takes just what she needs for managing a lovely home, having some guests, dressing to the nines . . . the cheerful worker who looks for a dream-worthy supplement to her life of labor in the stories and images. And I thought of you also, the exquisite women of the provinces in this century when there are practically no more provinces, you, those inexhaustible reserves of the grace, wit and art of Paris: I saw you, oh pretty lady of the place du Martroi, of the cours Gambetta, of the rue des Ursulines, decked out, nimble, sporty, running to your bookstore or the train station library, the day *Femina* comes out![13]

Prévost's comments point to a wider and more diverse audience than the exclusively upper bourgeois readership that the magazine's high-end advertisements seem to suggest.[14] Lenard Berlanstein has argued that *Femina*'s readership was mostly upper bourgeois, based upon the high-end advertisements and those who responded to surveys. Colette Cosnier also notes that the absence of pointers on household tasks (as in *Le Petit Echo de la Mode* or *La Mode Pratique*) presumes a reader who would not engage in such tasks. However, there is also evidence of other kinds of readers, including women in the work force. In December 1902, for example, novelist Gabrielle Réval wrote a piece on female stenographers that was explicitly solicited by readers—presumably stenographers themselves—after an article appeared about female phone operators. While the magazine certainly modeled a highbrow milieu, this did not mean that all readers actually lived in one. Beyond signaling who some of the actual readers might have been, Prévost's remarks underline the importance of the imaginary universe that *Femina* so actively created. Reading this piece assured the *chère lectrice* that she was in good company. Whether she was from Paris or the quickly receding provinces—or an exotic foreign land—mattered not. Of the highest echelons of society or laboring away but still finding time to admire, every woman had a reason to feel good about reading the magazine. Taking in Prévost's words, the less than well-off, hardworking provincial could fancy herself a high-class Parisian, and that Parisian could, in turn, feel good about serving as a model for the hard-working provincial. And thus, the simulacrum was complete: the woman reader was free to imagine herself among this cohort of peers, reading about a world of exceptional women, equally constructed; the magazine offered subtle tools to enable women to emulate these role models, and, as we shall see in a moment, invitations to participate in the magazine itself. Hence the celebrated glory and achievement highlighted in its pages ultimately served to enhance the reader's own sense of self-worth and possibility.[15]

This kind of self-enclosed and self-perpetuating female community constructed through women's magazines has been justly criticized in contemporary feminist criticism for putting unproductive and deleterious pressures on women, by circumscribing their roles according to conventional and sometimes oppressive feminine norms.[16] What interests me here, however, is the way similar pressures may have functioned in the 1900s as an expansion of women's worlds. In particular, the promotion of the ideal magazine reader as a thinking woman rather than strictly a consumer offered women a new, positive role model who successfully bridged public and private spheres. To the extent that she served as a figure to emulate, the pressures toward self-improvement that she generated were mostly constructive, pushing women towards new realms of achievement.

## *From Chic Parisian to Modern Woman*

Both *Femina* and *La Vie Heureuse* cultivated and updated the late nineteenth-century feminine figure that historian Lisa Tiersten has named the "chic *Parisienne*." This profoundly modern figure, initially denigrated as a vulgar consumer prone to reckless behavior, was rehabilitated in the late nineteenth century, and came to be seen as embodying a positively coded association between femininity and consumption. The chic Parisian woman signaled the rational development of taste as a learned, refined skill, giving bourgeois women cultural legitimacy and aesthetic authority, as art and commerce were happily reconciled. By the 1880s, this figure was depicted in women's magazines as "a devotee and practitioner of the arts whose avidity for high culture in no way precluded an ardent interest in fashion and decorating." Indeed, this double interest in fashion and culture made the Parisian woman "an artistic creator in her own right."[17] The editors of *La Vie Heureuse* signaled this alliance explicitly, arguing that art was a natural part of women's daily life: readers were thus invited to see their own flower arrangements and hair stylings as modest enactments of the works of famous painters or writers to be figured in the magazine's pages. Women, declared the editors, naturally transport art into life. "They arrange flowers, they adjust the drapes, they imagine an outfit, they knot and tie the supple mass of their hair. Art is their most familiar companion." In turn, reading the magazine promised to make their own lives more beautiful and more useful, as they learned ways to "embellish their lives" and "best occupy their time."[18]

Both magazines, then, clearly embraced the model of the chic Parisian as a supreme arbiter of taste (and therefore respectable figure) and played on her power as a consumer: being a reader of both magazines was tightly linked to a whole line of commodities for self and home. *Femina* was keenly aware of the commercial potential connected to the cultivation of an identification between readers and subject matter. In their introductory statement in the February 1901 inaugural issue, the editors promised that for the first two thousand subscribers, the magazine would essentially pay for itself. Those readers would receive "must-have objects" including perfume, gloves and soaps from the most fashionable and trendy Parisian shops.[19] For those first readers, then, buying *Femina* also constituted an instant makeover performed by the editors of the magazine themselves—one that ensured a shared level of aesthetic sophistication among its readership. The reader in this discourse was perfectly conflated with the consumer. That had been the model for British magazines, through which, as Ellen Gruber Garvey has compellingly demonstrated, the reader was gendered female primarily through her taste for consumption.[20] And so, like the *grand magasin* to which it was linguistically rooted, the magazine appeared at the outset to be a kind of department store, offering a panoply of tantalizing choices.[21]

Advertising was a key mechanism by which both magazines bridged the gap between reader and elite woman from the very beginning, as the Cinderella publicity attests.[22] Indeed, within *Femina*'s first pages, advertisements, text and image were often fluid; the editors themselves might include a letter or brief note promoting a particular product, using the same typeset as the rest of the magazine. In December 1904, for example, the editors devoted a full page to inviting their "chères lectrices et amies" to take advantage of a special offer on the Liane corset, featured at a special price at the Claverie shop in Paris (Fig. 1.4).[23] The first issue of the magazine included pictures of all the prizes to be awarded to the first subscribers, as well as the names of the stores they were from; the Janu-

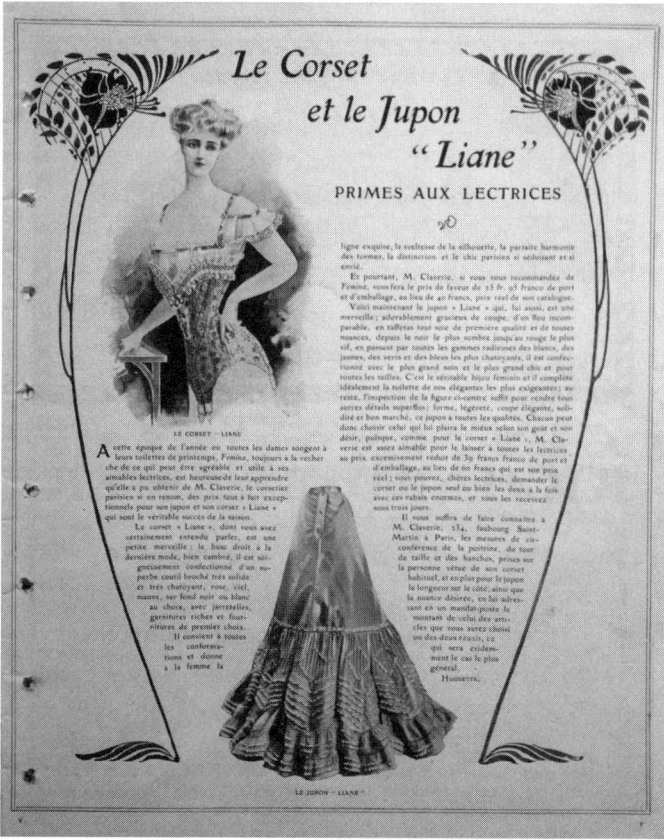

**Figure 1.4** *Femina* offer for Liane corset (March 1, 1905).

ary 1, 1902 interior cover pictured a strand of pearls to be awarded to one lucky reader, along with the name and address of the jeweler where the pearls were on display.

Within a few months, however, *Femina* appeared to be catering to the fuller, far more multivalent femininity it had originally promised, in which the female reader's purchasing power receded in large measure to the background (and the back pages). Those advertisements most certainly funded and ensured the magazine's success, but the *Femina* reader was no longer simply figured as a consumer of high-culture goods; rather, she was depicted and valorized as a consumer of culture itself—and not just to the extent of her fashion choices. By 1902 the *Femina* editors had slightly reformulated their mission, announcing their obligation to "introduce their female readers to the curious and useful manifestations of the female mind, with absolute impartiality."[24] By 1904 the magazine featured articles on women artists, writers, doctors and lawyers; essays discussing possible changes to the Civil Code; reviews of theater, art and literature; and surveys inviting readers to weigh in on everything, from women's education and their preferred career paths to the qualities of an ideal husband. Ultimately, *Femina* and *La Vie Heureuse* constructed a female reader who, while she was clearly recognized as a consumer, had many other facets to her identity.

Amidst the tributes offered to women achievers in its pages—doctors, lawyers, athletes, writers—*Femina* was the first to offer all women a rapid path to glory—not just through their purchasing power, but through their talent and skill. At the outset, *Femina*'s multiple contests were clearly meant as a pure marketing ploy, an effort to draw readers in and ensure their continuing fidelity to the magazine.[25] If they entered a contest, after all, they would need to keep buying the magazine to see if they had won. Contests based on speed, rewarding the first respondents, were juxtaposed with contests based on talent and ingenuity. In *Femina*'s first issue, for example, the page describing the rewards for the first two thousand subscribers was immediately preceded by a page describing an ongoing series of *concours*, similar to those found in other women's magazines. The first was simply a puzzle, or *devinette*: the magazine displayed several drawings of women in costumes from around the world, but the attire from each location was jumbled together on each figure. The winner would successfully assemble the various elements of these costumes (numbered in the images) in the correct order. The second contest was to create one's own original child's carnival costume. The winners of these efforts would receive gift certificates and have their names published in the magazine. They would also be eligible for the *concours d'honneur*, selected at random, whose prize consisted of the haute couture Ney Sœurs dress and hat featured on the magazine's cover.

Rather quickly, these *concours* began to involve opinion surveys—although they would not be regularly labeled under the more serious (and masculine, scientific) term *enquêtes* until 1903.[26] In 1902 *Femina* asked readers to name their favorite public figures; later that year they asked the ten qualities for female perfection; in 1903 they were asked to describe "the ideal life for a woman." These surveys were still described as contests: winners would be drawn at random from the submitted entries and rewarded with money, gift certificates or goods, as well as publication in the magazine. At the outset, then, the rewards were entangled in the magazine's spirit of conspicuous consumption. Eventually, however, these various ways of eliciting readers' responses took their own unique shape. By 1903, the *concours* were limited to puzzles and arts and crafts contests, listed in small print in the back pages, while the magazine began to contextualize its *enquêtes* in feature articles or essays. These were often on rather heady topics involving contemporary publications. A December 1904 *enquête*, for example, asked readers to comment on novelist Michel Corday's recent study of the relationship between playwrights and actors. "What is the role of the playwright versus that of the actor in the success of a play?" they asked, promising to publish their readers' most interesting responses in an upcoming issue. These kinds of surveys, increasingly frequent, represented a significant shift from the earlier contests, one that substantially blurred the lines between the roles of editors and readers. The invitation to comment on the relationship between actors and playwrights appeared in the very same issue as the appeal to readers to purchase Liane corsets. And yet, the shift did not mean a negation of the *lectrice* as consumer of high-culture goods and arbiter of taste. Indeed, that is the surprising point of *Femina*'s modern woman: she was envisioned as both the potential purchaser of corsets and the intellectually engaged woman fully capable of sophisticated commentary. To be a true *Femina* heroine it was no longer simply enough to look good—to be exclusively the feminine artist of everyday life. The *femme moderne* celebrated in the magazine had successfully taken on new roles, all the while balancing the older aesthetic ones.

These surveys and contests invited women from all over to take part in the world that the magazine created, further democratizing its new model of femininity. The chic, sophisticated Parisian was a figure women could emulate from far and wide, and the evidence shows that they did: Lenard Berlanstein notes that of 292 readers who responded to a March 1904 survey about what constituted the "good life," only 71 were from Paris; the others resided in the provinces, and not necessarily in major urban areas.[27] While the first questions posed by *Femina*'s *enquêtes* remained carefully distanced from politics, by 1906, *Femina* was asking readers about such thorny topics as suffrage, displaying the development of its relationship with its readers and its increasing comfort in dealing with complex, controversial issues—not to mention feminism.[28]

## Literary Rewards

Beginning in 1903, *Femina* began to have literary contests as well. These contests were even more significant in shifting women's notions of their own potential. They offered women the possibility of emulating one of the figures most often celebrated in the magazine's pages: the woman writer—an ideal female professional for the magazine in that she could do her job without leaving her home, and without necessarily or overtly challenging traditional gender roles. *Femina*'s announcement for its first "Poetry Tournament" in February 1903 declared, "What woman today is not a poet, after all?" Here we have, then, the magazine's ultimate elaboration on the democratized aesthetics of the chic Parisian: while in late nineteenth-century consumer culture every woman, by virtue of her femininity, was figured as a kind of artist of the self, in the thriving intellectual culture of Belle Epoque France, energized by an influx of newly educated women, every woman was figured as a writer, capable of rendering life as poetry. This is all the more intriguing when considered in light of the rather tortured history of the French woman writer, the *bas bleu* who in the nineteenth century had been associated with hysteria, prostitution and the rejection of traditional family structures.

*Femina* proposed an altogether different image, elevating the woman writer to the status of queen and princess. *Femina* tied its contests to the rise of women poets, and saw its literary contests as a way to coronate the next great female talent. Commenting on the increasing numbers of women poets, *Femina* insisted that its very role was to "encourage as many female talents as possible, all of whom surely would like to get noticed."[29] Like the opinion surveys, then, these contests were part of *Femina*'s energetic efforts to articulate a new kind of female reader, as they coaxed women into modern roles while assuring them of the appropriateness of these changes.[30] Similarly, while encouraging women readers to participate in their own first writing contest, *La Vie Heureuse* assured them it would not be too much work—that they would simply have to put down the magazine for a few moments and reflect a bit. And the prizes they would receive—well, just think of them not so much as rewards but as compliments.

*Femina* explicitly inscribed its "tournament" in a feminine courtly tradition dating back to the fifteenth century, when queens and princesses judged poetic jousts. In recognition of this, the magazine's cover featured a photograph of the "Poet Queen" Her Majesty Elisabeth, Queen of Romania, at her desk; she had recently published a poetry collection under the pseudonym Carmen Sylva (Fig. 2.13). (This image will be discussed in further detail in the chapter that follows, as an example of the new iconography of the woman writer.) *Femina*'s labeling of Queen Elisabeth in this way again literalized the metaphor for women's accomplishment: to write was to attain royal status—witness the woman writer as celebrity—a possibility open to all women. The paradoxical democratization of this elevated status is made vivid in the ways that her majesty the queen is brought down to earth: both through her taking of a pseudonym, and the image of her sitting at a modest desk, the folds of her thick silk skirt forming an unwieldy curtain around her as she toils like a lowly commoner. This only underscores the point: if all women are royalty, and all women are poets, then all women can be *reines poètes*. Writing becomes at once a great equalizer (like motherhood) and a lofty aspiration—eliciting the labor of the queen herself.

*Femina*'s first poetry prize would be judged by an impressive all-woman jury including Countess Anna de Noailles (another sort of Poet Queen) and Madame Alphonse Daudet, depicted in a photograph in her elegant home, next to her son Léon. The rewards, then, were no longer linked to high-end goods, but rather to the approbation of respected literary women, in addition to publication in the magazine. These first poetry tournaments led to "Les Prix Femina," a series of literary contests for published authors launched in December 1904. The original Prix Femina included six awards: Female Merit (awarded to an exceptional act of social justice or generosity); Teaching; Literature and Poetry; Fine Arts and Poetry. In their denomination these prizes built upon while slightly expanding conventional feminine realms. The prizes were presented as an explicit rearticulation of the magazine's mission, one that we can see as an elaboration of their 1902 promise to introduce readers to the "diverse uses of the female mind." Remarking once again on the ever-increasing accomplishments of women in all areas, not just art and literature but society at large, the editors took the opportunity of the prize's launch to carefully describe their own vision of the modern woman: "Certainly no one values domestic virtues more than us," they wrote, reminding readers that in this magazine devoted to "Women," any "feminism" (in quotes) "is strictly repudiated." However, they went on to explain, these domestic virtues were in no way incompatible with the development of a woman's "mind and personality." Thus, "the expansion of women's activities that characterizes the dawn of the twentieth century" should be not only celebrated but facilitated, and it would be *Femina*'s self-declared job to encourage women in this direction.[31] In selecting future winners, *Femina* immediately called upon "the collaboration of our countless readers," who would be asked to nominate candidates for these honors, after which juries of eminent women would make the final selections.

Two months later, in February 1905, Caroline de Broutelles announced that *La Vie Heureuse* would offer an annual prize for the best literary work of the year, to be awarded to a new author by a jury of his or her female peers. This prize was a response to the disappointments of the brand-new Prix Goncourt, which was established in 1902 and gave its first prize in 1903.[32] Despite the dramatic rise in popularity of women writers during the years of its establishment, and Broutelles' own ties to many of the writers involved, the Goncourt convened a jury of ten men, repeating the patriarchal structure of the Académie Française from which it was meant to be set apart.[33] Nonetheless, there was still hope that, given the increased visibility of women writers, a woman might soon receive its prize. In November of 1904, *Femina* published an article by editor Jacques de Nouvion entitled "Women and the Prix Goncourt," which discussed several female contenders; precisely because of the prize's newness and detachment from tradition (and thus its distinction from the comparatively archaic Académie française, which had repeatedly refused to elect women to its ranks), De Nouvion concluded that women had a good chance.[34] Based on interviews with several members of the actual jury, a determination was made that novelist Myriam Harry was the most likely candidate for her critically acclaimed *La conquête de Jérusalem*. It was soon revealed, however, that Harry would be excluded because of her sex.[35] Shortly thereafter, Léon Frapié was named the Goncourt winner for his novel *La maternelle*, which, as Margot Irvine has brilliantly demonstrated, was a more conventionally feminine text (told through a young woman's voice) than Harry's orientalist novel based on her father's life in Jerusalem.[36] It quickly became clear that the Goncourt would, *vraisemblablement*, not be recognizing women's writing.[37]

Within weeks of this announcement, De Broutelles had assembled a jury for her new prize, made up of twenty-two female stars of the women's press and presided over by Anna de Noailles, who presented the first award to Harry herself. The Prix Vie Heureuse has traditionally been recognized as the origin of the current Prix Femina, which remains a highly coveted honor to this day: the magazine's prizes (and juries) later merged, along with the magazines, for the Prix Femina–Vie Heureuse, only to become the Femina in 1919. The Prix Vie Heureuse's original structure, modeled on the Goncourt and much leaner than *Femina*'s complex process, would be the archetype for the eventual prix Femina.[38]

It would be a mistake, however, to discount *Femina*'s parallel, if not equally substantial, role in shaping the roots of the Prix Femina, as well as the democratic forces at its origins. The determining role of *Femina*'s readers reaches back to their participation in one of *Femina*'s very first opinion surveys in July 1902. *Femina* had asked its readers to nominate talented French women (living or deceased) who they felt would make "An Ideal Female Academy."[39] The editors received 8,277 postcards with suggestions. Of the top forty nominees, seven would become part of the eight-woman jury that judged *Femina*'s first poetry tournament; twelve would later be invited to the jury of the Prix Vie Heureuse. Many of the

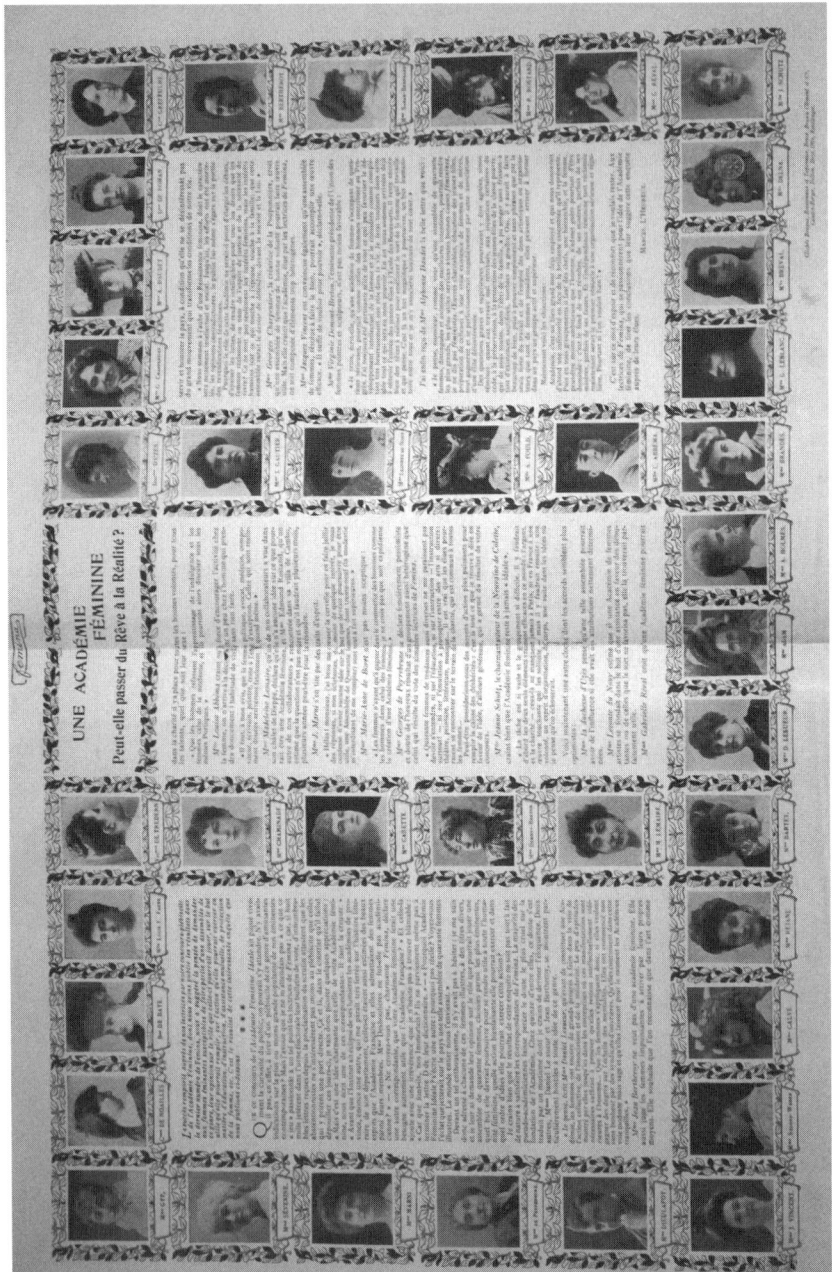

Figure 1.5 "A Female Academy: Could It Go from Dream to Reality?" *Femina* (October 15, 1902).

same women writers, including Anna de Noailles and Daniel Lesueur, served on the juries of both prizes; the female jury that remains the enduring legacy of the prize was a key element of *Femina*'s original prize series.[40] Perhaps more crucially, *Femina*'s prizes helped both to generate and solidify the female literary community and reader support that would be crucial to the success of the Prix Vie Heureuse and eventual Prix Femina. As it turns out, many of the famous women selected by these readers were not entirely in favor of the notion of a female academy, per se. In October, *Femina*'s editor-in-chief Marcel L'Heureux noted in an article that fifteen of them, when queried, offered deafening silence on the topic, while several, including Lesueur and Bertheroy, were notably hostile (Fig. 1.5). The opinion of readers, on the other hand, was overwhelmingly enthusiastic, and L'Heureux therefore preferred to end his article on a positive note, citing Madame Alphonse Daudet's encouraging remarks as a measure of hope and comfort for *Femina*'s *lectrices*, who themselves "were passionate about a female Academy."[41] Despite their hostility to the notion in 1902, just three years later Lesueur and Bertheroy went on to become members of the first Prix Vie Heureuse and eventual Prix Femina—as did Georges de Peyrebrune and Jeanne Marni, also less than favorable in L'Heureux's article. The strong response of the readership that Femina had worked so hard to cultivate thus appears to have been an influential factor in the creation of this enduring prize.

For *Femina*, success was always predicated upon readers' direct implication in their endeavors. "We are counting on you," wrote the editors in their description of the new prizes—simultaneously announcing their new offices on the highly chic avenue de l'Opéra, a sign both of their financial success and social standing. In a follow-up article responding to readers' questions about their awards in November 1905, *Femina* insisted it had no preferred candidates and reiterated the fact that the readers would play a direct role in selection: "Our readers will be effectively collaborating with members of the jury."[42] They had been even more explicit in declaring the readers' role as they announced the first literary contest: "Naturally, the names of subscribers will be published and will remain attached to the prizes, which they will have founded."[43] Despite their different model, *La Vie Heureuse* also ended up opening their contest to their readers. In August 1906, they invited readers to guess who the winner of the Prix Vie Heureuse would be from the list of nominees. The submission showing the greatest "literary finesse" would be awarded 500 francs.[44] Theirs, in general, was a less democratic model, and tended to emphasize editorial sophistication while similarly appealing to a reader who could mirror that sophistication. But like the *Femina* awards, the prix Vie Heureuse privileged the discovery of new talent over the coronation of well-established writers.[45]

## "A Femino-literary Victory"

In April 1909, *Femina* posed the question of a female academy again, this time receiving 6,700 responses. By this time, the question (to which we will return at the end of this book) had become particularly charged, due in part to the success of the magazines themselves. While the magazine was always loathe to make political demands, preferring to applaud women's accomplishments, writer Hélène Avryl waxed somewhat rhapsodic in pondering the beauty of this academy. Perhaps such campaigns would one day lead to—not a feminist victory, "heaven forbid!" but rather *une victoire fémino-littéraire*—a femino-literary victory.[46] Of course, this term never took hold, but it is worth pausing upon for a moment as we consider the feminist implications of these magazines even in their efforts to remain apolitical, and their espousal of a feminism that could not be named as such. Following the first award made by the *Vie Heureuse* prize committee to Myriam Harry, Jean Bertheroy did remark in that magazine: "Now that's the right kind of feminism."[47] Indeed, the literary realm turned out to be the domain in which the editors of both magazines felt most comfortable directly exhorting women towards change, the kind that would be "favorable to women's interests," offering benefits "on a grand scale that would include other realms."[48] Both *Femina*'s and *La Vie Heureuse*'s feminist leanings found their most natural outlet in this "femino-literary" realm—poised between public and private roles. My own terminology, Belle Epoque literary feminism, thus designates not just a mode and an ideology, but also the nature of female achievement for which the magazines most vividly and successfully advocated.

In her inaugural literary column in *Femina* in April 1908, Lucie Delarue-Mardrus (a member of the Prix Vie Heureuse jury from inception and throughout her life) marveled at the enduring power of the book amidst the ruins of modern society. She wrote that not only are books still of lasting value, their importance "increases every day. They are more than ever a social necessity." And while this in itself was surprising given the changes of modern society, perhaps even more unexpected was the role of *Femina* in ensuring this "supremacy." Indeed, the beautiful images dominating the magazine, wrote Delarue-Mardrus, "have not managed to change the fact that literature is being talked about here in a more regular and extensive fashion than would have been anticipated."[49] Similarly, in his May 15, 1906 "Survey on Women's Writing," journalist Maurice Laval interviewed several critics for their opinion on the current "expansion of women's writing," referring to the increasing numbers of women publishing in the early 1900s. Summarizing the diverse remarks of these critics, who included Catulle Mendès, Edmond Haraucourt and François Coppée, Laval noted that they were in agreement on one major point: "that the current success of women's writing is due in large part to the efforts and success of *Femina*."[50] Both Delarue-Mardrus's and Laval's comments call attention once again to a significant and too-often-overlooked aspect of the magazine: its strong link to the unprecedented success of Belle Epoque women's fiction. Moreover, I would suggest that not only was the success of women's writing linked to *Femina* and *La Vie Heureuse*, but the success of both magazines was due to their promotion of women's literature and its production. The editors of *Femina* must have realized the market appeal of this literary emphasis when they devoted a full page in their December 1903 issue to announcing that the magazine was "the most literary of all the illustrated magazines" and featured thumbnail images of upcoming contributors— a campaign perhaps elicited by *La Vie Heureuse*'s recent arrival on the scene and its promotion of a more overtly intellectual image.[51] Literary appeal was clearly selling magazines and keeping readers. This appeal was linked not only to these authors' writing but also very much to their celebrated and newly accessible public images, equally promoted through feature stories about their lives and lifestyles. As we will see in greater detail in the next two chapters, one real and fully documentable triumph of Belle Epoque literary feminism was its coronation of the woman writer as the ultimate *femme moderne*.

*Femina* and *La Vie Heureuse*'s literary appeal worked to the extent that it did because the publications invested in what was ultimately the most essential element to their success: the cherished *lectrice*, whom they never forgot to acknowledge. From the very beginning, this reader was given a fundamental role in participating in the intellectual parameters of both publications. *Femina*'s first poetry tournament was followed by dozens more, with nearly every issue of the magazine containing an announcement of a new contest or featuring winners of previous ones, their epic verse taking up page after page. "Mesdames and Mesdemoiselles who read us, delicious readership, the most desired in the world, we salute you" wrote Delarue-Mardrus, announcing her own literary column, "L'âme des livres," as a just reward for their efforts. Laval too, in applauding *Femina*'s success, recognized his audience, describing editor and reader as equals sharing the pride. This news, he wrote, "will, I hope, be as agreeable to you our readers as it was to myself." Recognizing their *chères lectrices* at every turn, inviting them into the exclusive world of the anointed literati, the magazine allowed each reader the possibility of feeling as special as real queens, princesses . . . and women writers. *Femina* and *La Vie Heureuse* did their best to convince readers that such a fantasy was indeed achievable and that a reflective, independent mind was an essential part of the new female ideal.

Cinderella had traded in her glass slipper for a golden pen.

CHAPTER 2
# BEYOND THE BLUESTOCKING
*Images of Work-Life Balance in the Belle Epoque*

"**WHAT** people don't say enough about George Sand is that she was a skilled housekeeper, often made little dishes for her guests, and was excellent with jams and cauliflower soup," wrote Marie d'Ourlac in a 1901 *Femina* article devoted to the celebrated author, marking the launch of an annual literary fête in her honor.[1] The article ends with a requisite nod to Sand's artistic prowess as the reason for her assured immortality, but not before devoting the bulk of its text to her unparalleled skills as a homemaker, devoted mother ("she herself had cut and sewn her babies' layettes") and grandmother.

*Femina*'s tribute to George Sand as domestic and literary heroine was part of the magazine's broader efforts to decouple the woman writer from her tainted past. Sand, far better known for her cross-dressing than for her mothering, was the most recognizable of the nineteenth-century *bas-bleus* or bluestockings.[2] When she was writing during the 1830s and 40s, her audacious sartorial choices only added fuel to a long-brewing misogynist fire, at a time when women writers were denigrated as mannish and chided for their careless abandon of proper feminine roles. By 1900, the terrain had shifted only slightly for the woman writer. The term *bas bleu* remained in wide circulation, while the writer herself had become one among many possible manifestations of troublesome women in the public sphere, embodied most often as the New Woman, or *femme nouvelle*. The fear-inducing New Woman was thus a descendant of the *bas bleu*, and a sister/alter-ego of the equally scorned feminist, imagined to have abandoned all semblance of femininity in her bold fight for new rights and some sort of vaguely defined "emancipation."[3]

In the article cited above, *Femina* references this association with

Figure 2.1 Feature on George Sand, *Femina* (October 15, 1901).

Sand ("She was heavily criticized for her masculine clothing during the first years of her literary career") before quickly moving on to the task at hand: proving that, in fact, George Sand was a profoundly feminine role model—kind, patient, caring and sensitive. In remembering Sand in this way in one of its first issues, *Femina* encapsulated the ambiguity at the heart of its ambitious efforts to remake the French woman writer. The magazine promoted the *femme de lettres* as a feminine role model in defiance of her tarnished nineteenth-century reputation at all costs—even if that meant a selective revision of history.[4]

We have already begun to see the privileged role given to women's literary expression in both *Femina* and *La Vie Heureuse*, in part through fostering readers' identification with women writers and their work. In what follows, I explore the elaborate ways in which both magazines directly confronted the troubling visual associations with female intellect by offering a carefully constructed image of the woman writer as a conventionally feminine ideal. The threat of the New Woman was tightly linked to the newly exploding mass media and its capacity to circulate images at an increasingly rapid pace.[5] In place of these persistent caricatures of modern women's roles, *Femina* and *La Vie Heureuse* presented a highly pleasing alternative: the woman writer was celebrated—in text and image—as the very definition of the *femme moderne*. The challenge for the magazines was to present the woman writer as modern and new while at the same time deeply familiar and thus non-threatening—someone who respected the past, while projecting the modern French woman into a more promising future. By expertly harnessing multiple mechanisms of journalistic innovation, including the joint forces of celebrity and mass culture, innovations in photography and contemporary artistic trends, *Femina* and *La Vie Heureuse* offered women readers iconographic evidence of a brand-new role model to emulate: a woman who could balance—with impeccable agility—tradition and innovation, femininity and feminism, work and family.

## *"At Home" Photography and the Woman Writer in Context*

Photography was a key ally in the magazines' efforts to reinvent the *femme de lettres*, ensuring the elevation of writer to celebrity, while also instantly normalizing her through reassuring visual cues.[6] (The Sand article, all of two pages long, featured eight images [Fig. 2.1]).

Both *Femina* and *La Vie Heureuse* relied heavily upon the relatively recent phenomenon of "At Home" photography, popularized in the 1890s by the photographer known as Dornac (pseudonym of Paul Cardon), who used portable cameras to capture famous figures in their own domestic spaces.[7] Dornac's images differed strikingly from previous portraits that focused entirely on the individual at close range, often with a few strategically placed symbolic objects.[8] Like the celebrity interview, another newly popularized genre, his wide-angle lens offered the public a whole new level of access to the casual details of the famous person's private world.[9] Dornac's series "Nos Contemporains chez eux," which appeared in *Le Monde Illustré* in the 1880s, featured dozens of these photographs of famous writers, artists and public intellectuals. By the early 1900s, there were endless photographers specializing in this genre, featured in newspapers and illustrated magazines; these intimate images of the famous were also sold to the public through postcards and albums.[10]

The visual immediacy of the photograph offered a shortcut to the message being conveyed by *Femina* and *La Vie Heureuse* about the compatibility between feminine and intellectual pursuits that bypassed more complex gender strategies during roughly the same time period. Mary Louise Roberts, for example, has described the "subversive mimicry" used by women writing for Marguerite Durand's *La Fronde* through their alternating between conservative and unconventional womanhood, reading that paper's quick demise as proof of "the potential weakness of parody as a subversive strategy."[11] Both *Femina* and *La Vie Heureuse*, on the other hand, exploited the straightforward power of the image to show women as both progressive and conventional, immediately normalizing, through pictures themselves and the accompanying text, any potential conflict. Like the female mountain climbers or women literally reaching new heights described in the introduction to this volume, photographs of women writers often created metonymic chains between the literary figure and conventional signs of femininity, visually fusing the natural relationship between woman and writer. A 1902 article on left-leaning journalist and devoted Dreyfusard Séverine—who might seem an unlikely candidate for celebration by these magazines given her outspoken socialist militancy—shows her seated beatifically, eyes closed, "in the hearth of the great fireplace" of her modest dining room, figured strikingly as part of the furniture, one with the home: *la femme*, quite literally, *au foyer* (Fig. 2.2), enacting the French expression for housewife.[12] Another unlikely candidate because she almost always dressed in male attire (even if for "good" reason: devotion to her husband Marcel, which impelled her to follow him to the army during the Franco-Prussian war and participate alongside him), Jane Dieulafoy is pictured in August 1902 sporting "the man's suit that she is never apart from."[13] This serves as a reminder that her pants were merely an expression of wifely duties. The caption below the image of Dieulafoy in her living room deliberately invites the reader to look away from her diminutive presence in the corner towards the rest of the stately, enormously high-ceilinged room in which "you'll notice the monumental fireplace which is a true marvel" (Fig. 2.3). Indeed. Covered with fleur de lys and regal insignia, it is the image of tradition, wealth, clear social strata, and all that her garb might appear to threaten.[14] And as with Séverine, Dieulafoy's audaciousness is tempered by the diversion of the viewer's gaze to the hearth, age-old metonym for feminine comfort and stability.

The images used by *Femina* and *La Vie Heureuse* insisted on the compatibility between femininity and authorship through the ease with

**Figure 2.2** Séverine quite literally in her foyer, *Femina* (October 1, 1902).

**Figure 2.3** Jane Dieulafoy in her salon, *Femina* (August 15, 1902).

which women's professional role could be assimilated with their domestic one, thus diffusing the threat most closely associated with the bluestocking as public woman, in the worst sense of the term. As *Femina* was quick to remind readers, the woman writer did not need to leave her home to take on her professional role. Interviewed for an article on women's literature, decadent author Catulle Mendès noted affirmingly: "Women, because of their sedentary nature, are in every way suited for fully sedentary professions and activities. Literature is a profession that requires no movement, that allows a woman to stay at home, and to oversee her household."[15] This comment is, of course, a reminder of the profound conservatism of the magazine in its support of conventional familial structures, a stance which made it willing sometimes to describe women in terms that seemed at odds with what we can now recognize as its more feminist objectives. But *Femina*'s particular twist

*Beyond the Bluestocking* 61

on the At Home photography of the woman writer countered this conservatism in important ways: the magazine almost always depicted the woman writer at her desk, aligning her with a visual trope associated with the authority of the *grand homme*.[16] Image after image picked up on this visual framework made familiar through Dornac's and other photographers' portraits of famous men that were a mainstay of the Belle Epoque press. Indeed, it is hard to find a picture of a male writer *not* at his desk between 1890 and 1910. In so many of these images, the esteemed writer or thinker is depicted deep in thought, surrounded by the trappings of an upper-bourgeois existence that serve to confirm his stature.[17] Dornac did photograph a few women writers, but these images were often strikingly different from those of their male counterparts. Anna de Noailles and Marcelle Tinayre, for example, are featured in soft lighting, with no visual reference to their profession. A series on "modern women" in the 1896 issue of the *Revue Encyclopédique* included dozens of photographs of exemplary women, with only one at her desk (the venerable Juliette Adam).[18] In their adoption of this familiar masculine trope, on the other hand, *Femina*'s images of women writers at their desks suggest intellectual parity and literary genius, while, as we will see, always, insistently, offsetting the associated threat to gender norms of such a suggestion through other kinds of visual and textual evidence of conventional femininity.

An early example of the careful dance between text and image is from an article on Daniel Lesueur, the first woman writer awarded the Legion of Honor, in a feature billed as "Women of Yesterday and Today." While the frontispiece to the issue had featured a hyperfeminized image of Lesueur in a richly ornamented dress, clutching a long necklace (not surprising, perhaps, for an author who had written on the relationship between feminism and beauty for *La Fronde*) (Fig. 2.4), the accompanying feature story showed her sitting at a rather austere desk, rows of neatly aligned books lining the shelves behind her (Fig. 2.5).[19] The image can be compared to a well-known Nadar image of Zola, in which the vertical lines of his extensive library work against the swirling florals of his tiny desk (Fig. 2.6).[20] Side by side, Lesueur seems every bit as *grand homme* as Zola—in fact, too much so. The curvy shape of the photograph slightly tempers Lesueur's somewhat brutish look and less-than-elegant attire. But it's the accompanying text that works most hard to compensate. The

**Figure 2.4** Daniel Lesueur, frontispiece to *Femina* (March 1, 1902).

**Figure 2.5** Daniel Lesueur feature story, "Women of Yesterday and Today." *Femina* (March 1, 1902).

**Figure 2.6** Émile Zola studio portrait by Félix Nadar.

subheading to the article promises to "introduce readers to the charming and unique woman that is this writer they adore." And then as if to literalize this promise, the first line of the article reads: "This decorated [with Legion of Honor] writer, former poet, is a *woman*," before going on to describe her joyful graciousness and beauty: offering, explicitly, a definition of femininity itself. Despite her forceful writing, Lesueur is not the least bit adversarial in person, the article assures. She loves movement and color, nature and horses. While her desk might look severe in the image, in fact she cannot write unless all of her *bibelots* are in place. Indeed, the article insists, Lesueur's femininity goes down to the very paper upon which she writes her books: "of the most tender and soothing blue color."[21]

Just a few months earlier, in October 1901, the playwright Jeanne Marni was pictured at her desk, pen in hand, facing outward (Fig. 2.7). The numerous knickknacks on every surface of the desk convey a healthy excess (compared with, for example, a barren desk in an image of the working-class Marguerite Audoux from *Femina*, July 1, 1910). With prac-

**Figure 2.7** Playwright Jeanne Marni at her desk. *Femina* (October 1, 1901).

tically the same language as the Lesueur feature, the caption declared *Femina*'s delight in introducing "the woman that is this enormously talented writer" (*la femme qu'est cet écrivain de grand talent*) to its *lectrices*; the somewhat awkward syntax of this formulation is an attempt to reconcile the *femme* with the always masculine *écrivain*. In this case, the photograph can avoid awkwardness entirely. Indeed, this seems to be the main objective of presenting Marni in this way: the image of woman writer at her desk represents the fusing of the very identities of woman and writer, the demonstration, that is, through the matter-of-fact evidence of the journalistic photograph, that she is both of these things without contradiction. The abundant lace billowing around her sleeves and collar matches the casual disorder on her desk, and these images somehow affirm her femininity.

Sometimes the desk seems to overtake, if not displace, the woman, as in the image of Madame Henry Gréville's *cabinet de travail* from the June 1902 issue of *Femina* (Fig. 2.8). Madame Gréville sits at her desk in the center of the photograph, pen engaged in one hand, cheek resting thoughtfully on the other. Her pensive gesture is a familiar trope (see, for example, the Dornac photo of Alphonse Daudet from 1891, Fig. 2.9).[22] But rather than the harsh lines of bookshelves behind her, a floral paper decorates the wall. Her oval face and patterned dress blend into the background of the cavernous room; every surface is adorned, from the overlapping Persian rugs covering the floor to the floral wallpaper, upon which a series of mirrors and paintings appear to be affixed. The recently deceased Madame Gréville becomes a decorative object herself, aligned with the blooming flowers to her right, and similar to the roses she passionately described in her writing, quoted in the article below. The room itself of-

**Figure 2.8** Madame Henry Gréville, *Femina* (June 15, 1902).

**Figure 2.9** Alphonse Daudet, from a Dornac photograph. From the series "Nos contemporains chez eux." *Le Monde Illustré* (1891).

fers far more visual interest than the diminutive writer, especially the desk, a weighty confection with swirling flowers carved into a dark wood in the same style as Nadar's Zola, but covered by a richly embroidered throw. As light streams onto her face, flowers, writer and desk thus form a metonymic chain of beauty, femininity and domesticity that steadily elide the potentially threatening intellectual gravitas of her professional role.

Images of women at their desk slowly evolve in *Femina*, with more visible feminine indices that visually reconcile the writer's femininity with the harsh angles of the furniture. Sometimes the potential dissonance of the upper bourgeois woman at her desk is diffused by reference to other more familiar domestic scenes. An article on Madame Alphonse Daudet, wife of the famous decadent novelist, shows her sitting at a small writing table, more befitting of a "*femme du monde* than would be a writer's desk" (Fig. 2.10). And yet it was there that she wrote her latest collection of poetry. Again, the desk itself works to assimilate the identities, to demonstrate the reconciliation of opposing forces: with her exquisite ostrich feather collar and heavy gold chains, Madame Daudet is no less a *femme du monde* than a brilliant writer, her genius having been "to have known how to describe the outside world with intensity, all the while maintaining her charm and feminine qualities."²³ The delicateness of her appearance and of the table itself, the fact that she is actually reading rather than writing, her gaze modestly averted from the camera, links her visually not to the trope of *grands hommes chez eux*, but rather to impressionist paintings like Berthe Morisot's 1877 *Girl Reading*. The curving border of the photograph further situates her in a feminized frame.

The shifting emphasis on décor allowed the viewer to see the desk as a decorative object, detached from its more audacious function as a link between these upper bourgeois women and the outside world of work and profession. In a rare and early appearance in the women's press, Colette, named Madame Gauthier-Villars, sits at a long table with her dog by her side (Fig. 2.11). The article followed the publication of her *Dialogue des bêtes*, and thus appeared just before her bitter divorce from the notorious Willy captured the French imagination, and three years shy of her scandalous lesbian kiss with Missy, her lover, on the stage of the Moulin

**Figure 2.10** Madame Alphonse Daudet at her writing table. *Femina* (January 15, 1903).

**Figure 2.11** Colette, known as Madame Gauthier-Villars, at her writing table. *La Vie Heureuse* (May 1904).

Rouge, which nearly caused a riot. Nonetheless, as if hesitant to subject this compelling female talent to too much scrutiny, the caption seemed to deliberately divert the reader's gaze away from Colette herself and towards the furniture, offering a view of what the camera does not capture in this case. "Within this Dutch austerity one finds a fleeting disorder of books strewn about, leafed-through magazines littering the thick red carpet. And the contrast is charming: that of the somber furniture with the bright Parisianism of the copperware that catches the light, and the cheerful flowers in their crystal vases and pots."[24] A charming contrast, indeed, and a gendered one as well: that of the severity of intellect (books, reading materials) with the lightness of the feminine ornaments and flowers. The contrast is in fact the crux of it all: a perfect display of the magazines' effort to show that all of these juxtapositions were not threatening at all, but rather nothing short of charming, and that femininity is never fully lost, even when momentarily displaced.

The clutter of papers and books, knickknacks and flowers only just past their prime that appears in so many images of *cabinets de travail* connotes a cheerful and natural feminine hominess, while nodding to the High Victorian decorative tradition.[25] Sometimes this ultrafeminine décor served to compensate for either the particular woman writer's lack of feminine traits or her audacious behavior. See, for example, the feature on Gyp in the November 1902 *Femina*. Born Sibylle Aimée Marie Antoinette Gabrielle de Riquetti de Mirabeau, in 1869, Gyp married the count Martel de Janville, with whom she had three children in rapid succession before becoming financially ruined and eventually estranged from him.[26] This controversial and prolific author was best known for her outspoken anti-Dreyfusard writings, famously declaring, at one point in 1899, her official profession to be "anti-Semite." Gyp, then, was hardly a role model for upper bourgeois young ladies, described in the article itself as having "the spirit of *La Fronde* and its writers, and a sharp sense of opposition."[27] And yet, iconographically, she is the image of bourgeois bliss. In the brief autobiographical sketch she herself offers in the article, she mentions her marriage without further commentary on its tumultuous history. An excess of ultra-feminized bourgeois interiors continue her own work of reframing, distracting the reader from prevailing gossip with their visual evidence of domestic stability. The very multiplicity of images—there are six on the first page alone, nine total—serves to efface this biographical context, offering a concrete visual alternative. She too is figured "at her writing table," but both books and flowers are overflowing around her, her flowing robe mimicking the floral lines of the furniture, making her appear to be almost a giant flower herself in the center of the photograph (Fig. 2.12). And while the caption indicates a desk, the image illustrates the perfect

**Figure 2.12** Gyp at her writing table, *Femina* (November 15, 1902).

conflation of At Home photography with the impressionist woman at her toilette trope. Writing table and dressing table are indistinguishable, a mirror peeking out behind Gyp's piles of papers. In a portrait by Louise Abbéma featured in the same article, the very presence of which reminds of Gyp's noble origins and the importance of her image to posterity, she is also seated at a writing table, framed by two large plants that mimic the floral scarf tied round her neck.[28] Once again, then, she is a picture of feminine beauty, propriety and upper class modern style. The composition of both images recalls Morisot's paintings of women in their private interior moments—whether at their toilette, easel or piano.

The 1903 cover image of the "Poet Queen" Her Majesty Elisabeth of Romania (Fig. 2.13) completes, in a sense, *Femina*'s metonymic work

**Figure 2.13** "A Poet Queen: Carmen Sylva, her majesty Queen Elisabeth of Romania." Cover of *Femina* (February 1, 1903).

of adopting At Home photography to fuse the identity of woman and writer in a perfectly feminine balance. The queen is seated at her desk, her luminous satin gown flowing to the floor; with one hand, she holds her pen to a manuscript in progress, while with the other she consults an open book. Her sidelong pose mirrors Mary Cassatt's "Mrs. Duffee, Reading" (1876): in both painting and photograph, the elegant woman is engrossed in thought, her billowing skirts softly draped against the opposing geometry of the furniture (Fig. 2.14). As an updated version of Cassatt's image, the Poet Queen's seamless flow from domestic leisure activities of the upper class to the At Home work of authorship is vividly displayed in the visual arc from seat to table, book to manuscript, reading to writing. And yet, as striking as this image seems to be, by the time

**Figure 2.14** Mary Cassatt, "Mrs. Duffee Seated on a Striped Sofa, Reading" (1876). Courtesy of the Museum of Fine Arts, Boston.

it had appeared in February 1903, the juxtaposition of the ornaments of aristocracy with the work of writing had become familiar in *Femina*: that the queen was a writer was clearly meant to elevate her capital among readers rather than diminish it, assimilating the unfamiliar royal with the numerous famous women writers already depicted in a similar stance.

## New Frameworks

The image of Colette at her desk is encased by vines of flowers, whose swirling lines call up the art nouveau patterns of Belle Epoque poster art. In fact, the repeated art nouveau motifs throughout *Femina* and *La Vie Heureuse* point to a connection that goes beyond the purely aesthetic.[29] The magazines not only reflect some of art nouveau's key aesthetics but also offer an overlooked expression of its core ideological tenets; the pen-and-ink frames reflect a shared means of framing ongoing social shifts through visual culture. As part of the democratization of luxury so crucial to the rise of consumer culture at the fin de siècle, art nouveau meant "the diffusion of taste and tradition from above, from an official institution of the cultural elite."[30] *Femina* and *La Vie Heureuse*, linked to the same highbrow *monde artistique et littéraire*, represented one such kind of institution and as such demonstrate the ways in which this refined taste was specifically deployed for women. Like the art nouveau movement, the magazines sought a way of updating, not French decorative objects but rather French women, while maintaining—and reviving—French artistic tradition. And like the magazines, art nouveau was preoccupied with domestic interiors, which, as Debora Silverman has argued, emphasized conventionally feminine forms so as to allay the New Woman's audacious forays into the public sphere, seen as a threat to the fundamental social structures of French society.[31] If art nouveau sought to restore woman as "queen of the interior," the women writers of *Femina* and *La Vie Heureuse* were depicted as new iterations of traditional French values, and this was done, more often than not, within elite domestic interiors themselves.

The very first issue of *La Vie Heureuse* showcased the beloved Countess Anna de Noailles in a magnificent five-page spread entitled "A Woman Poet Appraised by a Woman of Letters," written by the Baronne A. de Rothschild. Noailles herself was a felicitous choice, beloved for her social status as well as for her talents. Born Princess Anna Elisabeth

Bibesco-Bassaraba de Brancovan, she married Mathieu Fernand Frédéric Pascal de Noailles.[32] Well-connected to the literary and artistic elite, at the time of the article she had published two volumes of poetry, *Le cœur innombrable* and *L'ombre des jours*, both of which had received widespread critical acclaim.

In the image that introduces the article, Noailles is pictured in her sitting room, just off center in the photograph, her young son gingerly upon her lap (Fig. I.1). The extensive caption tells the reader exactly what she is supposed to see, narrating Noailles' decorative choices, from the furniture to the flower arrangements:

> A nearly white rug, the walls draped with a pale blue silk; no clutter, just precious objects; a veil of a beautiful point de Milan lace drapes the chaise longue; only carefully chosen and arranged antiques, which in this brightness take on a new light. The furniture was modern style at first. But Madame de Noailles could not live in the uncomfortable mixing of such sharp forms. She came back to the wing chairs and the medallion armchairs. In a vase, one finds branches of delphinium, flower of Old France (*la vieille France*).

This inscription, just beneath the visual evidence, provides almost more detail than the image itself, and its overdetermined narration underlines the significance of the countess's decorative choices to the story that is being told. Noailles is described here as having rejected "modern style" furniture in favor of carefully chosen antiques.[33] Yet old cannot fully win out over new: the antiques are rejuvenated by their context, just as Noailles herself, a member of the aristocracy, is part of a new poetic movement. Her poetry, details the article, exihibits "that something new that pervades contemporary women's writing."[34]

The image of Noailles is framed by a simple pen-and-ink series of rectangles, around which is laced a most delicate wreath of flowers—a subtle visual index of the still-nascent modern style of art nouveau, with its emphasis on nature, feminine floral lines and those intricate swirls that weave throughout the magazine itself. In the photograph, the decorative signs of French tradition anchor the *femme de lettres* in a familiar past while the stately furniture situates her in the confines of a museumlike interior. At the same time, the fluid, dynamic floral lines of the frame augur a change that is at once radical and natural. Situated in the sight line of the delphinium branches, Noailles seems meant to be read in parallel to them as a "flower of Old France," she herself, seen, literally, in a transformative new light as it streams through the window.

With these kinds of glimpses into the beautifully furnished homes of their stars, the magazines functioned both like the pavilions of the recent Exposition Universelle, displaying France's finest new home accessories, and like the more permanent collection of antique furniture gathered in the Louvre's Department of Art Objects in the late 1890s. Named the Museum of French Furniture in 1901 (thus coinciding with the birth of *Femina*), this installation also represented a key moment for art nouveau.[35] Influenced by the renewed interest in interior design that the exhibits at the 1900 Exposition Universelle had provoked, these popular collections were meant to bring visitors from all classes into close contact with the intimacies of aristocratic life, and thus shape their sensibilities. Visiting these interiors, stated Gaston Migeon, would be an uplifting experience for the masses.[36] Like the museum, on the other hand, the magazines, through their extensive photo spreads, invited readers into the homes of their women writers while presenting them as role models for a broader, not exclusively upper bourgeois or aristocratic audience. Echoing Migeon, the editors of *La Vie Heureuse* had asked in their first issue, in which the feature on Noailles appeared: "Isn't it good that those women who are burdened by hard labor catch a glimpse, as in a dream, of the lives of queens, princesses and Women who are the most refined specimen of the aristocracy of all races?"[37] One might think about the feature stories in these magazines and their use of At Home photography, then, as a visual experience that mixes the highbrow appeal of the Louvre's furniture museum, which reproduced homes without their inhabitants, with the mass marketing of the Musée Grévin, which featured celebrities in recreations of their interiors.[38] Like the museum's thick red ropes employed to maintain that fragile border between viewer and object, the delicate, highly feminized art nouveau pen-and-ink framing helped preserve and elevate the figures within, even as they were offered up for mass consumption.

Despite their ideological resonances with the mission of the magazines, however, the signature lines of art nouveau were visually associated with a model of femininity that did not always match *Femina* and *La Vie Heureuse*'s ideal. The early feature on Daniel Lesueur that appeared in the *Femina* series "Women of Yesterday and Today" (Fig. 2.5) betrays some of the initial difficulty in harmonizing a visually modern frame with a very traditional looking woman.³⁹ As an idealized example of the modern *femme de lettres*, Lesueur is presented in this feature as a woman of both the past and present, perfectly balancing the tradition of elegance with contemporary new roles. But there is also something rather jarring in this image: the "whiplash" lines surrounding the photograph of Lesueur had gained their familiarity largely through popular Belle Epoque poster art. In images by Alphonse Mucha and Paul Berthon, similar lines flow from the cascading tresses of women's hair, and were used most often to surround a hypersexualized feminine image, often of an actress. See, for example, the Berthon poster of the famous courtesan Liane de Pougy at the Folies Bergères (Fig. 2.15). Similarly, in this heading, two mermaidlike, mythical-looking creatures frame Lesueur's face.⁴⁰ Figured in black undulating, snakelike contours, their

**Figure 2.15** Poster of Liane de Pougy by Paul Berthon, 1895.

hair, while mimicking the curves of Lesueur's tightly knotted coiffure, suggest an unbridled sexuality that the accompanying photograph and article seem to flatly deny. The giraffe motif behind Lesueur's portrait demonstrates the entanglement of African imagery with art nouveau graphics. Along with the disembodied birds' feet clawing at the title, these images suggest a wild energy that the writer's image seems deliberately poised to work against.[41] The magazine both evokes and displaces in this way the threat of the New Woman and her seemingly dangerous sexuality, deliberately replacing such an image with a far more respectable alternative that feels, at the same time, strangely superimposed.[42] And yet, the image inscribes itself in a highly modern aesthetic. It thus presents its own idealized version of the professional woman—the *femme de lettres*—as both thoroughly modern *and* thoroughly traditional, split, like the mythical creatures, in two. This was, indeed, the challenge of the Belle Epoque woman writer attempting to have it all: within the context of the women's press, she must somehow be both "a woman of yesterday and today."

### Books and Babies

As Anna de Noailles sits with her baby delicately balanced upon her lap, the poet-countess balances feminism and femininity through the precise equilibrium of books and babies—offering, then, compelling visual evidence that writing need not be perceived as a threat to women's traditional roles. In the multipage feature story, Noailles' darling son is deliberately juxtaposed with passages of her verse. The image described above of the countess in her living room is matched with a slightly larger photograph on the facing page of Noailles in profile, a book open across her lap (I.1). In the first picture, the white of her son's clothing matches a blanket draped across the Louis XV chair, ready to receive the child. The loosely folded fabric of this makeshift baby bed corresponds to the folds of the countess's billowing skirt in the facing picture, which cradles not her child but her book.

In this, *La Vie Heureuse*'s visual emphasis differed from that of *Femina*. Unlike its rival, *La Vie Heureuse* rarely showed the work of writing. The editors' favored image was that of the writer on a well-appointed sofa, with her children in reach—a trope that, working in iconographic opposition to the pants and bicycles that conjured the New Woman, demonstrated to readers that authorship was in tension neither with motherhood nor an upper-class lifestyle. Moreover, we have here the beginnings of the visual mystification of modern motherhood as a female ideal. Aristocrats and upper-bourgeois women still rarely actually took care of their own children in Belle Epoque France; but the desire to recognize their contributions as mothers meant that they were increasingly photographed in this role. The images of women writers with their children, alongside those of queens and their babies, offer a pleasing image of maternity as yet another aspect of female achievement to be admired and emulated.

The juxtaposition of the Noailles images, while so carefully aiming to convey the harmony of maternity and intellect in parallel pursuit, also ironically captures their inevitable tensions: the baby in the first image looks to his left, through the open window but, if you follow his gaze, also to his mother in the facing picture. Noailles, on the other hand, faces left as well, leaving her gazing outward, to the extra-maternal realms suggested by the open volume on her knees. The next two images, however, bring mother and child back together in unity. In a dramatic portrait, the parallel gazes of mother and son aim directly at the reader, while below the last paragraphs of the article we see the countess in profile again, this time playfully holding her young son beneath her (2.16). As if growing out of this last image, itself circled in an egg-like oval, are hand-sketched branches of a flowering tree—those of a *pied d'alouette*, flower of Old France, perhaps?

The images in *Femina* and *La Vie Heureuse* are hardly ever left to speak for themselves, and this article makes no exception. The accompanying

**Figure 2.16** Anna de Noailles playing with her son, *La Vie Heureuse* (October 1902).

text, both in the captions and in the articles, reminds of the important critical work being done to create harmony where there was once dissonance. The Baronne de Rothschild describes holding Noailles' "beautiful book" upon her knees, enchanted by "the beating of this *Vast Heart* [*Cœur innombrable*, the title of her poetry collection]." She devotes the bulk of the article to extensive analysis of the countess's poetry, having charged herself to "demonstrate the ways in which this book was very new for us." Then, in her final paragraphs, she finds herself face to face with Noailles, interrupted by the entrance of *un petit poème vivant*—a little living poem— her son. She notes, "in her delicious maternal expression that fruitiness that came so strongly for me out of her work," thus confirming, once and for all, that initial link between literary and procreative products.[43] The erudite literary criticism that preceded (Rothschild inscribes Noailles in literary history between the "genius" of Marceline Desbordes-Valmore's melancholic poems and those of the eighteenth-century romantic poet André Chénier) evaporates in the baby's presence. At the end of the day, it all boils down to this, really: the countess is a profoundly feminine talent. Books and babies are just two different forms of her poetry, two ways to infuse the world with maternal beauty.

The women writers celebrated in the pages of *Femina* and *La Vie Heureuse* had more or less impeccable bourgeois reputations. Their novels, on the other hand, often treated complex, controversial subjects. Reviews in both magazines regularly indicated if a novel was "not for everyone," or not for young women.[44] Often part of the work of the photograph was to disassociate the writer from her characters or subject matter. Children were extremely effective towards this end. In October 1903, Gabrielle Réval, best known for her treatment of female education in the 1900 *Les Sévriennes*, was pictured picnicking with her son: "In the paths of the Bois de Boulogne where she writes her novels Madame Gabrielle Réval spends her moments of relaxation teaching her son Jacques to read."[45] Again the magazine creates the perfect symmetry, demonstrating the harmonious relationship of books and children. When Réval is not writing about education, rest assured that she is busy educating her own child.

An article in *La Vie Heureuse* from May 1903 pictures Gérard d'Houville, wife of novelist Henri de Régnier and author of the best-selling novel *L'inconstante*, with her son, nicknamed Tiger (Fig. 2.17). Although not a member of the actual nobility, d'Houville, christened "the youngest of

M^ME DE RÉGNIER, assise au coin de la cheminée de son petit salon, menace d'un doigt léger et d'un geste charmant, le fils qu'elle a baptisé Tigre. Et elle ne se souvient assurément plus qu'elle a écrit, à la page 201 de l'Inconstante, cette phrase que Tigre, bien heureusement n'a pas pu lire : « Au fond, les parents les meilleurs sont tous mis dedans, et c'est parfait ainsi. »

# La Plus Jeune des Femmes de Lettres
## GÉRARD D'HOUVILLE ET « L'INCONSTANTE »

*IL Y A DEUX MOIS*, parut un roman que l'auteur, qui est une jeune femme, avait dédié « à sa chère maman »; elle-même avait pris pour pseudonyme, pieusement, le nom d'un aïeul. Ce n'est cependant pas pour ces sentiments de famille que nous le citons. Ce n'est pas non plus pour ce qu'il contient, et nous n'en conseillons pas la lecture aux jeunes femmes. Mais l'auteur est fille et femme de poète. Elle a fait elle-même de beaux vers, qui ont paru dans la Revue des Deux Mondes, avec trois étoiles pour signature. L'anonymat est un plaisir, à condition qu'il dure peu. Une femme serait déçue si, voulant rester inconnue, personne en effet n'arrivait à la connaître. L'auteur de l'Inconstante n'a pas subi longtemps cette épreuve. La Revue a mis son nom à la table des matières, et au lendemain de l'apparition du livre, un journal, justement informé, nomma Mme Henri de Régnier.

❋ ❋ ❋

DEPUIS de longues années, M. J.-M. de Hérédia reçoit le samedi : maintenant dans son appartement de bibliothécaire de l'Arsenal, rue Sully, et naguère dans son appartement de la rue Balzac.

Les réceptions sont en quelque sorte doubles. Dans son cabinet de travail, arsenal de bibliophile, l'auteur des *Trophées* est entouré de poètes, d'historiens, d'écrivains. On fume ; on puise le tabac dans une boîte ouverte et on roule des cigarettes ; le maître de la maison offre ses cigares. Lui-même fume la pipe. A quatre heures on lui apporte du lait et des biscuits.

Tout à coup, apparaissait une jeune fille grande, svelte, brune. Le poète posant sa pipe suivait sa fille et allait saluer une admiratrice quelquefois créole dans le grand salon clair où recevait Mme de Hérédia.

Or, parmi les écrivains qui fréquentaient rue Balzac, il y avait un jeune homme grand et mince, au sourire aimable et languissant, que toute la jeune littérature salue comme le prince des vers fluides et des belles images, M. H. de Régnier. C'est ainsi qu'il devint le gendre de M. de Hérédia, dont les deux autres filles épousèrent, comme on sait, M. Pierre Louÿs, écrivain attique, et M. Maurice Maindron, qui connaît le XVIe Siècle.

Mme H. de Régnier publia des vers, qui furent une révélation. M. de Hérédia était ravi. « Jamais, disait-il, je n'ai fait de pareils vers. » Puis tandis qu'elle arrivait, comme naturellement, à la gloire de poète, voici qu'elle a laissé brusquement la poésie, pour écrire en prose : et le piquant, c'est qu'elle a malicieusement caché son jeu. Elle a fait son premier roman sans en parler à personne. M. de Régnier n'en savait rien. M. de Hérédia l'ignorait. Mme de Régnier écrivait son livre sans le silence de sa pensée. Présenté à la *Revue*

GÉRARD D'HOUVILLE

de Paris, M. Ganderax tourne et retourne le manuscrit, l'épluche, gémit et admire, et, après le terrible examen qu'il fait impitoyablement subir à toute espèce de manuscrit, fût-il d'Anatole France, il publie l'œuvre. On l'envoie à M. de Hérédia. Le poète a la surprise de reconnaître, dans le nom de l'auteur, celui d'un parent d'autrefois. Il lit, et revoit sa vie d'enfance à Cuba, les nuits parfumées et divines, les luxuriantes forêts, les étés torrides et poussiéreux, la magie des souvenirs créoles, tout un passé évocateur et vivace. M. de Hérédia n'en revenait pas, ni M. de Régnier non plus. Il fallut se rendre à l'évidence. Nous avions un poète ; ce fut un prosateur qui nous vint.

On a dit : Le style, c'est l'homme. Ici le style, c'est la femme. Mme de Régnier est une femme charmante. Sa prose est comme son caractère : très crâne, très franche, aimablement familière. Sentimentale bien, avec l'aisance féminine qu'elle a dans ses manières, dans son allure mondaine. Elle a ceci de particulier pour une femme de lettres, c'est que son talent est bien elle, et bien à elle. On ne dira pas d'elle ce que disait Boileau à Racine fils, qui lui soumettait de vers : « gloria patri ». M. de Hérédia ne donne à sa fille ni une pensée ni une rime. Il est là simple admirateur, le plus étonné de tous. Mme de Régnier écrit ses œuvres sans presque y songer. On peut même affirmer qu'une fois finies, elle n'y songe plus.

Étrange femme, un peu énigmatique, parlant haut, bon camarade et bon garçon, adorant les fleurs, les parfums, les livres et les bibelots, l'esprit littérairement saturé de toutes les nombreuses et curieuses conversations qu'elle a entendues, pas romanesque, pratique, spontanée, indépendante.

❋ ❋ ❋

CETTE JEUNE FEMME, qui a écrit des vers charmants, efface autour de ses bibelots, comme elle le dit elle-même, le cerne de poussière que chaque heure reforme autour de chaque objet.

DANS UNE ALLÉE, l'ombre des arbres verse une inspiration heureuse et naturelle. « J'aime les arbres, dit Marion dans l'Inconstante ; ils me gardent et ils me consolent. »

**Figure 2.17** Gérard d'Houville with her son, Tiger. *La Vie Heureuse* (May 1903).

the *femmes de lettres*" in the article's title, has the advantage—like many of the elite writers featured in the women's press—of being a member of the literary aristocracy. In addition to being the wife of a famous writer, she is the daughter of one as well: J.-M. de Heredia, adding even more interest to her celebrated role. And yet the article worked hard to depict her in a nonthreatening light. d'Houville and her son are seated in another lush domestic interior, lined with adornments like the fans and candlesticks arranged atop the mantle. The wide-angle shots pioneered by Dornac to give a sense of "milieu" are exploited here to normalize the writer and visually inscribe her in typical upper-bourgeois existence. Light bounces in seemingly from a window beyond the photo's frame, drawing the eye between a flower-filled vase, d'Houville herself in the center, and her contrite-looking son seated on the sofa, chastened by his mother's supposedly wagging finger. The caption reads: "Madame de Régnier, sitting by the edge of the fireplace in her small sitting room, threatens the son that she has nicknamed Tiger with a slight and charming wag of the finger." It seems that d'Houville's novel contained something of a suggestion of parental impropriety. The photographic evidence, combined with the textual explication, thus works to negate any hint of parental neglect or resentment suggested by d'Houville's literary work that might conjure Daumier's woman writer as negligent mother. Each comment is offered in a delicate and careful effort to maintain a precarious equilibrium: d'Houville's disciplining finger is "slight" and constitutes a charming gesture. In the article itself, she is described through this hybridity: "Strange woman, a bit enigmatic, she speaks loudly, a good buddy, real good kid who loves perfumes, books and knickknacks."[46] We see here competing journalistic urges: the impulse to show d'Houville's eccentricity, as was often the case in feature stories about male writers, and the desire to affirm her conventional femininity. Again, the charm of juxtaposition is invoked. Any sense of anxiety surrounding the troubling personality is alleviated if not effaced by the accompanying images of a familiar bourgeois existence. In one, "the young woman who wrote such pretty verse" is figured dusting those same adored *bibelots*.

While it might seem patronizing to modern eyes, the insistent distinction between writer and subject matter, I would argue, worked to women's advantage in the literary sphere. It proved, through example after example, that women could explore controversial topics in their writing without implicating themselves in the process. In this sense, the magazines performed a crucial gesture that helped foster the women's writing they supported in the same pages. Even as women's domestic roles seem immensely circumscribed in these photomontages, then, their imaginations were liberated.

## *Novels and Children*

Looking at these magazines with twenty-first century hindsight, some obvious cultural critiques beckon. Indeed, Roland Barthes famously deconstructed a similar phenomenon in his *Mythologies*: "If we are to believe *Elle* magazine," he wrote, "which some time ago mustered seventy women in one photograph, the woman of letters is a remarkable zoological species; she brings forth, pell-mell, novels and children."[47] Barthes was referring to a double-page image in the November 22, 1954 issue of the magazine, under which a headline declared "Women Writers Make Their Presence Known!" Accompanying the photograph to which he refers, a caption identifies the featured writers according to their credentials. Number 15, for example, reads "Marguerite Yourcenar (5 novels)." Witness, however, number 31: "Hélène Parmelin (2 children, 2 novels)" or number 34: "Nicole Dutreuil (2 sons, 4 novels)."[48] Playfully but incisively deconstructing these captions, Barthes reads the 1950s woman writer as circumscribed by her procreative function, only permitted to write to the extent that she performs her feminine duties:

> Women, be therefore courageous, free; play at being men, write like them; but never get far from them; live under their gaze, compensate for your books by your children; enjoy a free rein for a while, but quickly come back to your condition. One novel, one child, a little feminism, a little connubiality. (50)

It is hard to argue with Barthes' cynical reading, certainly as far as *Elle* 1954 is concerned, and impossible not to see the parallel with the message that *La Vie Heureuse* was sending. But when we historicize Barthes' critique, we see that this conscientious construction of a new model of feminine achievement in the Belle Epoque—limited as it might have been—was not meant as a retrenchment of women's roles but rather as an expansion of the ways in which women could be equal. In 1903, in other words, novels and children was a response to a denigration of the woman writer, and part of a wider effort to broaden the scope of a feminism that was associated with (even if unfairly) a necessary rejection of all things conventionally feminine. The message conveyed in these photo spreads is repeatedly formulated throughout *Femina* and *La Vie Heureuse*: women's achievement does not mean abandonment of conventional feminine roles—and thus widespread denigration as some sort of unnatural being. Femininity can be conjugated with authorship, these photo spreads prove, and to glorious and exemplary ends. To be a woman writer, according to *Femina* and *La Vie Heureuse*, is no longer a contradiction in terms.

Indeed, the editors of both *Femina* and *La Vie Heureuse* seem strikingly conscious of the conflict between the beautiful image of achievement they are constructing and the image of reckless depravity that still clung to the *femme de lettres*. "Small, brown-haired, slim and pale, her expression always changing, Madame Marcelle Tinayre is certainly the absolute contrary of what men a bit disdainfully call a woman of letters," reads a 1903 profile of Tinayre from *La Vie Heureuse*.[49] Similarly, a *Femina* article on "Women's Works" from 1905 explicitly describes the images included as a challenge to Barbey d'Aurevilly and his legacy: "Barbey d'Aurevilly, who hated those he called bluestockings and haughtily maligned them with the most venomous traits, would himself wave the flag of surrender before such diverse, effervescent talent."[50] In this sense, then, what looks like a naïve and exploitative affirmation of patriarchal norms in 1954 can be seen, in 1903, as a deliberate embrace of convention intended to push further open the feminist umbrella, and thus to expand the ways through which Belle Epoque women could challenge gender roles.

### *Staging Work-Life Balance*

For the most part, *La Vie Heureuse* emphasized the perfect conjugation of woman and writer through visual emphasis on her domestic fealty, while *Femina* situated the woman writer in a visual space parallel to her male counterparts by depicting her at a desk or writing table. One particular image stands out, however, in displaying both desk and child and thus beginning to express a new kind of ideal. In their 1903 feature "En Visite chez Marcelle Tinayre" (directly evoking the *visite au grand homme* trope popularized throughout the nineteenth century), *La Vie Heureuse* showed the emerging novelist at her desk, one arm posed gingerly next to a closed manuscript, the opposite hand linked to her impeccably groomed young daughter, who gracefully met her mother's gaze (Fig. 2.18).[51] Everything

EN VISITE CHEZ
Sa Maison

MARCELLE TINAYRE
Ses Romans

Entre le manuscrit commencé, et l'enfant à qui elle donne la main, Madame Tinayre, tout en composant de beaux livres, a gardé l'esprit même de la vie féminine, un cœur tendre, l'amour des tout petits, le goût d'orner sa maison.

Une assez petite personne, au regard vif, étonné et charmant, qui discourt d'une voix menue et facile, a eu cette année un très grand succès, un des plus grands assurément de l'année, en publiant la Maison du Péché. On reverra le roman à la scène. L'auteur avait deux fois droit qu'on parlât d'elle. Elle réconcilie les lettres avec la nature. Elle écrit spontanément, par l'effet d'un don heureux, qui lui fait dire net et juste, et peindre avec bonheur la figure des choses et le mouvement des passions.

A TROIS KILOMÈTRES environ du bourg de Montfort-l'Amaury, campé sur une hauteur au bord de la ligne de Paris à Rambouillet, la route étroite qui mène au village du Gros-Rouvre s'abaisse brusquement, dessine un coude et descend, rapide, vers une vallée. Des prairies, plantées de pommiers, la bordent d'un côté, et des arbres pressés dans la profondeur cachent des masures de chaume. Juste au tournant du chemin, une maison s'élève contre un massif de châtaigniers et de chênes. On voit d'abord une barrière à claire-voie, puis un mur que dépassent trois tilleuls en charmille. Sur un côté de la cour, un escalier de pierre monte à un petit jardin en terrasse ; de l'autre côté, à l'entrée du bois, un châtaignier de trois cents ans dresse son tronc rugueux et ses énormes branches. Toute blanche, longue et basse, sous son toit de vieilles tuiles assombries par le temps, la maison semble sourire au soleil. Elle n'a qu'un étage, de larges poutres solides forment le plafond, le sol est carrelé ; elle a l'âme simple, paisible et bonne des demeures très anciennes où vécurent des hommes d'esprit calme et de conscience pure. Derrière elle, comme pour l'abriter de regards curieux, grimpe une colline boisée. On devine l'église dans la masse moutonnante des frondaisons et plus loin, baignée d'un air transparent, la plaine s'étend jusqu'à l'extrême horizon. C'est là qu'habite et travaille toute une moitié de l'année Mme Marcelle Tinayre ; et c'est là qu'elle a fait vivre, aimer et souffrir cette délicieuse et charmante Fanny Manolé, l'héroïne de son livre.

Petite, brune, mince et pâle, le visage sans cesse changeant, Mme Marcelle Tinayre est bien le contraire le plus absolu de ce que les hommes appellent un peu dédaigneusement une femme de lettres. Profondément artiste, éprise du silence bienfaisant de la nature, d'une sensibilité vive et frémissante, elle est avant tout une femme. Une jolie toilette l'enchante, et elle aime la fièvre des grands magasins qui renferment tout l'artifice frivole et exquis de la beauté. Ses doigts ont cousu les courtines

Mme Marcelle Tinayre.

claires qui pendent aux fenêtres de sa rustique retraite, et c'est elle qui a cherché chez les antiquaires de Paris et chez les paysans de nos provinces les meubles qui remplissent les chambres.

Elle ne méprise point la cuisine, et collabore fièrement à la préparation des repas. Elle a trois enfants, deux fillettes et un garçon, qu'elle adore. Est-ce à dire qu'elle possède toutes les vertus ? ce serait un éloge qui ne lui plairait point : elle affirme simplement qu'elle a les qualités et les défauts des femmes.

Elle avait épousé très jeune, à dix-sept ans, je crois, un graveur qui s'est fait une solide et juste réputation : M. Julien Tinayre.

Elle appartenait à une famille du centre de la France où les dons de l'intelligence et du goût remplaçaient la fortune. Sa grand-mère se distrayait à composer des vers lamartiniens, et sa mère est une femme supérieure. Elle-même, tout enfant, commença à écrire : à cette époque elle ne comprenait point qu'on pût être autre chose que poète. Elle se maria ; elle rappelle aujourd'hui en riant avec quelle inexpérience elle dirigeait son ménage. La gêne d'argent y était terrible. Bravement, elle lutta. Elle essaya de donner des leçons et n'en découvrit point ;... elle porta des nouvelles à des suppléments de journaux quotidiens, on lui en prit quelques-unes ; elle lut et annota des manuscrits de trente mille lignes et plus, pour des concours. Le courage redoublé par la dure nécessité, elle restait joyeuse et confiante.... Son troisième enfant naquit.... Elle portait des robes usées, des chaussures fatiguées. Elle continuait bravement son rude apprentissage de l'existence. Elle avait enfoui au fond d'un tiroir un roman écrit durant la première année de son mariage : Avant l'Amour ; elle le revoit, le porte à un éditeur qui le refuse sans même le lire. Tout de même, Mme Adam, à qui il avait été remis, le publie dans la Nouvelle Revue ; il paraît en librairie, mais passe inaperçu.... Elle ne désespère pas. Le Temps prend son second roman, la Rançon, mais le public ne l'achète pas plus que le premier. Courageusement, elle dépose

Figure 2.18 Marcelle Tinayre with her daughter. *La Vie Heureuse* (March 1903). © Bibliothèque Marguerite Durand/Roger-Viollet.

about this image reveals an expertly staged, carefully crafted symmetry. The subtitles on either side of the image: "Her Home," "Her Novels" balance each other perfectly. Their equivalence is paramount: the equal emphasis allotted to these potentially competing elements of her life, house and novels, ensured her celebrated place in the magazine. The image itself is circular, and its shape makes it look as if we had peered through a peephole to catch a glimpse of their life *en medias res*. A pen-and-ink floral pattern surrounds the circular photo—that art nouveau framework that sets the image apart and elevates it, like the museum's red rope. In this case, the flowers appear to be blooming out of this domestic-professional arrangement, gorgeous proof of its proliferating fruitfulness, reconfirmed by the fact that Tinayre's daughter clutches a baby doll herself, repeating, then, the maternal role modeled by her mother.

In combining the prevailing iconography of both magazines, this image brings the workspace vividly into dialogue with the domestic feminine life. As such it is suggestive of a much longer, more complex narrative than the simple equation described by the caption, which insistently continues the work of the photograph, as if still uncertain of its blatant power: "Between the started manuscript and the child to whom she gives her hand," it reads, "Madame Tinayre—even while composing wonderful books—has maintained the very spirit of feminine life—a tender heart, love for little ones, the taste for decorating her home."[52] In its staged equilibrium, the photograph itself begins to announce the challenges that lie ahead for the *femme moderne*: the questions of work-life balance that are only vaguely hinted at through Tinayre's somewhat awkward, and surely untenable, pose.[53] Within *La Vie Heureuse*'s perfectly constructed page layout, on the other hand, there is no room for uncertainty. Instead, we can clearly see all the magazine's mechanisms—celebrity At Home photograph, elegant art nouveau frame, explicit text—doing the imaginative work of Belle Epoque literary feminism, and launching a new fantasy of female success. This was the woman writer as *femme moderne*: novels and children, work and home in beautiful synchronicity, she was truly queen of the interior—her once-tainted reputation a distant memory—with her desk chair as her new throne.

# CHAPTER 3
# THE "ORIENTAL" AUTHORESS
*Myriam Harry and Lucie Delarue-Mardrus*

FOR the first three years or so of their existence, *Femina* and *La Vie Heureuse* almost always pictured women writers through the domestic images I explored in the previous chapter. They stayed insistently on message, demonstrating how this modern figure could succeed, seemingly without having to alter anything else about her lifestyle. Around 1904, however, two new figures, Myriam Harry and Lucie Delarue-Mardrus, emerged as favored media darlings of the women's press, and the iconography associated with the woman writer expanded in accordance with another visual trope tightly linked to female celebrity during this time: the exotic Orient.[1]

Born in Jerusalem to European parents, Harry grew up in Ottoman Palestine before moving to Vienna as an adolescent, finally ending up in Paris.[2] Her 1903 autobiographical novel *La conquête de Jérusalem* (and its sequels) captured the attention of a French audience already captivated by the Orient and further seduced by the grain of authenticity Harry's true-life experience promised.[3] This novel was the partial impetus for the first Vie Heureuse literary prize, which she was awarded once it became clear that she would be excluded from the Prix Goncourt because of her sex.[4] Delarue-Mardrus, on the other hand, was the young wife of the Egyptian doctor Joseph-Charles Mardrus, who was celebrated for his translation of the *Arabian Nights* into French.[5] His savvy negotiations of Parisian literary circles ensured Delarue-Mardrus's quick rise to fame, especially after the publication of her third collection of poetry, *Horizons*, in 1904, after which he circulated photographs of her visit to Tunisia. While she is remembered chiefly through her affiliation with "Sapho 1900" and the lesbian subculture of the Belle Epoque, remarkably (if not surprisingly), no sign of this facet of her identity is visible in the women's press.[6]

Images of both Harry and Delarue-Mardrus mapped on to an orientalized and theatricalized aesthetic made popular through actresses like Sarah Bernhardt, herself a staple of both publications.[7] Like Bernhardt and Cléo de Mérode, Harry and Delarue-Mardrus were women celebrated in part for their performance of otherness through photographic spectacle.[8] These images ensured their success, demonstrating the potency of this early model of celebrity in a domain that has remained almost entirely out of the critical spotlight. But Harry's and Delarue-Mardrus's costume changes are even more interesting when considered in light of what the magazines energetically refrained from suggesting about these potentially controversial women. As Emily Apter has shown, orientalism functioned "as a theatrical conceit in turn-of-the-century feminist performance."[9] During this time, women were "empowered or accorded sexual license through association with the dominatrix characterologies attached to exemplary princesses, queens, seductresses, or women leaders of the East" (139). In the pages of *Femina* and *La Vie Heureuse*, on the other hand, the seductive powers and associations of the East were harnessed in ways that needed always to keep the threat of such unconventional femininity at bay, in keeping with efforts to present the woman writer as a figure to be admired and imitated. The magazines, I argue, sought to extract from orientalism its attention-grabbing visual appeal while denying the implicit sexual undertones of these acts of cultural transvestism through an insistence on the writers' bourgeois familiarity. Harry's and, to a lesser extent, Delarue-Mardrus's, free-spirited, adventurous personalities and exotic origins were cautiously balanced by repeated reminders that the exotic Orient served as a costume that could be put on and taken off, one of many landscapes these writers inhabited. At the same time, the magazines exploited the pleasing trope of orientalized otherness to diffuse the potentially troubling aspects of these women writers' challenges to gender norms, masking in this way the traditional threats associated with the woman writer.

### *Becoming Parisian: Myriam Harry*

Harry appears on a remarkable cover of *La Vie Heureuse* from April 1904, sporting an elaborate Chinese costume: every part of her is adorned, from the three-corner hat on her head, replete with hanging tassels, to the strands of beads that hang over her silk flowered robe, to the sinuous faux finger nails she displays on her right hand, and the figurine of a similarly clad Chinese woman she holds in her left hand (Fig. 3.1). The photograph is brought into stark relief by the dramatic orange background on which it sits—the color in itself both a signal of the exotic culture represented within and a preview of color photography, still in its early phases. Inside the magazine, four contrasting images dominate a one-page article on the author: in the photograph stretched above the title ("Madame Myriam Harry"), Harry is shown in Saigon, clad in white European clothes (although white is described as the "the universal costume of the country"), driving an English carriage for a morning promenade;

**Figure 3.1** Myriam Harry in oriental garb on the cover of *La Vie Heureuse* (April 1904). © Bibliothèque Marguerite Durand/Roger-Viollet.

a Malaysian peasant, also dressed in white, sits behind, holding a parasol over her (Fig. 3.2). Their parallel luminous figures are linked by the white of the parasol and draw the eye to the power structure embedded in their perfectly colonial relationship of French traveler to *indigène*. Then, on the bottom left of the page, the full image from the cover appears, the caption offering additional details that were obscured by the black-and-white photography: we learn that the tunic is light blue and that Harry's "theatrical hair style" is made of red satin incrusted with fragments of mirrors. Just to the upper right of that image, Harry is shown as a baby in her mother's arms, a photograph taken, we are told, in an Armenian convent in Jerusalem, the city where Harry was born. And finally, on the bottom right, perfectly symmetrical with the image of Harry in Chinese garb, the final photograph depicts Harry "having become Parisian" (*devenue parisienne*). This is the "real" Harry, we are meant to believe, Harry the writer. Dressed in the conservative apparel of the upper bourgeoisie, she is described as contributing to the *Journal*, publishing with Calmann-Lévy, and working on a new novel about the island of Ceylon.

What are we to make of this dizzying array of images, each one offering another captivating but alternative version of the exoticized author? On the one hand, photographs of Myriam Harry as a *bonne bourgeoise* in the women's press seemed to secure her ability to don the other looks with impunity. An article announcing Harry's receipt of the Prix Vie Heureuse in 1905, for example, juxtaposed an image of her in a veil with one in bourgeois attire (Fig. 3.3). The first photograph offers an alluring image "in oriental costume"; the second, her "true" domestic self.[10] The irony, of course, is that Harry was born and raised in Jerusalem. Her identity as Parisian *bonne bourgeoise* was just as artificial as her exoticized Asian performance—if not more so. The careful balance between fantasy and reality suggested by these alternating images was of course fundamental to these magazines' success: readers must at once admire women like Harry, one of the "brilliant destinies" depicted, and identify with them, in order to believe on some level that if they were to buy the expensive creams and corsets advertised by the magazines, they themselves could achieve some version of such good fortune.

But the depiction of Harry draws on several other narratives as well, her attraction connected somehow to the natural fluidity of her identity—her ability to perform multiple iterations of Belle Epoque femininity.

A SAIGON, dans les allées du jardin botanique, Mme Myriam Harry conduit sa charrette anglaise. Elle est vêtue de blanc, selon la coutume universelle du pays. Le canotier blanc et le choix de la voiture indiquent la sortie matinale. Un groom malais élève au-dessus de sa maîtresse un parasol japonais, et deux chiens chinois, d'une race très rare, deux humanités se combattaient, et leur lutte faisait la grandeur nouvelle du tableau. Mais le style gardait sa qualité première : la perfection de l'image.

## Madame Myriam Harry

IL Y A QUELQUES ANNÉES, ce nom parut sur un recueil de nouvelles : pages singulières, à sentiments directs, à silhouettes étincelantes, sentant le sable et le désert. En 1900, un nouveau livre évoquait, à Saigon, un menu peuple fatot et jaune. Il y a quelques jours enfin, paraissait la Conquête de Jérusalem. Hélie Jamain aimait et mourait dans la cité sépulcrale. Au loin les montagnes de Moab paraissaient comme le signe d'une vie libre et naturelle. Deux esprits, deux humanités se combattaient, et leur lutte faisait la grandeur nouvelle du tableau. Mais le style gardait sa qualité première : la perfection de l'image.

IL NAQUIT A JÉRUSALEM, de sangs divers et de races complexes, une petite fille dont Mme Myriam Harry a plusieurs fois dit l'histoire, et qui lui ressemble. Elle parlait alors l'allemand, qu'elle mêlait d'arabe ; en se promenant avec sa nourrice, elle avait aussi dérobé des mots grecs, russes, italiens, qui lui faisaient un langage merveilleux et bariolé. A treize ans, elle écrivit un roman, qui fut publié dans un grand journal allemand. Elle en publia encore d'autres qui étaient tout pleins de fureurs et de passion, et c'était une petite fille extrêmement intelligente. Puis elle se mit à écrire en anglais. Elle vint à Paris, et ne voulut plus savoir que le français. Elle étudia passionnément le mécanisme et l'esprit de notre langue. Il y eut alors dans sa vie un moment tout à fait étrange. Elle se trouva n'avoir plus de langage propre : l'anglais et l'allemand effacés bien loin derrière elle, et le français, encore rebelle et mal assoupli, et qu'elle ne pouvait pas manier. Il fallut qu'elle cessât d'écrire.

Ceci dura cinq ans. Entre temps, elle suivait les cours de l'école des Hautes Études à la Sorbonne, et ceux des Langues orientales. Elle étudiait l'archéologie de la Palestine. Elle savait l'araméen et le nabatéen. Puis elle voyagea. Connaissant déjà l'Europe et la Méditerranée, elle parcourut l'Extrême-Orient. Elle vécut à Saigon. Elle poussa jusqu'à Port-Arthur. Revenue en France, sans relations littéraires, le hasard d'une nuit de Noël lui fit publier un conte sur Bethléem. Et tout de suite il parut qu'elle écrivait admirablement. Un volume de nouvelles et deux romans l'ont fait connaître. C'est une jeune femme, blonde avec des cheveux crépelés, le teint vif et les yeux clairs ; un mélange extraordinaire, l'air d'une fille du Rhin baptisée dans le Jourdain ; une vivacité, une curiosité qui sont les signes de l'écrivain ; un langage chantant et passionné, où roulent tous les accents, et qui bouleverse de mille sentiments opposés le visage mobile qui le reflète. Tout cela fait un être unique, parisien et sauvage, violemment antiféministe, mais surtout prodigieusement vivant. Son dernier livre, la Conquête de Jérusalem, est un hymne à la vie : la vie souveraine, telle que des tombeaux de Jérusalem, on l'imagine dans le libre désert ; la vie avec sa beauté naturelle et la splendeur de sa force. Cette liberté magnifique fait un écrivain précis et coloré, passionné et fort, comme on n'en a point vu depuis Maupassant.

MME MYRIAM HARRY enfant, sur les genoux de sa mère. La photographie a été faite au couvent arménien de Jérusalem.

LE COSTUME EST CHINOIS, et formé d'une tunique bleu pâle, sur une autre robe d'une soie plus foncée. La coiffure de théâtre est de satin rouge incrusté de fragments de miroirs.

DEVENUE PARISIENNE, Mme Myriam Harry collabore maintenant au Journal, publie des livres chez Calmann-Lévy, et en prépare un sur l'île de Ceylan.

**Figure 3.2** "Madame Myriam Harry," *La Vie Heureuse* (April 1904). © Bibliothèque Marguerite Durand/Roger-Viollet.

# LE PRIX VIE HEUREUSE POUR 1904

## LE JURY

NOS LECTRICES connaissent déjà Mme Myriam Harry, à qui a été attribué le prix de la Vie Heureuse. Elles savent que cette jeune femme, blonde avec des yeux bleus, par un de ces destins qui se plaisent parfois à composer un écrivain, est née à Jérusalem, a étudié l'araméen en Sorbonne, et a parcouru l'Extrême-Orient. L'histoire de son langage, qui est le français le plus pur, n'est guère moins singulière : enfant, elle parlait un mélange d'anglais, d'allemand et de la langue de sa nourrice, qui était une

MME MYRIAM HARRY
*En costume oriental.*

TOUS LES MEMBRES du Jury de la *Vie Heureuse* présents à Paris avaient eu à cœur d'assister à cette importante séance où le prix de cinq mille francs devait être décerné. Et l'on fut exact. Dès trois heures, le salon de la Comtesse de Noailles se remplissait de l'élégant aréopage qui siégeait en cercle sans préoccupation d'âge ou de préséance. Vraiment on se sentait dans une atmosphère de cordialité qui fait le plus grand honneur aux lettres — et aux femmes.

La Comtesse Mathieu de Noailles, encore assez souffrante, prie Mme Dieulafoy de la remplacer aujourd'hui et de diriger les débats à sa place. Mme Dieulafoy déclare aussitôt la séance ouverte et donne lecture de l'ordre du jour. On discute quelques projets de modification aux statuts proposés par des membres absents qui n'ont pu prendre part aux votes antérieurs. A l'unanimité on décide que le Bureau ne sera pas rééligible chaque année, mais tous les trois ans seulement afin de permettre à chacun des membres de la Compagnie d'occuper tour à tour ces fonctions et d'y apporter plus spécialement ses lumières. On convient également que le vote par correspondance sera admis, mais seulement pour les membres qui auront assisté au moins à six séances durant l'année révolue, et de cette façon auront pu se tenir au courant des travaux et des lectures qui feront l'objet de ces réunions mensuelles.

On adopte ensuite le règlement intérieur, très sagement élaboré, et l'on arrive enfin au vote principal, le plus émouvant, celui du Prix. Un grand nombre de volumes a été examiné par chacune des « auteuresses » présentes, et l'on est d'accord pour reconnaître que la floraison des œuvres féminines a été particulièrement brillante ces douze derniers mois. Il est donc tout à fait à propos d'attribuer pour la première fois à un livre de femme le prix que la Maison Hachette vient de fonder.

Le silence se fait. Le vote est secret, et chacune de nous griffonne des lignes sur un petit bout de papier. On passe la corbeille. La Comtesse de Noailles se rapproche du bureau pour dépouiller le scrutin. Et un nom revient, presque toujours le même, à chaque bulletin dé-

## LA LAURÉATE

bédouine. A quatorze ans, elle composait des romans en allemand ; elle en fit d'autres en anglais, avant de découvrir le français qui est devenu son vrai et parfait moyen d'expression. Elle a publié dans notre langue trois volumes, dont le dernier, la Conquête de Jérusalem, met en scène les forces de la vie en lutte avec l'esprit de discipline, de crainte et de restriction. Et le livre lui-même, animé d'un beau ciel et de la perspective infinie du désert, est comme un hymne au libre élan de la vie.

ployé : Myriam Harry, la Conquête de Jérusalem. Sur 21 votes exprimés — dont 5 par correspondance — 17 sont allés à Mme Myriam Harry, 2 aux *Ailes brisées* de Mme Jacques Fréhel, et 2 à *l'Ombre de la maison* de Mme Ivan Strannik.

Mme Myriam Harry est proclamée pour cette année lauréate du Prix de la *Vie Heureuse*. La plupart des membres présents lui envoient leurs compliments.

Une adresse de félicitation est aussi votée à la Maison Hachette qui a si généreusement renouvelé la tradition des Mécènes et qui, en outre, ajoute à ses largesses pour l'année prochaine la publication à ses frais d'un manuscrit de la Compagnie aura à choisir parmi ceux qui lui seront adressés.

Enfin on remercie de grand cœur et par acclamation Mme Dieulafoy qui, avec une courtoisie et une logique admirables, a conduit les débats, parfois un peu mouvementés, et ne les a pas laissés un seul instant s'égarer dans les digressions inutiles.

Il serait injuste de ne pas citer quelques-uns des volumes les plus remarqués à la suite des œuvres de grande valeur dont il a déjà été fait mention. C'est d'abord le *Choix de la vie*, cette admirable œuvre d'art due à la plume de Mme Georgette Leblanc ; puis *Sibylle-Femme*, de Mme René Tony d'Ulmès ; *Terres de lumière* de Mlle Yvonne Vernon ; enfin deux ouvrages de poésie de deux jeunes filles qui portent des noms célèbres : *Des héros et des Dieux*, par Mlle Nicolette Hennique, et *Flammes de la vie*, par Mlle Jeanne Sienckiewicz.

Les mains se tendent et se serrent. On se sépare. Voilà du bon féminisme, et nous sommes loin du temps où chaque fois qu'une femme prenait la plume, le pinceau ou l'ébauchoir et offrait au public le fruit de ses efforts, il ne manquait pas de se trouver quelqu'un pour insinuer spirituellement : « Ce n'est pas mal, mais par qui donc l'a-t-elle fait faire ? »

Ces propos ne se tiennent plus maintenant que dans les provinces les plus reculées.

JEAN BERTHEROY.

MME MYRIAM HARRY,
*Qui a obtenu le Prix Vie Heureuse pour son volume* la Conquête de Jérusalem.

C'EST chez Mme la Comtesse Mathieu de Noailles qu'a eu lieu la réunion où a été décerné le prix de la Vie Heureuse. A l'extrême-gauche, de profil perdu, Mme Marni, puis Mme A. Daulet ; la Comtesse de Noailles assise, cause avec la Baronne de Pierrebourg en corsage clair ; Mme Daniel Lesueur, Marcelle Tynaire, Arvède Barine ; au premier plan, près de la table, Mme Judith Gautier puis Mmes Dieulafoy, de Broutelles.

**Figure 3.3** An article announcing Myriam Harry's award of the first Prix Vie Heureuse, later to become the Prix Femina. *La Vie Heureuse* (March 1905).

As the "coiffure de théâtre" suggests, the layout of the 1904 piece mimics the popular photo spreads of actresses frequently featured in the magazine, often clad in costumes from their various productions. Harry, the article seems to propose, is just another sort of actress, a European playing with more exotic identities. The article acknowledges her complex and fascinating identity, that of "a daughter of the Rhine baptized in the Jordan River," who has traveled through several languages before conquering French; a woman at last both "wild and Parisian."[11] Her actual Middle Eastern ties are offered as a fascinating but distant detail that makes her better able to perform exotic otherness as she gallivants in Far-Eastern lands. In addition to the references to China and Vietnam within the article, the facing article is entitled "Coréens et Coréennes." The East functions here as a generic pole of otherness—China, Vietnam, Korea—their geographic multiplicity elides the specificity of each individual location, and signals nothing more than a shared landscape for uninhibited exploration and orientalizing mimicry that always inevitably reinforces existing power structures.[12] We see this trope of playful European mimicry throughout the magazines: in an article on Pierre Loti's elaborate "Chinese party," where actual Chinese emissaries found themselves appearing "less Chinese" than the French guests;[13] in images of Miss Alice Roosevelt visiting Japan, her gaze off in the distance as Japanese royalty look up to her;[14] in the endless features on the famous artist Sada Yacca of Japan (and the fashion trends she inspired); and in rapturous descriptions of Moroccan beauty (Fig. 3.4).

There is, however, another layer to these representations of the woman writer in oriental costume, in which the Orient serves as a filter that at once masks gender subversion and makes it more powerful. Within the pages of *Femina* and *La Vie Heureuse*, part of the pleasure of these images of white women in costume, I would suggest, lay in the apparent removal of Western gender hierarchies from the orientalizing performance. The "European" woman in costume suffers none of the humiliations of the non-Western world (she is never dressed, for example, as part of the harem). Rather, her oriental adornments indirectly applaud women's more powerful roles in Western civilization. In a 1907 *La Vie Heureuse* article describing Harry's travels to Tunisia, Harry is pictured in a striking pose behind a billowing veil, her eyes peering out above a dark cloth, her eyebrows joined in a dark double arch that is repeated in

**Figure 3.4** "A Type of Moroccan Beauty." *Femina* (October 15, 1907). The caption describes her as "of such admirable purity and delicacy that she could take part in the International Beauty Contest with a reasonable chance of success."

the graphic frame of the photo (Fig. 3.5). Despite the dramatic pose and the reference to the strictures of Islamic law in the caption, Harry's gesture is one of liberty rather than submission; her naked arm gently rests on the grate behind her, and her exposed flesh lies in stark contrast to the reams of fabric that shield the rest of her from view. We see this same casualness with respect to Muslim headgear throughout the magazines, in multiple images of Arab women wearing alluring, gauzy coverings over their faces.[15] The 1904 image of veiled Harry "in oriental costume" is in fact nearly identical to a picture that accompanied a 1903 short story by G. Dorys in *La Vie Heureuse*. That image, in turn, matches those featured in a four-page article on Turkish women in the same issue (Fig. 3.6). Entitled "Princesses, Grandes Dames, Bourgeoises," it described

**Figure 3.5** Myriam Harry "veiled as Islamic law requires." *La Vie Heureuse* (September 1907). © Bibliothèque Marguerite Durand/Roger-Viollet.

**Figure 3.6** A story on Turkish women, *La Vie Heureuse* (April 1903).

one such veil "of a light silk that beautifies more than it hides." The very fact of these photographs' existence becomes in itself a subversion of the subjugation the veil should signify, proof of the different valence it was meant to have in this altered context. Under a smaller image of a Turkish woman covered by another sheer silk facial wrap, the caption reads: "With the passing of time, the strictest proscriptions are alleviated, and, despite the laws of the Koran, this Turkish grand dame poses in a veil for the photographer, which only adds to the mystery of her dark eyes."[16] In other words, the veil is but an accessory, a sign of femininity and mystery being actively harnessed and deployed. It is thus also, by definition, a metonym for the Orient itself.[17]

As if to prove a point, underneath the image of her, fully cloaked, Myriam Harry is pictured with her dark-skinned servants in two photos that confirm the joint fact of her freedom and European power in startling explicitness. In one of them, "Zorrah" serves her tea, and in the other, a nameless "little Negress, pretty and bright" is described as playing with her "like a domestic animal."[18] In addition to reinforcing Harry's powerful position, these images deter the reader from focusing on the sexual suggestiveness of Harry slipping out of her full body covering while confined haremlike behind the grated wall. The domestic images and their captions frame Harry in a "safe" and familiar environment: one of female domesticity.

In these photo spreads, West dramatically confronts East, in service, I would propose, of the woman writer's power and authority.[19] As the accompanying article makes clear, the Orient serves as Harry's muse—as it did for so many of her European peers—feeding her reveries, inspiring her next novel. If she is at home here, it is not as a native but rather as a colonizer and thus a figure associated with power and dominance. Through this very different set of "charming juxtapositions" than the ones in the domestic iconography of the woman writer, the magazine demonstrates the power of the French woman through the unambiguous fact of her opposition to the colonial woman. Indeed, the thinking French woman depicted in these pages, a powerful and potentially subversive figure of modernity, is removed from her traditional opposition to the French man whose role she always implicitly threatens to usurp, thus drawing attention away from her subversion of traditional gender roles. The importance of this displacement becomes clear in the text of the magazine, as Myriam Harry, *devenue parisienne*, is described as "violently antifeminist," despite the fact that she is also portrayed as courageous, independent, free-spirited and a prolific and talented writer—a partner to her husband, rather than a helpmeet.[20] The fact of her unconventionally feminine power can be masked, just as she herself is, through its exotic dislocation. Cultural subversion, it seems, is more easily accepted than gender subversion—and unlike the latter, in itself a desirable enterprise.

The European woman visiting the East, then, is undeniably and joyfully free, and her visual representation here adds another dimension to the conservative feminism of the women's press. In Myriam Harry, the complex stance of the woman writer reflects not only ambivalence surrounding French gender roles, but also that surrounding its complex relationship with the Orient. Rather than a source of anxiety, the relationship between France and the Orient is—at least on its surface—a pleasurable, desiring one that upholds the magazines' objectives of downplaying the threat of shifting gender roles. In describing French women's donning of the veil in the nineteenth century, Marni Kessler writes that "the veiled Parisian woman's face became a site for several levels of imperial mastery, for not only was her appearance a reminder of the inhibitions imposed on colonial women, but it also represented her own status as a 'colonized' being within France" (102). Decades later, and in a different visual context, Harry's veil signifies something more ambivalent: in addition to demonstrating European superiority over the colonial woman, it reminds both of Harry's femininity and of her freedom to choose that role—to choose, in a sense, her 'colonized' status. Compared to the women of Vietnam and Tunisia, Turkey and Korea, the *bonne bourgeoise* is a figure of power and authority; at the same time, through her association with the Orient, itself highly feminized, she emphasizes her own femininity. The powerful nature of the woman writer is normalized through her opposition to the passive Orient, while at the same time, her willingness to veil herself reminds that she has not entirely rejected femininity either, even in some of its most troubling dimensions. Indeed, as in the graphic surrounding "Daniel Lesueur, woman of yesterday and today," a certain dissonance comes through in these images and their accompanying text, one that likely only fueled Harry's popularity.

## Stranger in a Strange Land: Lucie Delarue-Mardrus

Harry's dear friend Lucie Delarue-Mardrus offers a slightly more complex case, the contradictions of which were also likely factors in her popularity. She was a favorite of both magazines, initially depicted as a mysterious and bold adventurer, accompanying her husband on his travels and producing exceptional poetry. In her memoirs, she writes of how the pictures her husband took of her made her into a literary sensation even as she remained thousands of miles from the Parisian literary epicenter: "I can say that, well before my novels, I owe the beginning of my fame to that collection of pictures on horseback and on camels, of silhouettes under cork trees and in the Sahara, and of portraits juxtaposed against white cityscapes or surrounded by Arab faces."[21] These unfamiliar images "of a Parisian woman off so far away," notes Delarue-Mardrus, were in high demand, and both *Femina* and *La Vie Heureuse* seemed eager to capitalize on the visual intrigue of this exotic and talented new figure on the literary scene.

But their efforts to impose the same feminized narrative on Delarue-Mardrus, or to offer any sort of consistent narrative at all, seem forced; the striking differences among images only call attention to the young writer's performance, making it difficult to identify the "real" Delarue-Mardrus. Adding to the confusion is the question of Delarue-Mardrus's own role in the manipulation and circulation of her image: in the photographs, she appears by turns complacent, ill at ease, smug or purposefully vacant in expression: almost inviting the viewer to interpret her very inscrutability. The fact that her domineering husband, a man sometimes referred to as "Oeil" (Eye), took them, further complicates our understanding of these images meant to launch a woman's lucrative literary career.

Delarue-Mardrus is first introduced in *Femina* in 1905 as "the young wife of Dr. Mardrus" in a demure photograph, her chin resting gently on fingers, above a selection of her verse (Fig. 3.7).[22] The youthful poet, coiffed in what would be her distinctive hairstyle, offers an expression that appears both neutral and guarded. Seven months later, in October, the same demure guise—and hairstyle—appear in the exact same layout, only this time she is cloaked in a tunic, perched on what seem to be Roman ruins, bearing a slightly less complacent expression in her eyes; she looks, in fact, ill at ease, uncomfortable, like a child forced to pose for the camera, waiting for the moment to pass (Fig. 3.8). Her new volume of poetry, the caption suggests, "evoked new emotions in Madame Delarue-Mardrus's

Mme LUCIE DELARUE-MARDRUS.
*La jeune femme du D<sup>r</sup> Mardrus, le traducteur des « Mille et Une Nuits », vient de publier un nouveau recueil, Les Horizons, où s'affirment définitivement les qualités lyriques qui caractérisent son beau talent.*

## POÉSIES DE FEMMES

A PROPOS D'UN NOUVEAU VOLUME D'UNE JEUNE FEMME POÈTE. — DEUX POÉSIES EXTRAITES DES HORIZONS DE M<sup>me</sup> DELARUE-MARDRUS. — QUELQUES VERS INÉDITS DE M<sup>me</sup> LA BARONNE DE ZUYLEN DE NYEVELT ET DE M<sup>me</sup> AMÉLIE MESUREUR.

\* \* \*

### PRÉSAGE.

Dans l'été rembruni du finissant mois d'août,
L'automne déjà flotte avec un peu de brume,
Et, dès aujourd'hui, mêle à l'impérial goût
Des roses, son austère et dolente amertume...

Reviens-nous une fois encor, belle saison,
Seule saison des inconsolables natures !
Tu berceras tragiquement sur l'horizon
Ton agonie en flamme et tes noires ramures,

Et nous irons asseoir notre grave bonheur
Dans le soleil taché d'ombre où tu nous accueilles,
Pour entendre tomber au fond de notre cœur
La mort blonde, dansante et douce de tes feuilles.

Lucie Delarue-Mardrus.

### LES CORBEAUX VOLAIENT EN CRIANT.

« ... Et les corbeaux volaient en criant sous la lune... »
L'infini d'une phrase évoque tout le Nord,
Gouffres -les bleus glaciers où s'attarde la mort
Et cimes d'argent froid que la bise importune.

Les troncs d'arbres flétris posent leur tache brune
Dans la neige, crissant et craquant sous les pas,
Le ciel vide s'étend comme un gris canevas,
« ... Et les corbeaux volaient, en criant, sous la lune... »

Les fjords aux phoques lourds et glissants, l'azur froid
Des sommets, et les champs que la montagne écrase,
Tout cela, grâce au bref cliquetis d'une phrase
Que je lis au hasard, dans le jour qui décroît.

...Et je voudrais m'enfuir vers le Nord simple et rude,
Vers les froids que sillonne un éclair de patins,
Car, loin des rives d'or et des vergers latins,
On y savoure en paix l'altière solitude.

Près des monts, revêtus de leurs brillants linceuls,
Où l'on vient à pas lents se soumettre et se taire,
O Nord ! enseigne-nous ta force volontaire
Et le calme de ceux qui savent chanter seuls,

De ceux que n'émeut pas la tristesse commune
De n'être point aimés, ni connus, ni compris
Et passent sans regrets sous le ciel bas et gris
Où les corbeaux joyeux vont criant vers la lune.

H. de Zuylen de Nyevelt.

### D'ÉTÉ.

Le jardin vague et vert contre la vitre aqueuse
Y figure un immense et trouble aquarium
Qui contient l'océan du ciel ; et l'onduleuse
Frondaison où s'étoile un vif géranium
Y berce des rameaux avec toutes leurs ombres
Au rythme submergé des madrépores sombres.

Prise par l'attirante illusion des eaux,
Je poserai mon front sur la vitre marine
Et serai la sirène enroulée aux coraux
Noués par mille bras à sa pâle poitrine,

Qui, prisonnière, rêve à la félicité
D'avoir royalement troué l'immensité,
Pour surgir au soleil couchant qu'elle salue,
D'un signe de sa tête humide et chevelue.

Lucie Delarue-Mardrus.

### PETITE, PRENDS GARDE A TON CŒUR !

Les grands yeux sont d'un bleu céleste,
Profonds et purs comme les cieux ;
D'un bleu tendre et délicieux
Avec un regard, je l'atteste,
Plus doux que nul n'en a rêvé,
Et dont le souvenir vous reste
Dans le cœur, à jamais gravé.

La fleur du lin ni la pervenche,
Ni l'humble bleuet qui se penche
N'ont leur ineffable couleur.
C'est le pâle azur du ciel même.
Sans le vouloir, avec candeur,
Ils semblent dire : je vous aime.
— Petite, prends garde à ton cœur !

La paupière qui les protège,
Transparente, est rose et de neige
Voilant leur éclat séducteur.
Langage des yeux touche l'âme,
Il est papillon et toi fleur.
L'amour est prompt comme une flamme,
— Petite, prends garde à ton cœur !

Amélie Mesureur.

101

**Figure 3.7** Women's poetry, featuring Lucie Delarue-Mardrus. *Femina* (March 1, 1905).

# Poésies de M^ME Lucie Delarue-Mardrus

M^me LUCIE DELARUE-MARDRUS.

*M^me DELARUE-MARDRUS RENTRE A PARIS APRÈS UN VOYAGE EN ORIENT ET EN RAPPORTE UN VOLUME DE POÉSIES.*

※ ※ ※

Soucieuse de la beauté des lignes et de l'harmonie des formes, M^me Lucie Delarue-Mardrus est une des poétesses les plus éloquentes de notre époque. Les lectrices de *Femina* déjà connaissent son précieux talent et son inspiration émue.
Partie en Afrique avec M. le Docteur J. C. Mardrus, son mari, orientaliste fameux qui traduisit les *Mille et une Nuits*, elle connut pour la première fois cet Orient qu'elle pressentait. Mais la grandeur des ruines et des cités mortes, l'apparition soudaine à ses yeux éblouis de tant de paysages nouveaux, suscita dans l'âme ardente de M^me Mardrus des émotions nouvelles.

### Brise.

Au soleil d'aujourd'hui, le vent qui vient de terre
Rebrousse doucement la mer et la moisson.
La Méditerranée est lourde du mystère
Des couleurs; elle brille et vit comme un poisson,
Comme, étalée au cœur des caps, une méduse
Qui se rétracte un peu sur la roche qu'elle use
Et prolonge le bleu de ses bras assoupis
Jusqu'au milieu de l'or terrien des épis.

Et, mitoyenne, seule et grande, tu te poses
Entre les horizons mêmement ondulés,
Pour, debout sur la houle identique des choses,
Goûter le sel des eaux et le sucre des blés.

### Soir Punique.

Mes mains et mon esprit te cherchent à tâtons
Devant la mer qui vit ta grandeur et ta perte,
Ville qui dors sous l'orge verte
Et la parole de Caton !

L'ombre éternelle tourne autour des mêmes cimes :
Seule, je viens m'asseoir au milieu des cactus,
Sur la ruine des ruines,
Pour pleurer comme Marius.

Or, la nuit tombe. Un ciel orageux échelonne
Ses nuages le long des quatre horizons clairs,
Et, tandis que le flot roule encor des colonnes,
Le couchant reconstruit Carthage sur la mer.

### Utique.

Le bonheur monotone et grave de l'espace
Nous laissa souvent seuls avec les horizons
Où rôdait au couchant notre âme jamais lasse
De voir le beau soleil sombrer dans les moissons.

Le soir nous attirait vers les plaines d'Utique
Où les blés infinis se mouraient de chaleur,
Où, le long des sentiers, le sol trois fois antique
Ne nourrissait plus rien que des chardons en fleur.

Et, quand la nuit subite avait éteint la plaine,
En rentrant on voyait dans le faux poivrier
Qui longe la maison solitaire, briller,
En face du couchant fini, la lune pleine...

### Cimetière.

Le cimetière avec sa flore d'abandon
Et le silence heureux de la mort musulmane
S'ouvre parmi l'odeur d'épices qui émane
De la belle Tunis, la ville d'amidon.

Ils ont clos pour jamais leurs yeux mélancoliques,
— Néant si simple sous la mousse ou les épis ! —
Tous ceux-là qui vivaient en rêvant, accroupis
Dans les plis éternels de leurs manteaux bibliques.

Sur leur vie et leur mort un immuable été
Plane, faisant du tout une seule momie...
— Je veux vivre comme eux et mourir, endormie
Dans le grand linceul blanc de la fatalité.

**Figure 3.8** Lucie Delarue-Mardrus and her poems, *Femina* (October 1, 1905).

passionate soul"; she is depicted as Dr. Mardrus's ingénue, naïve, "her eyes dazzled" by the exotic world around her, even if her assured poetry suggests a more mature voice. Several excerpts of her poems are included, without further commentary.[23] Indeed, there is a startling disjunction between the photograph, the poems, and the caption. Delarue-Mardrus's next appearance in the magazine is on the cover of the April 15, 1907 issue, in an elegant profile, in honor of her playing Sappho in her own play, *Phâon Victorieux* (Fig. 3.9). The magazine neglects to mention, of course, that the original title was "Sapho désespérée," changed for reasons of propriety.[24]

*La Vie Heureuse*, by contrast, proposed a rather different image of the writer during those same years. A feature story from September 1905 entitled "Madame Delarue-Mardrus aux Pays Arabes" offered the requisite juxtaposition of Delarue-Mardrus in "costume" with the real

**Figure 3.9** Lucie Delarue-Mardrus on the cover of *Femina* (April 15, 1907).

Delarue-Mardrus, but to an entirely different effect than the Harry images. At the top of the piece, two images of Delarue-Mardrus in Kroumirie, Tunisia, are balanced around the same delicate profile of her that would later appear on the *Femina* cover (Fig. 3.10a). But rather than appear in feminized oriental garb in the Kroumirie pictures, Delarue-Mardrus wears riding clothes that suggest a subversive autonomy; indeed, the feminine European Delarue-Mardrus of the center image contrasts with the mannish Delarue-Mardrus of the East. Instead of recalling the beautiful costume changes of Harry or Bernhardt, these images of the poet in pants call to mind another common feature of the women's press: eye-popping human interest stories on eccentric feminine identities, like "Les Cowgirls" from *Femina*, October 1906.[25] Taken out of context, the image on the right of the triptych, in which a cigarette hangs from a confident, almost smirking Delarue-Mardrus's mouth, signals as much New Woman as adventurous traveler. On the following page, Delarue-Mardrus is pictured in a traditional European dress, surrounded by dignitaries, but the central image shows her in pants once again, staring directly at the camera with a decidedly neutral expression (Fig. 3.10b).[26] Delarue-Mardrus's exotic costume changes, then, take her consistently into masculine and not typical orientalized attire, while her husband, notably, sports the loose skirts of Egyptian men in an accompanying photo.[27] In Delarue-Mardrus's case, the geographic displacement seems to allow a level of audacity that would be anathema to *La Vie Heureuse* in any other context. Within the text of the article, one senses the elusiveness of Delarue-Mardrus's identity: "she hates and scorns socializing (*le monde*)," notes the journalist; and her poetry is singular, difficult to classify, exhibiting "a strange energy."[28] Like the country she visits, Delarue-Mardrus is fundamentally other; her bourgeois clothing appears to be as much a costume as any of her other sartorial changes.

Images of Delarue-Mardrus again dominate an issue of *La Vie Heureuse* from July 1906. The cover shows Delarue-Mardrus perched on the hump of a camel (Fig. 3.11). As in the images of Harry, the Bedouin in the background and Delarue-Mardrus's veil-like cloak remind of where she is, as well as of the inherent power structures that put her in a position of authority, despite her femininity. The image also accentuates the gender-neutral aspect of certain colonial garb through the pleats of the Bedouin's tunic, his pants cut off by the frame of the photo. On the one

**Figure 3.10a (above) and b (over)** "Madame Delarue-Mardrus in Arab Lands." *La Vie Heureuse* (September 1905).

## MADAME DELARUE-MARDRUS 173

une noblesse naturelle y ajoute l'horreur de l'hypocrisie, et l'impatience du joug; la vie y gronde avec force ; et enfin, les nerfs de la femme, qui font tout le talent de tant d'autres, ajoutent à celle-là, mais ajoutent seulement des émois, des inquiétudes, le sentiment de la vie, des choses, la mélancolie des saisons d'hiver.

Cette année, *Horizons* a paru. C'est une nouveauté et un enchantement ; et c'est le plaisir que donnent ces livres de femmes, quand ils ne sont pas un simple déchet littéraire, d'y suivre une pensée nuancée, contrastée, qui se retrouve et qui se contredit. Ici, tous les thèmes des deux premiers livres reparaissent : le thème de la Normandie, le thème des saisons, le thème de la pitié, le thème de l'inquiétude, le thème de la peur de vieillir, le thème de l'amour des roses... Mais ils sont singulièrement assourdis et espacés. Ils ne font plus au fond du poème qu'un accompagnement et une réminiscence. Toute la symphonie est, au contraire, baignée d'un sentiment nouveau, calme, apaisé.

Les volets sont déjà fermés, la nuit est faite,
Et tendrement, autour de la lampe, s'apprête
L'heure de tous les soirs, ineffable et secrète.

Si douce ! où l'on se serre un peu l'un contre l'autre,
Pour lire ou pour causer un moment côte à côte,
Mais presque bas, craignant le bruit de la voix haute.

La bonne épaule s'offre au front câlin qui plie;
On sent qu'on va pleurer de tout ce que vous lie...
Ah ! comme on s'aime bien ! Quel charme que la vie !

Il fait calme, Il fait chaud. L'âme heureuse se laisse
Aller. La lampe est douce ainsi que son jour baisse.
— Cette heure est le bonheur et toute la sagesse.

DANS LES JARDINS de la Marsa, qui est le palais d'été d'un Bey de Tunis, Mme Delarue-Mardrus, causant avec la Princesse Nazéli.

une cloche ancienne. Le mouvement qui est ordinairement très ample, se ralentit quelquefois et n'est plus qu'un petit battement imperceptible à la manière de Verlaine. Cette crise de verlainisme qui reparaît quelquefois dans les rythmes et dans les émotions, est tout à fait curieuse. Elle marque cette nature, sans la caractériser. Mme Delarue-Mardrus a dit un jour qu'elle écrivait en mineur. Il serait intéressant d'avoir l'avis d'un Fauré ou d'un Reynaldo Hahn. A première audition, elle donne exactement l'effet contraire. La poésie n'est ni soupirée, ni modeste, ni défaillante, ni hésitante et retenue. Elle dit ce qu'elle veut dire, et elle le dit avec éloquence.

Par la nuit dramatique et le jardin amer,
Montant les toits, cognant aux murs, sifflant aux fentes,
La tempête d'octobre, obscure et véhémente,
Déferle avec l'éclat d'une mauvaise mer.

Pourquoi faut-il du fond de moi qu'une Gorgone
Ruée aux vitres, cherche à sortir, à sortir !
Pour ajouter l'horreur de sa face à l'automne,
Et hurler, et rouler au vent et s'en vêtir ?..

On n'est pas surpris du tout qu'elle chevauche les paysages de Kroumirie, vêtue en machacho ; on perçoit à travers le dédale et la délicatesse des sentiments féminins, une netteté, une ardeur, une pitié, qui sont le propre de son tempérament poétique. Il y a une étrange énergie dans des vers comme ceux-ci, qui célèbrent le printemps, et qui sont admirables :

Je reviendrais contente et la feuille à la bouche,
Avec une âme fraîche et simple d'animal.

Car c'è en soi, s'il doit en être de plus folles,
Rien ne vaudra la paix de ces ténèbres molles,
Et ce seul regard, et ces quelques paroles.

Cet apaisement a gagné l'esprit. De beaux vers calmes célèbrent un motif nouveau, singulièrement grave et solennel : le goût de la mort.

Notre course au fond d'elle s'est élancée
Comme un oiseau de l'œuf ouvert au creux du Nid,
Chiffre infini comme le rien est infini,
Seul le Zéro clorait la course commencée.

Mais nous fuyons le Rien, nous qui voulons le Tout.
Vertigineux, vers lui, de partie en partie,
Nous montons, sans vouloir envisager au bout
Le néant primitif d'où la Vie est sortie.

Archange, Ah ! laisse-moi sur la terre. J'ai peur !
A quoi bon m'être mise en route pour le nombre ?
Je n'atteindrai jamais le but. Je suis une ombre !
Le nombre est éternel, et je viens d'où l'on meurt.

Les thèmes anciens eux-mêmes sont transposés sur un mode plus égal et plus doux. Si la mort n'est pas haïssable, la vieillesse même s'accueille avec mélancolie, mais non avec colère. Et si quelque tourment de l'ancienne verdeur renaît, dans ce livre qui a, exactement la beauté de son titre, une strophe suffit à le calmer :

Et cela suffit sans doute
D'être une femme tendre au bras de son ami,
Qui marche dans la vie en rêvant à demi,
Sans plus sentir ses pieds ne meurtrir sur
les routes...

LES MONTAGNES DE LA KROUMIRIE...

Elle hait et méprise le monde : « Il ne vient rien de bon, dit-elle, que des sincérités, qu'on trouve dans un coin obscur des pauvres âmes. » Mais elle ne se retire pas dans l'orgueil de la montagne sereine. Il lui faut entendre, comme elle dit, « les cris ivres de la terre ». Elle aime la vie, le mouvement et la douleur de l'homme.

Elle a souvent comparé sa maison à un grand navire tourné vers Paris, et d'où elle entend, comme la mer, cette rumeur tragique que fait la Ville. La Ville demeure multiple et mystérieuse ! La poétesse paraît aux yeux, au fond de son appartement aux couleurs fines et aux meubles nets, appuyée contre une fenêtre, où les doigts de sa main quadruplement baguée tiennent soulevé le rideau. Et elle regarde au loin, elle écoute la souffrance des misérables qu'elle plaint, qu'elle aime et dont elle prédit quelque terrible retour. « Mon anxiété est sans cesse vers la ville. » Elle ressent vraiment la douleur humaine. Nulle non plus n'a dit, en vers plus poignants, l'horreur de vieillir.

Mais je vous voyais hâler votre jeunesse rose,
Hâtive, vous goûtier, avant que d'en mourir,
Au bonheur de souffrir et de faire souffrir,
Car votre chair n'était qu'une fugace rose.

Vous saviez bien qu'avec les fleurs longtemps écloses,
Et les jours longtemps clairs, qui sombrent dans le soir,
Qu'avec l'automne vient la douleur de déchoir,
Et que la Femme est brève entre toutes les choses....

Ces strophes, qui sont parmi les plus belles qu'on puisse lire, nous donnent peut-être l'intelligence de cette âme, si elle est toutefois déchiffrable. Il faut y placer d'abord la pitié et l'amour :

**Figure 3.11** Lucie Delarue-Mardrus on the cover of *La Vie Heureuse* (July 1906). © Bibliothèque Marguerite Durand/Roger-Viollet.

hand, the reams of fabric meant to cover Delarue-Mardrus from head to foot parallel the Muslim headdress worn by Myriam Harry in 1907; like Harry's, only part of Delarue-Mardrus's body is covered. On the other hand, however, in contrast to Harry's unclothed and decidedly feminine arm reaching out, Delarue-Mardrus's masculine pants and boots disrupt the cloak's full coverage; her wardrobe, like that of the Bedouin, is startlingly androgynous. A few pages later, the frontispiece of the same issue shows her at the helm of a ship's wheel in an enigmatic scene that disrupts the colonial visual discourse seemingly at play, while reminding us of her femininity (Fig. 3.12). Although her dress is described in the caption as Asian, its simple toga-like drapery, lacking the embroidered adornment seen in Fig. 3.8, also conjures ancient Greece. Indeed, she might be one of the Fates, as the enormous structure at which she stands suggests

**Figure 3.12** Lucie Delarue-Mardrus, frontispiece to *La Vie Heureuse* (July 1906). © Bibliothèque Marguerite Durand/Roger-Viollet.

that she steers a wheel of fortune rather than a ship. Such a mythological subtext is alluded to in the caption's description of her round bracelets as "prophetic" (*fatidiques*) as well as in her comparison to "one of Ariel's sisters." These vague allusions to an unsettling feminine power contradict the status of the photograph as amusing travelogue that was suggested by the cover shot of Delarue-Mardrus on a camel. The caption, with its ambiguous language, fails to guide the viewer, who is left entirely unsure of what to make of Delarue-Mardrus peering forward with her mysterious gaze: she is clearly in costume, yet it is unclear what role she is supposed to be playing, or where she is traveling to and from.

Finally, in December 1907, Delarue-Mardrus is pictured in her French writerly persona, her profiled face in hand; engrossed in a book, she is turned away from the camera now, refusing in this sense its frame (Fig. 3.13).

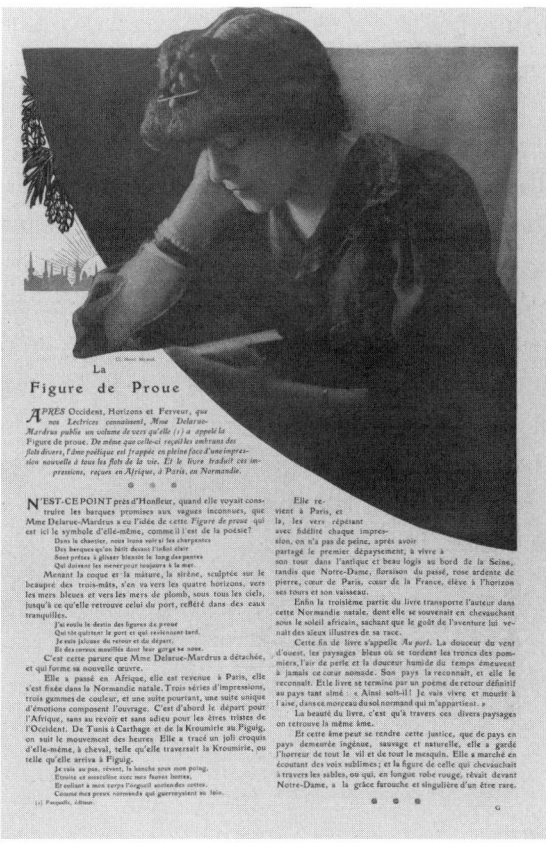

**Figure 3.13** Lucie Delarue-Mardrus announcing her new poetry collection, *La Figure de Proue, La Vie Heureuse* (December 1907). © Bibliothèque Marguerite Durand/Roger-Viollet.

A cut out triangular image takes up more than half the page—behind her elbow, the sketches of oriental turrets beckon under a distant sun—a reminder of the enhanced appeal of this otherwise visually mundane figure. Unlike Harry, Delarue-Mardrus's costumes throughout the pages of *Femina* and *La Vie Heureuse* ultimately seem more suggestive than imitative—less a sign of the times or an ode to the Orient than a sign of a free spirit unable to be circumscribed by convention. The repeated disjunction between her expression and the role her costumes suggest that she is playing add to Delarue-Mardrus's allure as an inscrutable and therefore compelling figure. The images of the demure, conventionally feminine, "true" writerly Delarue-Mardrus fail to convince in comparison: we have already seen too much.

There was, of course, much more to both Delarue-Mardrus and Harry than these captivating images. In both cases, their enthralling personae were matched by widely acknowledged literary acumen. Harry's novel *La conquête de Jérusalem* was so compelling and widely acclaimed that it helped launch the Prix Vie Heureuse, later to become the Prix Femina. The talented Delarue-Mardrus, poet, novelist, sculptor, was only in the beginning of what would make her one of the most prolific and successful women writers of her generation.[29] Their important iconographic presence in *Femina* and *La Vie Heureuse* demonstrates how the magazines were able to participate in and even exploit one of the most visually powerful tropes of their generation, to the extent that it authorized (even as it masked) their own feminist agenda. In the next chapter, we will examine the emergence of Delarue-Mardrus's own authorial voice—equally staged—in the pages of *Femina*, and how the magazine enabled this woman writer to harness her own celebrity in service of Belle Epoque literary feminism.

## CHAPTER 4
# THE WRITER WRITES BACK

AT a 1907 banquet honoring publisher Pierre Lafitte's recent nomination to the Legion of Honor, Daniel Lesueur offered a toast (reproduced in the February 15 issue) in which she applauded his accomplishments in creating *Femina*. The magazine, she said, introduced young women to a newly multivalent life, opening before them "an active, intellectual, modern existence."[1] For women writers, she added, it had special significance, dramatically changing the response of readers to their work, producing thoughtfulness and creativity in the letters they received, and a whole new engaging set of questions. Above Lesueur's remarks were the answers to *Femina*'s most recent opinion survey—on favorite professions for women. The winner: "Femmes de lettres," with 7,645 votes.

Women writers were of course major stakeholders in Belle Epoque literary feminism—those for whom the magazines' glorification and promotion of their chosen profession had rather direct consequences. And yet, despite the myriad dazzling images of so many literary darlings of *Femina* and *La Vie Heureuse*, we know little of the role they might have played in their self-presentation within the magazines' feature stories, or in the manipulation and circulation of their own images. We can safely surmise, if simply from the sheer number of the images of Tinayre, Noailles, Harry and Delarue-Mardrus, that they were willing participants, and in some cases their expressions give a bit of indication as to their own agency.[2] While some of these women published memoirs and autobiographical writing, they say frustratingly little about the magazines or their own role in what the publications accomplished (or awareness of the impact of these accomplishments at all).[3] Even after the establishment of the Prix Vie Heureuse, we are left with little more than matter-of-fact descriptions of proceedings and results rather than personal reflections or behind-the-scenes accounts that might give us more of a sense of any challenges or conflict they might have faced.[4] Moreover, the accumulation within the magazines of gorgeous images of these thinking women—while elevating their lot—has the unfortunate result of disempowering them as individuals, making them appear too often as decorative objects to admire rather than voices to be heard.

As the magazines gained their foothold and established their identity, however, many of their favored female literary celebrities shifted from being the object of study and fascination to being regular contributors, and their perspectives and own voices came into clearer focus. Two of the most successful of these writers—Marcelle Tinayre and Lucie Delarue-Mardrus—betray, in their efforts to speak directly to their *chères lectrices* (both within and beyond the magazines), a deep understanding of the influence of these publications on women readers, and an awareness of their own potential role therein. In examining some of their own words, we see a little of how these writers bridged the gap between reader and celebrity in order to make the work of the magazine more personal, relevant and compelling. Their writing gives indication of their relationship, not just to new ideas surrounding modern femininity, but to their sense of the magazines' role in manipulating or shaping these ideas. Although intimately connected to the magazines, Tinayre and Delarue-Mardrus were not simply mouthpieces for its work, but rather, subtle commentators on it, each in her own way.

In October 1904, *Femina* published a multipage feature story on Tinayre, replete with images of her home, children and husband, and heartwarming details about the nature of her domestic life. "With her great talent as a writer," we quickly learn, "Madame Tinayre combines a lovely modesty. She leads a simple life out of public view, split between her study and her children's games."[5] The chief concern of the article was to diffuse any anxiety readers might have about Tinayre's lifestyle given the nature—and title—of her best-selling and critically acclaimed novel, *La maison du péché* (*House of Sin*). Centered between the italicized paragraphs of this introduction is a photo of Tinayre in profile, standing outside next to a haphazard-looking rock formation, demurely holding her hat. Underneath, the caption reads: "La maison du péché," followed by the explanation: "Madame Marcelle Tinayre in her garden, near a little stone cabin that her kids have named The House of Sin" (Fig. 4.1). The subversive title of the book is thus transformed, quite literally, into child's play. Lest we miss these less-than-subtle messages, however, the article concludes: "Thus this house where *The House of Sin* was born is a house of happiness."

The interview with Jacques de Nouvion, who signs the article, is full of Tinayre's adorably charming interjections, and a desire to address the reader herself: "Tell them that I love my children," he quotes her as saying, in her self-effacing way, "and that I'm a good mom, even if I don't know how to wash up a child or teach them to read." As the questions continue, she offers to write the piece herself, and the rest of the article is the "lovely note" that she sends instead. In this way, then, Tinayre takes hold of her own image and its surrounding narrative, writing of the careful distinctions between her identity as a writer and the nature of her characters, and her own sense of the creative process. Those all-too charming earlier interjections, in this context, seem like nervous efforts to control the story that would be told.

In the part of the article that she writes, Tinayre describes a forthcoming novel that is especially dear to her heart. She had been in the midst of writing a different one, she explains, "but then I wasn't free to

**Figure 4.1** Feature story on Marcelle Tinayre, "next to the stone hut that her children have nicknamed 'La maison du péché.'" *Femina* (October 1, 1904).

choose." She ends up finishing what was at the time tentatively entitled *Le Cœur de Josanne* but which later would become *La rebelle*. As it turns out, *La rebelle* is a novel about a woman working at a magazine similar to the very one in which Tinayre is introducing it. Indeed, Tinayre's independent-minded protagonist Josanne de Valentin works for *Le Monde Féminin*, which bills itself as "the greatest magazine in the world" and serves as a central character in her drama.[6] The novel describes a large-format photographic magazine in which the editors "touted babies and tutus, elegant charities and athletic feats, the domestic virtues of queens, the modesty of women poets and the marriages of actors" (44). In her novel, then, Tinayre shines a not-always-favorable light on the inner workings of the publications so central to her own career success.

While her official job is "associate of the associate editor," Josanne is also "the do-it-all employee" filling in everywhere from editing to writing to printing. Some days this includes answering phones, including one caller who threatens to switch to *Femina* and *La Vie Heureuse* if not reimbursed for a missed issue. Early in the novel, these referents signal to the reader *Le Monde Féminin*'s peer publications. The magazine's cofounder, Madeleine Foucart, "the prettiest woman in Paris," is the image of the *femme moderne*, although in this case, happily accepting the feminist label. In fact, she was likely modeled after the founder of *La Fronde*, Marguerite Durand, known by this very epithet.[7] Tinayre provides in these pages a tongue-in-cheek description of the office in which Josanne works. In the hustle and bustle of deadlines and print media, expediency regularly wins out over truth. Rushing to get his fashion designs to press, Monsieur Foucart reminds a young staffer that these images need have little to do with art or nature. Minutes later, Josanne is negotiating a debate about whether a nude baby picture of a famous actress can be used for their series "Great Young Actresses" (42). The narrator continues, echoing precisely the opening statement of *La Vie Heureuse*, while mocking both its elitism and the naiveté of its readers: "In *Le Monde Féminin*, all the women were pretty; nearly all were virtuous; all the men were 'talented' . . . Men and women, they were all rich. Within suave interiors, they displayed high-fashion attire from the biggest *couturiers*. And their images, their life stories, all their fame and glory, would trouble the hearts of little provincial subscribers, those Bovarys from Limoges and Quimper-Corentin" (44–45).

Tinayre echoes this discomfort with the magazine's manipulation of its readers once again when Josanne is charged with answering their foolish letters, seeking advice about looking younger and slimmer. Writing these letters, she is brought to tears by the sheer inanity of her work: "What a life, my God, what a life!" (36). In another scene, Josanne watches as her editor, the unmarried dowdy feminist Mademoiselle Bon (who, incidentally, while a brilliant contributor, is hidden in a back office so that subscribers might never come across her embarrassing inelegance in person) allows her photographer to arrange a picture of a charitable home for unwed mothers so as to hide their pregnant bellies; later, discouraged by the story of one of these mothers who has abandoned her child to return to her abusive partner, she asks Mademoiselle Bon whether she is discouraged by "this trade of deception that you do! . . . Lift up women, educate women, liberate women" (129).

And yet, the readers of *La rebelle* were, in large measure, also likely readers of *Femina* and *La Vie Heureuse*—as the De Nouvion piece would ensure. Josanne, we saw from those comments, was a figure close to Tinayre's heart—indeed, it's hard not to see her as a direct reflection of the author. How then to read Tinayre's comments on women's magazines—the very organs in which she was not only celebrated as queen of her own "suave interior," but through which she had reached out to her readers to comment on a novel in which she would paint a critical portrait of these magazines and their readers?

Perhaps this ambivalent stance was one of the reasons for Tinayre's commercial success, one of the reasons that she was adored by these very readers. Tinayre's criticism of the women's press is all the more significant because of Josanne's need for what it might potentially offer: while she is a member of the editorial staff, she also represents a certain kind of reader of these magazines: she struggles not just to balance work and love, but to define herself comfortably through this balance. This desire reminds us of the heroine of Camille Pert's *Leur égale* and her fantasy of a women's magazine that would offer a forum for discussing issues addressing contemporary women. Like Pert's Thérèse, Josanne is looking for something more from these magazines—eager not (just) for the *mondanités* and fashion that draw in readers, but for "the philosophy and social issues."[8]

As much as Josanne/Tinayre criticizes its artifice, *Le Monde Féminin* also offers Josanne an important forum—the possibility of commenting on the work of her eventual love interest, feminist author Noël Delysle: she will review his treatise *La Travailleuse*, an event that launches their love affair. The magazine thus becomes for her both an intellectual outlet and a conduit to deeply ambivalent romance, one which will lead her to embrace feminist partner Noël as her "master," while insisting that such a gesture does not compromise her feminism (we will discuss Tinayre's version of the "new man" in greater detail in the next chapter). Josanne's love story demonstrates precisely the magazine's twist on the modern Cinderella. Her ending, although not quite a fairy tale, is sappy and romantic. While she insists on her feminism, the label seems at odds with her embrace of a decidedly traditional female role. The key, I would argue, is the struggle to get there, the fact that her critical acumen is what leads her to love, that her golden pen, as it were, replaces the glass slipper.

But let's not ignore Tinayre's criticism either. By turning a sharp eye to the women's press even as she embraces its possibilities, Tinayre both points a finger and winks at her readers. Don't be seduced, she reminds. Read the magazines, for who can resist, but not just for the glossy photos; read the book reviews; read the novels; be mindful, be self-aware. There are no easy answers. The modern woman is a bundle of contradictions. We are all Bovarys of Limoges, prey to the seductive powers of consumer culture, and to the desire for romance and self-fulfillment through love, and that doesn't stop us from being sophisticated readers as well. As in Prévost's description of *Femina*'s *lectrices*, the magazine symbolizes a collapse of boundaries, not just between reader and celebrity role model, but between kinds of readers—sophisticated Parisian, provincial worker. Tinayre reminds us that just as the *provinciale exquise* can momentarily fancy herself a Parisian sophisticate, so the sophisticated Parisian can become, for a moment at least, a Bovary of Limoges—just as we all do, dear reader, when we pick up *People* magazine in the supermarket and take pleasure in ogling someone like Tinayre herself.

### *"An Attentive, Trustworthy Friend"*

While Josanne was initially frustrated with certain aspects of the feminism promoted by the magazine for which she worked, as a contributor she not only benefited from the intellectual community it provided, but had an opportunity to reach readers directly. Lucie Delarue-Mardrus's own turn as a columnist for *Femina* offers an even more explicit example of how a woman writer herself could participate in the imaginative work of *Femina* and *La Vie Heureuse*. Beginning in 1908, Delarue-Mardrus contributed a regular literary column entitled "L'âme des livres" for *Femina* in which she promised to be for her readers "an attentive, trustworthy friend." While speaking to bourgeois women readers in their own idiom, Delarue-Mardrus proposed sophisticated—and sometimes subversive—ideas about what they should be reading, and, more significantly, what they themselves might consider writing. Here we see the feminist influence of *Femina* staged explicitly, as the newly minted authoress encouraged women to push themselves further as readers and writers. Delarue-Mardrus's confident, feminine voice in these columns conformed neither to the earlier images of the poet as demure European ingénue nor to those of her as a smug cross-dressing amazon; and yet her familiarity as a media icon authorized her role as a trusted friend and confidant for thousands of readers.

If Delarue-Mardrus's role in manipulating her earlier photographic images was not clear, her expertise in exploiting her verbal authority was, by contrast, manifestly so. In her inaugural column, Delarue-Mardrus posed the question of what readers look for in a book, as a means of calling attention to *Femina*'s unanticipated role as promoter of literature. The enduring value of the book against all odds, she noted, was brought into relief in the magazine through the simple fact that literature took up such a prominent place. *Femina* itself, remarked Delarue-Mardrus, was proof of the "supremacy of the book," for in the magazine "the beautiful images didn't end up preventing us from being drawn to talking about literary works in a more extensive and regular fashion than had been anticipated."[9] She herself of course was one such example of how this came to be true.

While Delarue-Mardrus's column was meant to guide female readers toward appropriate literary choices, it also steadily urged those readers to consider themselves as writers. In the first column, Delarue-Mardrus commented on the fact that it was a natural instinct to remark to oneself, "What a great novel I would write about this or that experience I've had, if I were a writer!" This, she concluded, meant that "everyone contains within them the instinct of a book (*l'instinct du livre*)." The pleasure and continuing dominance of the book, she argued, stemmed not from a readerly instinct but rather a writerly one, from the thrill of finding on paper what the reader herself might have written, had she known how to go about doing so. Indeed, when you love a book, wrote Delarue-Mardrus, it is because you have found in it, without realizing, "the work that you were carrying around obscurely in your own head or heart." Delarue-Mardrus then went on to recommend books to readers of different ages, but stopped to meditate on the lack of works for adolescent girls, those "creatures of transition" between girlhood and adulthood. Books fail to treat the young woman in her reality, but rather only as a "gamine attardée," or a "future woman." Perhaps, she wrote, young women themselves should be the ones to fill in this gap, for they themselves could capture the reality of the experience. Only they could "naturally fascinate their female readers and compensate for the books they are not allowed to read."

It is unclear in those last musings whether Delarue-Mardrus had her metaphorical tongue planted firmly in her cheek, for she went on to note that the same could be said for children, who would also be best equipped to captivate their peers if they could write. But she picked up the thread once again several months later in November, when she used her column to declare—this time far more explicitly: "It's time women told their own stories." Women's true experiences need to be written, she explained, to offer "a counterpart to this growing pile of volumes of male ink on the Woman in Love."[10] Delarue-Mardrus's argument here offers a clear example of Belle Epoque literary feminism, which advocated for women's rights to traditional male roles through an emphasis upon what made them uniquely feminine and through literary channels. Men have written well about women, Delarue-Mardrus conceded, using *Madame Bovary* as a central example. But women could do even better. "Men, after all, only have their heads to enlighten them [on the subject], but women have their whole being." And women as "suffering creatures" have all sorts of miseries that only they can recount. They also have the leisure time at home to reflect. "There is no more captivating enigma than that of woman," wrote Delarue-Mardrus, urging women themselves to be the ones to unveil this mystery. She thus used the very same notions of feminine difference that were deployed throughout the nineteenth century in order to exclude women from professional roles, to make a case in *favor* of women writers. In doing so, she implicitly questioned the logic of the traditional thinking that young women's reading led to hysteria.[11] These same qualities—inscrutability, propensity to illness and reverie—now became a reason that women should both read and write.

Delarue-Mardrus's editorial presence, then, traces *Femina*'s clear path in leading women from reading to writing, as well as the role of the famous woman writer therein. In her essays, Delarue-Mardrus guided readers from being passive admirers of captivating women writers to imagining themselves as that very thing—the visual evidence making the possibility all the more evident and compelling. Delarue-Mardrus passed into the powerful second person in this piece, as she urged women directly: "Reflect, ladies, and write for us what you find." Calling out to her "dear sister reader," she mocked the male-authored typology of the "misunderstood woman" and appealed to women with increasing fervor, concluding on a note of female empowerment: "But tell me. What do you think of all this? If men with their mindset had to go through a quarter of women's troubles or physical pain, if they had to run the same risks as them, would they have the *heart* to think about anything but moaning and taking care of themselves? Would they think only about love? Despite all of that male braggadocio, which ones, men or women, are ultimately the most courageous?"[12]

## *Cross-dressing in Kroumirie, Redux*

Delarue-Mardrus's regular column was short-lived, but she continued to appear as a regular editorial and visual presence, and served on many of the prize juries of both magazines. (The July 1, 1911 issue of *Femina* featured another elaborate photo spread of Delarue-Mardrus in Egypt, evoking the earlier images.) In August 1910, firmly established as an editorial presence, Delarue-Mardrus revisited some of the photographs that had established her authority; in so doing, she raised the question of the modern woman's apparel that was a subtext to those earlier images. We know from Delarue-Mardrus's memoirs that the pictures were her husband's idea, and she seems to have been little invested, at least initially, in their symbolism. The fact that she was thousands of miles away from where they were being published makes this startling claim a little more plausible. Her comments in the 1910 essay, on the other hand, make the complex relationship to her own image sometimes suggested by her shifting facial expressions finally more transparent, as she deploys a carefully constructed editorial voice that draws upon her now-established celebrity, both as a writer and cultural icon, with a distinctive visual identity. Manipulating both text and image, Delarue-Mardrus explicitly takes control over her visual representation.

Like the wordy captions that appeared in early issues of the magazines, Delarue-Mardrus's essay provides an extensive commentary on the cover image of her, guiding the reader in what she was meant to see. This image of Delarue-Mardrus in Kroumirie had, in fact, first appeared in *La Vie Heureuse* in 1905, in the feature "Madame Delarue-Mardrus aux Pays Arabes" (Fig. 3.10a and b). In the photo, she sports pants and what appeared then to be a Muslim headdress but in another context could pass for a boyish cap (Fig. 4.2). The accompanying caption, while not entirely explicit, allows the reader to think that this image was of

**Figure 4.2** Delarue-Mardrus on the cover of *Femina*. (August 15, 1910).

Delarue-Mardrus's native Normandy, where she regularly wore pants for their facility during her excursions: "Madame Delarue-Mardrus, who relaxes from her hard work as a writer in the green plains of her native Normandy, wears this picturesque accoutrement for her long hikes around Honfleur."[13] Her essay, entitled "In Normandy" and part of the series "Travel Impressions," describes the pleasures of dressing *en garçon* while on vacation and makes an argument for women wearing pants—naming, then, what the cautious cover caption refused to name. The voice is tongue-in-cheek: the delightful, cultivated charm of the "attentive, trustworthy friend" who knows just what her readers want and where they are coming from. Indeed, while the photograph first appears to depict the exotic travels of a mysterious figure, the voice heard is that of one *bonne bourgeoise* to another. Wearing pants is not a political statement, Delarue-Mardrus assures with delightful charm, but just a simple necessity, and perhaps even a fashion statement. Referring to the pants readers might have seen in earlier photo spreads of herself in the Orient, she notes that they are just as essential to her excursions in the mountains of Normandy as they were in her Tunisian travels. But while Normandy is described for Parisians as being equally exotic to Kroumirie, Delarue-Mardrus also intimates the process by which the exotic becomes familiar—you simply get accustomed to the idea. If you wear pants on vacation, *chères lectrices*, "people will be surprised at first, but they'll get used to it," she writes. In support of this concept she reminds readers that her famous hairstyle had seemed strange and unusual ten years ago, while now it was very much in vogue. Delarue-Mardrus's logic is a *mise en abyme* of the strategies of the magazines themselves: through their iconographic insistence, *Femina* and *La Vie Heureuse* helped French women get used to the idea of the beautiful, adventurous woman writer as the embodiment of feminine success—an image radically different from both the bluestocking that had preceded and the more contemporary caricature of the New Woman.

While taking this bold sartorial position, Delarue-Mardrus was careful to circumscribe her comments. "I'm not claiming any male rights (I abhor feminism), but it's in the interest of convenience, I daresay, that I speak."[14] In her study of *Femina*, Colette Cosnier reads this comment as an explanation for Delarue-Mardrus's visibility in the magazine, despite her known association with the lesbian *demimonde* and figures like

Renée Vivien and Natalie Barney. Her avowed antifeminism, Cosnier claims, secures her place.[15] But we have seen a far more complex game of shifting performances here. While I would agree with Cosnier that the magazines generally promoted women who conformed to bourgeois norms, rejecting feminism in no way guaranteed entry.[16] Provided she did nothing overtly scandalous, Delarue-Mardrus's captivating, shape-shifting and mysterious image itself seemed to be what ensured her early success, combined with an ability to speak to her colleagues in their own idiom. This success is a testament to the power of celebrity culture in Belle Epoque France. Indeed, I would argue that it was her status as admired, recognizable, but not-quite-knowable wife of Joseph-Charles Mardrus, and her secure place in the *monde littéraire*, rather than any ideological stance, that initially allowed Delarue-Mardrus to secure her place. One has the impression that she slipped in, in costume, before anyone could quite realize the extent to which she was breaking all the rules.[17]

We must also consider the history of Delarue-Mardrus's presence in *Femina* and the ways in which her 1910 statements stood in contrast to her earlier timidity. In this later iteration, Delarue-Mardrus has reinvented herself. The use of an old photograph enacts this shift: she is literally providing a new reading of an old image. Her rejection of feminism, like that of Myriam Harry, continues the work of displacing gender subversion onto less contentious oppositions, like that between France and the Orient, Paris and the provinces. These clothes are not men's clothes, the article seems to suggest; they are Tunisian clothes. Not to worry, dear sister reader, none of this has anything to do with feminism. Like Myriam Harry's, however, this disavowal was backed by an entirely different message, indeed one that implicitly undermined it: that of steady feminine progress towards change, and the promotion of a persuasive, intelligent female voice. That it was a performance is not in doubt. In her memoirs, Harry describes Delarue-Mardrus's impressive ability to charm the members of the literary elite. She describes attending together committee meetings for the Prix Vie Heureuse at Caroline de Broutelles' estate, where they would sit across the room from each other so as to balance each other out. Harry writes that her friend "had a seductive manner of approaching them, always knew something lovely to say [ . . . ] calling them, 'charming friend' or 'my beauty.'" At the same time, Delarue-Mardrus freely expressed her own opinions, and, according to Harry, would curse her colleagues in Arabic if they disagreed with her.[18]

Delarue-Mardrus's fascinating intervention thus encapsulates the potentially subversive side of Belle Epoque literary feminism in its subtle indoctrination to new forms of femininity. By packaging what might be deemed frightening or threatening (women wearing pants) in familiar bourgeois codes (what Parisians should wear on vacation), the magazines made them more palatable to certain kinds of women who might otherwise be reticent toward change. Just as significantly, Delarue-Mardrus's comments highlight the success of these magazines by 1910. Whereas a few years earlier the work of the magazines had been to depict—pictorially as much as textually—the woman writer herself as safe and familiar, now her accepted role as authority figure for this specific audience allowed her to advocate—none too aggressively—for other social shifts. *Femina* was using, then, the power of the celebrity it had fueled to steer its bourgeois readers in significant ways. This kind of power harnessed and deployed by the mass press has been generally recognized in terms of consumption, and certainly women needed to purchase the magazine in the first place. But as a corollary, Delarue-Mardrus's writing shows how *Femina* urged women towards independence and intellectual exploration.

At the same time, there are important reminders that these subtle social shifts were taking place for a particular audience, in a particular journalistic context. In her essay, Delarue-Mardrus refers in passing to a caricature of herself in pants by the famous artist and actor Sacha Guitry. The image, she writes, was meant to be mean-spirited, but she did not take it that way: "it's actually very nice to see," she says of her likeness in pants, supporting her own claims that women look good and feminine in them.[19] Her comments are a subtle reference to what we will soon see to be a fierce disconnect between the women's press and the mainstream media around the public image of feminine achievement, and particularly that of the woman writer. What would be a caricature in the mainstream press could very well serve as the norm in *Femina* and *La Vie Heureuse*. And yet, these comments also demonstrate that by 1910, *Femina* offered a new kind of armor against similar attacks, a space in which women could see changes considered socially suspect in other contexts in a fundamentally positive light.

Finally, Tinayre's and Delarue-Mardrus's own commentaries shed light on the ways that *Femina* and *La Vie Heureuse* exploited the performance of femininity as a feminist strategy, in service of the *femme moderne*. Delarue-Mardrus's writing for *Femina* puts her in a parallel position to some of the magazine's male editors who took on women's voices to model a certain kind of interrogation of modern female roles. She was, in many ways, no more a *bonne bourgeoise* than Henri Duvernois or Fernand Vandérem; but, like them, she used this performance to support the expansion of women's worlds and world views. Tinayre, on the other hand, was closer personally to the ideology of the *femme moderne*, but was keenly aware of the challenges of realizing such an ideal. Despite her own implication in the publicity machine of the women's press, she was skeptical of the means by which *Femina* and *La Vie Heureuse* glossed over the new conflicts in women's lives, and her own novels offer a more sobering engagement of that precise territory.

As we move to the next half of my discussion, we will explore further the gap between the magazines' own highly constructed sense of their work and audience, and how *Femina* and *La Vie Heureuse* were perceived in a wider context. On the one hand, we will see that Belle Epoque literary feminism extended beyond the parameters of the magazines to a web of popular women's fiction, through which writers engaged in complex issues surrounding changing social mores in more subtle and complex ways than the magazines allowed. In these novels, feminism emerges once more as something much more complex than a yes or no identification, and having it all—work, love, children—seems at once tantalizingly within reach and just beyond the modern Belle Epoque woman's grasp. On the other hand, we will also see that much of the work of Belle Epoque literary feminism could not be assimilated beyond its carefully circumscribed domain, and that outside of the range of the magazines' devoted female readership, its work was often unrecognized if not radically misunderstood.

# PART II
# TEXTS AND CONTEXTS

## CHAPTER 5
# A NEW MAN FOR THE NEW WOMAN?

*Belle Epoque Literary Feminism and the French Marriage Plot*

READERS of *La Vie Heureuse* were not happy with the ending to Colette Yver's *Princesses de science*. In this 1907 novel, Yver told the story of the star medical intern Thérèse Herlinge, who early in the novel accepts an offer of marriage from the charming doctor Fernand Guéméné. Delighted, Fernand wonders aloud whether his future wife will regret the bright future that her career in medicine had promised. "But, I don't have to give up medicine to be your wife!" Thérèse exclaims, astonished.[1] And thus the trouble begins.

Thérèse and Fernand do manage to marry, her soaring career intact. But Thérèse quickly overshadows her husband's accomplishments, becoming a highly pursued internist as he naively seeks a cure for cancer. Tensions are already running high when she becomes pregnant. He is thrilled, assuming she will now retire. Thérèse, however, is devastated by the prospect of giving up a career so crucial to her very sense of self. She does manage, at least for a while, to juggle both baby and career. Then, tragedy occurs: because Thérèse is unable to nurse while she is seeing patients, her nanny adds water to the baby's milk, causing his sudden death. Anguished by this terrible loss, Thérèse still remains uncertain as to the proper balance of work and family, and struggles to find a role model in the women around her. Finally, with the threat of her husband's imminent betrayal looming before her, Thérèse gives up her beloved medical career; her emotionally wounded husband "broken, heartsick," would be her last patient.

Readers of *La Vie Heureuse* would have none of it.

Who says a woman cannot manage an ambitious career while maintaining a satisfying family life, asked writer Camille Marbo in a two-page editorial that appeared in the magazine a few months after the book's publication. Holding up none other than Marie Curie and her impeccable *ménage* as an example, Marbo insisted that women could and did achieve such things, with regularity, and all while remaining perfectly feminine, or, as she put it, *femme tout court*.[2] The next issue of *La Vie Heureuse* contained Yver's reply, where she justified her novelistic choices, arguing that while there was no reason why women should not be doctors, such a demanding field was simply incompatible with a happy marriage, for either spouse. This response by the novel's author, however, was already but one voice in an ever-expanding discussion. Following Yver's piece, the magazine invited readers to participate in one of its many opinion surveys, polling male readers (presumably relatives of the magazine's *lectrices*) on the possibility of marital harmony with a female professional. "Men, would you marry a woman who works?" a boldfaced headline demanded. Thousands answered, and the discussion continued, far beyond the parameters of Yver's finely circumscribed plot.

Belle Epoque literary feminism found its most powerful and fully realized voice in the relay between *Femina*, *La Vie Heureuse* and their surrounding network of fictional texts. The magazines shaped the way that certain popular women's novels were read in the 1900s, and the novels in turn offered a more open forum for pursuing the kinds of discussions launched within the magazines. Yver's richly recounted novel, which was awarded the Prix Vie Heureuse in 1907, was part of a far-reaching discussion surrounding the redefinition of marriage during the Belle Epoque. The possibility of modernizing marriage was of particular concern to the *femme moderne*, as a new, updated model of marriage would provide a way to safely hinge the modern woman to traditional family structures, even as her particular role within them evolved substantially. In this chapter, I will consider novels by Marcelle Tinayre and Louise Marie Compain alongside Yver's work.[3] We will see that the discussions of modern marriage that circled from the magazines into these novels and back again reveal a rather coherent set of identifications and concerns shared by large numbers of women readers. These ideas challenged conventional gender norms in ways that do not conform to traditional categories for recognizing feminist expression during this time period, but, I argue, were perhaps as crucial to shifting social norms in the Belle Epoque as any proposed legal reforms. Moreover, the particular relationship of women's novels to the magazines that responded to and debated them helps us to further define the crucial discursive space of Belle Epoque literary feminism, which extended beyond the physical pages of *Femina* and *La Vie Heureuse* in productive and fascinating ways.

## The Marriage Crisis

By the end of the nineteenth century, the institution of marriage was widely considered to be "in crisis,"[4] a situation stirred up in large part by the Naquet laws of 1884 through which divorce was reinstated, injecting a measure of choice into an institution which had long left unhappy wives with few options.[5] Because the Naquet laws allowed divorce only under particular conditions, they almost immediately elicited calls for further reform. Writers and feminists began seeking to make divorce easier for women on the heels of the legislation, gaining momentum and visibility especially in the early 1900s; frequent public opinion surveys on the topic began to appear in the press, and numerous plays were produced, eliciting widespread debate.[6]

 *Femina* and *La Vie Heureuse*, on the contrary, were highly—and, more to the point, visibly—invested in promoting marriage, even as they recognized women's changing roles. They devoted numerous articles to discussing the future of the institution, which *Femina* described in 1903 as being under violent attack "during this time when pitiless moralists probe the wounds already gnawing away at the ancient institution."[7] Although divorce was a topic of great interest, it did not dominate the discussion. Indeed, the magazines seemed more concerned with imagining a modern relationship between husband and wife. The one-hundred-year anniversary of the Civil Code in March 1904 contributed to this sense, particularly as the government set up numerous extraparliamentary committees to consider its reform.[8] In an editorial entitled "Should the Code be Modernized?" *La Vie Heureuse* commented on the vast social changes of the past century that resulted in a very different notion of marriage than what the writers of the Code had envisioned. The article described modern wives as "associates, equals, sometimes true geniuses," who deserved the rights they had been denied.[9] Despite this seeming openness to reform and the very modern notion of the wife as an equal, the article went on to conclude that reforming the code would be too difficult, given its importance in sheltering family and property, and the risk, quite simply, of making things worse.[10] The commentaries offered in *Femina* echo this double stance. In response to playwright Paul Hervieu's proposal that a mutual obligation of "amour" be added to the infamous Article 213, which mandated that women obey their husbands in exchange for their husbands' protection, *Femina* polled several prominent women intellectuals, including Marcelle Tinayre and Daniel Lesueur.[11] Everyone agreed that love was critical to successful marriage. But the women were far more ambivalent about what Lesueur described as its unnecessary legal codification, or "cristallisation légale."[12] Meditating on the distinction between sentimentality and the law, Tinayre affirmed that love should never be codified; to do so would be naïve. The article concluded that as long as love itself remained "undefinable," any law would be impossible.[13]

And yet, despite both magazines' resistance to fighting for explicit legal change, it would be a mistake to ignore the contribution of Belle Epoque literary feminism to marital reform, in the context of promoting a radical shift in the relationship between husband and wife. Much of the magazines' work was focused precisely on that kind of change, as they advocated for new kinds of women—modern, independent, free-thinking, professional—to inhabit traditionally feminine roles as wives and mothers. *La Vie Heureuse*'s editors said as much in the mission statement that introduced their opening issue. Speaking of their publication, they promised to "show everyone that a more intelligent, active woman is also a better mother and a vital, charming and strong link to the family." The domestic sphere, rather than the public sphere, was the target of some of their most important work, a fact which helps explain both the resistance to any "cristallisation légale" as well as why much of this work remains unrecognized in its feminist import.

While featuring women in all sorts of new venues, both magazines never ceased to remind readers that marriage was healthy ("Marriage Prolongs Life," *La Vie Heureuse*, April 1904) and necessary ("At What Age Should One Marry?" *Femina*, December 15, 1905).[14] To this end, both magazines were filled with images of happy modern couples. *Femina*'s series "Ménages célèbres" and *La Vie Heureuse*'s "Ménages d'artistes" charted the seamless relationships between talented pairs living the dream of egalitarian partnership. Feature stories documented their travels; photographs fetishized their shared workspace at home.[15] Through these articles, a new conjugal ideal was vividly promoted, capitalizing on the smooth, appealing veneer of celebrity culture, as famous couples were held up as exemplars of modern marriage. A perfect marriage became one of the featured celebrity's many accomplishments, as well as an opportunity to offer an updated definition of the institution. A 1904 *Femina* piece entitled "Ménages de poètes," for example, described the harmonious arrangements of several married poets at the heart of the literary *Tout Paris*, including Monsieur and Madame Catulle Mendès, Monsieur and Madame Henri Régnier (also known by her pseudonym Gérard d'Houville), and Monsieur and Madame Edmond Rostand (Fig. 5.1). The *femme moderne*, declared the article, has beautifully transformed and updated the traditional role of muse: "Not satisfied with simply inspiring the poet, she also wanted to imitate him [by becoming one]." Out of this mimicry, the article announced, a new kind of marital arrangement had emerged that was in itself a kind of art: these "exquisite couples" were "living poems of calm, simplicity, concord and harmony."[16] The article emphasized the reciprocity and interdependence of these couples at every turn, and was accompanied by photographs of the collaborating poets that affirmed this sense of absolute balance and partnership.

Central to the redefinition of marriage promoted by these set pieces was a vision for a new kind of wife, at once modern and traditional, one for whom equality did not conflict with requisite devotion and selflessness. An article from *La Vie Heureuse*'s very first issue offers this description:

Neither queen nor slave, in our time [a wife] keeps in her heart all the reasons to devote and sacrifice herself that have been developed little by little over time. But she inhabits them with a new dignity. As her husband's associate, reciprocal love is the very bond of this relationship.[17]

*Femina*'s description of the modern wife is striking for its similarity. The magazine often celebrated women for their exemplary embrace of their role as "associate," emphasizing the husband's obligation to treat his wife as a respected partner during this time when "women are becoming equal to men." Despite this equality, women were not meant to "act like men" in their marriages, but rather, to be the "complement to the man to whom they are tied."[18]

**Figure 5.1** "Poet Households," featuring Monsieur and Madame Edmond Rostand, Monsieur and Madame Catulle Mendès, and Monsieur and Madame Auguste Dorchain, in *Femina* (June 15, 1904).

### LE GLACIER
#### par M. Catulle Mendès.

Les lacs où, le matin, passent des brouillards bleus
Se couvrent en hiver d'étincelantes glaces ;
Les hardis patineurs, aux jambes jamais lasses,
S'élancent en troupeau vers les monts nébuleux.

Mais les lacs n'aiment point que leurs belles surfaces
S'écaillent sous les pas de ces rustres frileux ;
Souvent le clair miroir se dérobe sous eux,
Puis les glaçons disjoints reviennent à leurs places.

Tel est mon cœur, glacier sur des volcans éteints !
Le doute, les remords, les espoirs incertains,
Le déchirent sans cesse avec de durs patins.

Parfois il baille, alors tout s'abîme en un gouffre
Qu'emplit l'exhalaison d'une mare de soufre ;
Et toi seul, cœur profond, tu sais ce que je souffre !

CATULLE MENDÈS.

---

### SONNET
#### par M<sup>me</sup> Auguste Dorchain.

A M<sup>me</sup> Arnould-Plessy
en sa retraite de l'abbaye du Quartier.

Celle à qui vont les vœux de notre amour profonde,
Et qui, près de nos cœurs est si loin de nos yeux,
Fut l'artiste sublime, au front délicieux,
Qui versait l'harmonie et la joie à la ronde.

Puis, quand elle eut quitté la scène où sans seconde
Elle brillait, et reine et muse, elle aima mieux
Par un nouvel exil et par d'autres adieux
Se détacher aussi du théâtre du monde.

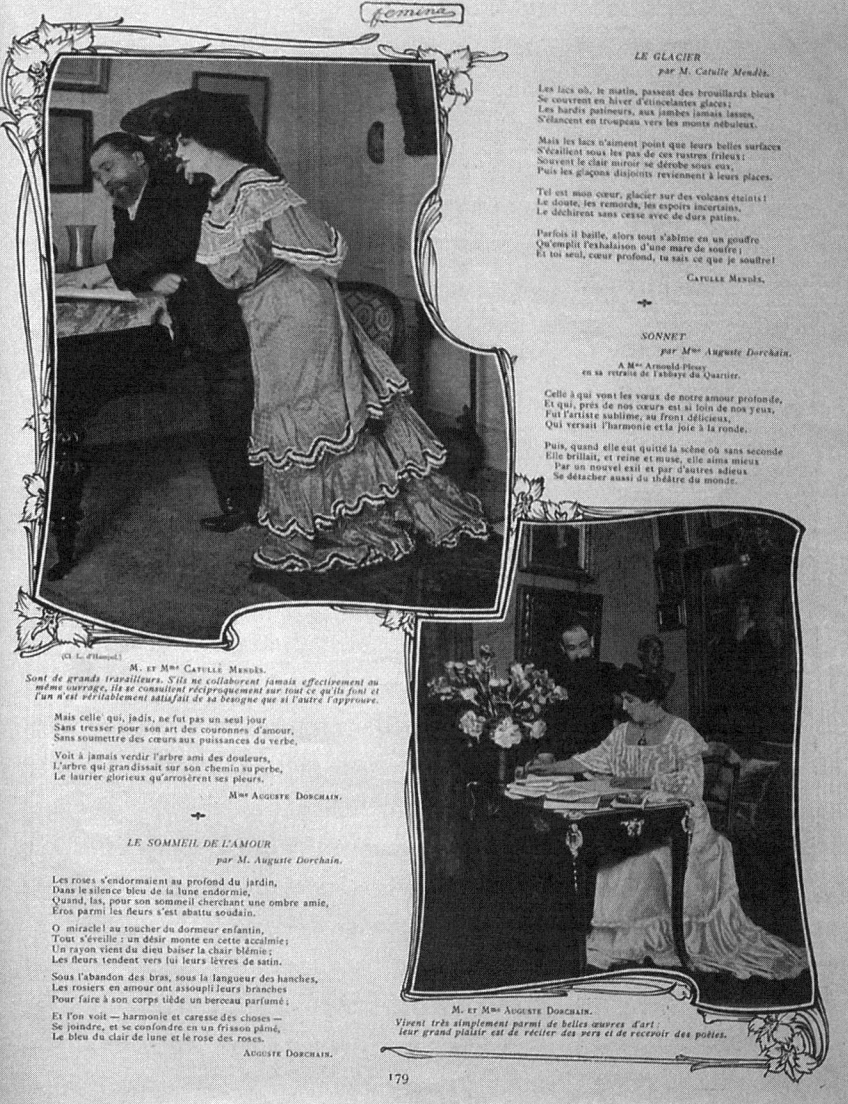

M. ET M<sup>me</sup> CATULLE MENDÈS.
Sont de grands travailleurs. S'ils ne collaborent jamais effectivement au même ouvrage, ils se consultent réciproquement sur tout ce qu'ils font et l'un n'est véritablement satisfait de sa besogne que si l'autre l'approuve.

Mais celle qui, jadis, ne fut pas un seul jour
Sans tresser pour son art des couronnes d'amour,
Sans soumettre des cœurs aux puissances du verbe,

Voit à jamais verdir l'arbre ami des douleurs,
L'arbre qui grandissait sur son chemin superbe,
Le laurier glorieux qu'arrosèrent ses pleurs.

M<sup>me</sup> AUGUSTE DORCHAIN.

---

### LE SOMMEIL DE L'AMOUR
#### par M. Auguste Dorchain.

Les roses s'endormaient au profond du jardin,
Dans le silence bleu de la lune endormie,
Quand, las, pour son sommeil cherchant une ombre amie,
Éros parmi les fleurs s'est abattu soudain.

O miracle ! au toucher du dormeur enfantin,
Tout s'éveille : un désir monte en cette accalmie ;
Un rayon vient du dieu baiser la chair blêmie ;
Les fleurs tendent vers lui leurs lèvres de satin.

Sous l'abandon des bras, sous la langueur des hanches,
Les rosiers en amour ont assoupli leurs branches
Pour faire à son corps tiède un berceau parfumé.

Et l'on voit — harmonie et caresse des choses —
Se joindre, et se confondre en un frisson pâmé,
Le bleu du clair de lune et le rose des roses.

AUGUSTE DORCHAIN.

M. ET M<sup>me</sup> AUGUSTE DORCHAIN.
Vivent très simplement parmi de belles œuvres d'art leur grand plaisir est de réciter des vers et de recevoir des poètes.

## Experiments in Feminist Marriage

If, through their emphasis on famous couples, the magazines risked presenting modern marriage as an ideal only available to the happy few, popular women's fiction offered a way to test the fantasy, as well as a terrain through which to explore the challenges a couple might face in attempting to assume a more modern partnership.

One concern that male writers mentioned repeatedly within *Femina* was that while new generations of young, educated bourgeois women were steadily reimagining their conjugal roles, scoffing at the antiquated structures specified by the Civil Code, their spouses were not nearly as quick to relinquish their legally grounded authority. In his *Lettres à Françoise mariée*, which appeared in serial form in *Femina* in 1908, novelist Marcel Prévost commented on this discrepancy, explaining to young Françoise that while women were known to giggle at the obligatory recitation of Article 213 in civil wedding ceremonies, husbands "find a clear advantage in the regime of Napoleonic law."[19]

Tinayre and fellow novelist Louise Marie Compain address this difference between modern, bourgeois men's and women's expectations in their novels, in which they try to imagine not just what a feminist marriage might look like but how a modern couple might achieve such a feat.[20] Like the social experiments conducted in Zola's novels not long before, these writers worked through the challenge of updating modern marriage by staging the process through which these changes might happen, as individual men and women (or temperaments, as Zola would say), from different backgrounds (or milieus, in Zola's terms) were confronted with shifting expectations.[21] What happens, for example, when an open-minded young man who has written a feminist treatise on women workers falls in love with an independent woman who challenges all his preconceived ideas about feminism and femininity? What happens when two earnest, well-meaning intellectuals try to balance career and family? In Compain's 1903 *L'un vers l'autre* and Tinayre's 1905 *La rebelle*, one can clearly see the continuation of discussions regarding marital roles already under way in the magazines, as well as fictional responses to questions that the magazines had not yet explicitly posed.

*L'un vers l'autre*, published in 1903, was Compain's first and most successful novel. After the publication of its sequel *L'opprobre* in 1905, she devoted her energies more exclusively to the feminist movement, serving as a founding member of l'*Union française pour le suffrage des femmes*, writing extensively on the rights of women workers and publishing regularly in the feminist newspaper *La Française*.[22] Little is known about Compain's personal life, which she kept extremely private; her husband is thought to have committed suicide after being accused by his mother-in-law of causing the stillbirth of their only child.[23] Tinayre, on the other hand, became something of a celebrity following the publication of her breakthrough novel *La maison du péché* in 1900, which received widespread critical acclaim. Though she wrote dozens of novels on a variety of subjects, we know that she identified personally with *La rebelle* and its subject matter.[24]

Both Tinayre's and Compain's novels are feminist fables, distinct for the nature both of their conflict and for their happy endings, which hinge on the male partner's claiming the woman's feminist sensibilities as his own. In their shared revision of the British courtship plot, they bring their couples together quickly, only to discover an obstacle to their continued union: the man's patriarchal prejudices.[25] Both Tinayre and Compain construct their male protagonists as exceptional and promising figures, such that their failure to satisfy their partners is somewhat unexpected. In Compain's *L'un vers l'autre*, we are quickly introduced to the handsome, sensitive and thoughtful Henri, who, upon graduating from the École Normale, "hardly thought of marrying" until he met Laure, whose "mind equaled her beauty."[26] With all the promise of the best sentimental hero, he readily gives himself over to the passion he had once rejected. As Henri gazes into Laure's adoring eyes, he appreciates all the qualities that an avid reader of the women's press would presumably want her husband to seek in a spouse: unpretentious beauty, maternal instincts, and vibrant intelligence.

It is hard to imagine a more auspicious partnership; yet Tinayre's *La rebelle* far surpasses Compain's tale in the feminist courtship fantasy of Josanne Valentin and Noël Delysle: she is a struggling, independent-minded young widow making ends meet by writing for *Le Monde Féminin*; he is the author of the feminist treatise *La Travailleuse*. Long before meeting him, Josanne encounters Noël's book while browsing a bookstore on a rainy day, where she reads of "the female rebel" who, the author sympathetically explains, acts not in defiance of morals but rather in search of "the right to think, to act, to love whomever she pleases, this right that men had always taken for themselves, and always refused her."[27] Josanne of course immediately recognizes herself in this figure. "Who is this man who remains unblinded by prejudice?" she asks, smitten (15). They finally meet after an exchange of letters following her review of his book and proceed, thoughtfully yet passionately, toward becoming lovers.

Despite these promising beginnings, in the second phase of both novels, the couples face intense conflict over the terms of their relationships. While Noël and Josanne fall quickly in love, Noël is plagued by the existence of Claude, Josanne's son through her previous lover, the child being an eternal reminder of Josanne's sexual past.[28] As it turns out, the author of *La Travailleuse* is limited by a feminism that was, as he admits, "a bit theoretical" (167). Henri, on the other hand, balks when his wife seems to privilege career satisfaction over family, leading to her departure. Both authors then stage a complex psychological process through which feminist values become personalized, allowing the man to reorient his entire sense of familial structures according to this new feminist perspective.[29] In the process, a new feminism emerges: one explicitly set in opposition to the organized feminist movement referenced in both texts; one allowing a balance between female independence and conventional heterosexual roles; and, importantly, one defined by male participation.[30]

## Beyond the New Woman

Both Noël and Henri are blinded, albeit only temporarily, by received ideas about the women of their generation and the limits of existing frameworks through which to analyze these ideas. Indeed, as the couples in both texts attempt to work past patriarchal prejudices, they also work to move past the rigid categories through which resistance to gender norms had been defined for them. With no accepted term through which to describe the apolitical stance of the *femme moderne*, Tinayre's and Compain's characters struggle independently to reconcile what appear to be competing ideologies: French marriage, as dictated by the Civil Code, presents itself as a betrayal of core feminist values; the feminist, on the other hand, is presumed to have shed her femininity.

Tinayre's Noël, for example, is puzzled by Josanne's conventional femininity. "You are so womanly!" he exclaims, noting her love for jewelry and home decor. In response, Josanne chastises him for expecting to see "the new woman" (notably the French says "la nouvelle femme" and not "la femme nouvelle") and then being surprised to discover "the eternal woman."[31] The lack of appropriate terminology, however, only seems to reflect the lack of consistent ideology, as women struggle to find a balance between equality and convention, new roles and old habits. Josanne is troubled by the modern professional women she meets, whom she describes as "the female elite, the 'liberated ones,' 'the rebels'" (130)—(and not *les femmes nouvelles*). While in their places of work these women are fiercely competitive, they also inevitably succumb to "romantic servitude" in their personal lives. Indeed, despite all their gains in the public sphere, on the home front "the old order re-establishes itself," complains Josanne, and these women are no different from their mothers (130). As much as she criticizes them, however, Josanne sees herself caught in the same contradiction, split between these two ways of being: "There were in her two women: the one from 'on high'—proud, valiant, the rebel who wanted to be liberated and healed and to live in chaste solitude; and the other, inferior, subjugated, who still, in her blood and in her nerves, held on to the ancient poison, the need for tears and caresses, the morbid taste of the sufferings of love" (134).

Describing Josanne in this way, Tinayre pits independence explicitly against love, making the latter eventuality sound like a failure of will and strength. She also makes clear the feeling that the feminist movement left no room for love or for traditional gender roles. Mademoiselle Bon, Josanne's friend and mentor at *Le Monde Féminin*, never married and frequently invites Josanne to meetings of the Fraternité française: "a small feminist association, socialist and revolutionary, where fat mustachioed women and scrawny enlightened ones heroically called themselves 'citizens'" (132). Josanne is admonished by one of their members for her libertine ways. Tinayre's caricature of these mannish women and their dedication to political causes echoes the disdain for organized feminism announced in *Femina*'s mission statement. Tinayre searches here to articulate a different kind of feminism where love and liberation are both possible. Immediately considered a roman à clef despite Tinayre's denial that it corresponded to any particular individuals, *La rebelle* rings of another kind of truth: her portrayal of Josanne's confusion offers a rare glimpse of the kinds of questions facing Belle Epoque readers of the women's press who sought to identify their modern femininity in a less ideologically rigid positioning than the feminist movement seemed to offer.

In Compain's novel, circulating stereotypes about modern women are also invoked as blinding. During the heat of his breakup with Laure, Henri's rant echoes the worst of the Belle Epoque antifeminist backlash. He tells his wife: "the woman who wants to be superior ends up losing the qualities that appeal most to men; she thereby loses her power without acquiring that of the opposite sex" (108). Compain channels here an authentic and widely circulating Belle Epoque idea of the *femme nouvelle*. By the end of the novel, however, Henri is able to distinguish between widely circulating ideas and the needs of the woman he truly loves. In a pivotal scene, Henri stands back while colleagues discuss a feminist speech one of them has just attended. One argues that women should pursue careers instead of men (husbands or lovers), while the other worries about the consequences for men of such behavior, which make women "ugly, sick, unfit for love" (295). Henri retreats, suddenly aware of the progression of his thinking. His realization, which leads to the rehabilitation of his marriage, turns on the recognition that feminism must afford women equality without forcing them to choose between work and love. This realization addresses the gaps on both sides of the feminist debate; it is explicitly posed as a third, as yet unarticulated term, an alternative to both feminism and its critics.

## Love and the Law

In both novels the Civil Code itself is posed as an explicit barrier to women's happiness. At the same time, both Tinayre's and Compain's happy resolutions are not a result of legal change, which remains elusive, but rather follow from the process of questioning and discussion around proposed reforms. *L'un vers l'autre* directly explores Article 213 and the gap between protection and obedience, exactly the gap that threatens to subsume the promising marriage between Henri and Laure. Laure had nervously brushed away her suspicions regarding the demands of the Code on the eve of her wedding. But when she becomes pregnant, Henri takes the liberty of resigning her position as schoolteacher without consulting her; all of this comes explicitly back to Article 213, which Henri invokes to justify his act: "I promised you aid and protection, he had told her one day, and you promised me obedience." Laure rejects this and leaves Henri for several months, a difficult period during which he combats anger and depression. Finally, after a degrading encounter with a prostitute, he comes to the realization that just as he was meant to act as a protector for his wife, invoking the Code once again, she served a parallel function for him: "as a protector against all that is base; a guide towards all that is noble and pure" (299). He also comes to realize that Laure needs his support at home in entering a brutal work force, and that their marriage can sustain and nurture her in both the public and private sphere. This symmetry is the platform for their resolution and approximates the definition of modern marriage as an "association" of equals articulated in the women's press: "this association of two minds, two hearts, two wills, each depending on the other, each one bringing their own qualities, and completing each other."[32]

Compain's novel ends with a fantasy of legal change, as the newly reunited happy couple dream of a day when "they will make laws that will prevent the oppression of wives, and arbitration will come between separated spouses, as between hostile nations" (309). Such a fantasy is voiced more explicitly in Tinayre's novel, in Noël's rewriting of the Civil Code in his feminist treatise. As he imagines it, "The terms of the conjugal contract will be changed such that women will be able to live without men's help, raising children on their own. They will no longer ask for protection and will not promise obedience. And the husband will have to treat his wife as one equal to another—even better, as companion to fellow companion, friend to friend" (15). The resonance of Noël's writing with the descriptions of modern marriage found in *Femina* and *La Vie Heureuse* is not surprising, given that, in the novel, Josanne reviews his treatise for *Le Monde Féminin*, a publication described explicitly as a rival to these magazines. *La rebelle*, in turn, would be reviewed and discussed in both *Femina* and *La Vie Heureuse*, where Tinayre was both a frequent contributor and media darling, featured in the adoring photo spreads we have already examined.[33]

This reflexive relationship between novels and magazines suggests why specific legal changes—the eschewed *cristallisation légale*—as much as they were an object of discussion—were not necessarily seen as essential to the process of modernizing marriage for Belle Epoque women readers. More immediately relevant, even on the most practical level, seem to be the discussions regarding such change that took place in novels like *La rebelle* (and the magazine depicted within it) but also continued in the pages of *Femina* and *La Vie Heureuse*. In both Tinayre's and Compain's novels, actual change is linked to open dialogue and the kind of questioning the magazines promoted: Henri and Noël shift their behavior and attitudes partly in response to conversations that they overhear. Ultimately, any legal change was imagined by both authors in a distant fictional future, one in which the Code might finally reflect the facts on the ground. But progressive couples need not wait around for new legislation. After all, as Noël wrote in his treatise, "Already there are many couples where the husband treats his wife as his associate, his confidant, a collaborator on his work, a devoted partner for all of his ambitions" (15). And glorious evidence of such couples was nowhere more evident than in the pages of *Femina* and *La Vie Heureuse*, where, the editors insisted with tantalizing photographic evidence, despite "current customs," there are already numerous exemplary "associations" that have realized a "new and enviable ideal."[34] This all helps to explain the deeper significance of a Henriot cartoon that appeared in *Femina* in 1904. "The Civil Code?" asks a well-dressed woman in her home. "Here's my husband's. I made a piano bench out of it . . . to sit on" (Fig. 5.2). Behind the playfulness of this comic lies a serious commentary expressed in part through the very situation of this joke in *Femina*, where so many discussions of marriage reform were taking place—suggesting, then, the extent to which the pages of the Civil Code were secondary to the very pages women held in their hands.

**Figure 5.2** "The Civil Code? Here's my husband's: I made a piano bench out of it . . . to sit on." Henriot cartoon in *Femina* (December 1, 1904).

## *Happily Ever After?*

With their grueling emotional work done, Noël and Henri find their way back to their partners in sentimental happy endings that clinch these stories as feminist fantasy. Henri returns joyously to Laure, announcing: "I have shed all my prideful judgments and the bad influences of heredity, don't you see that I am a new man?" Laure too is renewed and announces her realization that solitary independence is not a path to happiness, as she believes that women's "true place is in the home, but we can't live there unless we are honored." As in the magazines, any tension between equality and conventionally gendered roles is elided in this ideal. As the feminist fable comes to an end, husband and wife are reunited as a glimpse of nothing less than a new, happier world order: Laure and Henri are described as "a chosen couple, founders of a new race"; with marriage revitalized, "humanity will finally be unified and blissful" (309–10).

Though certainly more modest, Tinayre's novel is also a realization of a feminist fantasy of male transformation. Tinayre's protagonist is named Noël after all, the name of Tinayre's oldest son and thus perhaps of her own hope for the future, and his evolution dramatizes the cavernous gap between lofty feminist ideals and real lived experience. At the end of the novel, it seems hopeful that the chastened feminist author would now be better able to realize, in his own marriage, the changes in the marriage contract that he argued for in his own book.

Yet Tinayre's resolution is also decidedly more complex than Compain's, echoing the conservatism of Compain's text without the seamless application of gender advances in the public sphere to those in private realms. By the end of the novel, Josanne has come to terms with her opposing internal forces, embracing both equality and a highly gendered difference. Contemplating Mademoiselle Bon's warning that "as in the husband, in the lover there is a master" (301), Josanne reframes her feelings for Noël:

"My master! My dear master! [ . . . ] It's our shared desire that I be your respected equal before the world, before your mind and your friendship. But the rebel in me rebelled against an unjust society, not against nature; she didn't rebel against the eternal law of love" (304).

Coming not long after these startling declarations, the ending to Tinayre's *La rebelle* has struck some modern readers as serving to undermine the subversive promise of the novel's title. As the novel closes, Noël murmurs tenderly "my dear wife," and Tinayre writes: "The victory was in love, which had not weakened, had not lost hope—in a love strong like life itself" (372). Josanne's embrace of Noël as her master, however, must be understood in its proper context: as part of an effort to carve out a feminist stance beyond that of the organized feminist movement and the caricature of the *femme nouvelle*. "And that does not stop me from being feminist, from claiming my rights to freedom, justice and happiness," she concludes, affirming her feminism while preserving a sexual space where traditional power structures dominate (306).

Here we are, then, in the contradictory ideological terrain of Belle Epoque literary feminism—a place where a self-declared feminist can also declare her partner to be her master, if this also means the possibility of reconciling love, marriage, feminism and femininity without having to choose between them. Moreover, for Tinayre it meant, as the editors of *Femina* and *La Vie Heureuse* knew best of all, making feminism palatable to a wider audience—not just of women but of the men who loved them. In a review of the novel that appeared in *L'Illustration* in March 1906, journalist Emile Berringer thanked Tinayre for having written it, noting that had a man criticized feminist rebellions in favor of love, he would not have been trusted. "But how nice this proof becomes when it's a woman who writes it, and what a comfort these confessions offer to our threatened egos!"[35]

Because of the way in which discussions of marriage in women's magazines and fiction directly promoted new behavior and attitudes during this marriage crisis, they should be seen as more than simply a reflection of or window onto social norms. Instead, I would argue, the magazines and their related novels had the potential to act directly upon these norms, in no small part by challenging some of the master narratives of French literature.[36] Particularly in the nineteenth century, fictional women who steered from bourgeois norms were systematically punished, from Flaubert's Emma Bovary to Zola's Nana.[37] French women writers were just as cynical as their male counterparts in this regard, creating compelling feminist heroines who were nonetheless almost always denied satisfying conclusions. Tinayre's and Compain's romantic happy endings, on the other hand, stand in stark opposition to so many of their independent-minded female literary forbears: their heroines do not retreat to solitude, as does Madame de Lafayette's Princesse de Clèves (1678); or willingly choose spinsterhood, like Françoise de Graffigny's Zilia (1741); or die a noble but lonely death, like Germaine de Staël's Corinne (1805); or retire to a convent, like Claire de Duras's Ourika (1823); or jump off a cliff, like George Sand's Indiana (1832). And, perhaps more to the point, they are able to reconcile intellect and ambition with love and marriage, unlike Camille Pert's Thérèse in *Leur égale*, the 1899 novel in which the young heroine fantasizes about a women's magazine (aptly titled *La Femme Moderne*) which would offer a forum for exploring such a possibility while remaining separate from the politics of the feminist movement.[38] Less than a decade after Pert's novel, this sector of the women's press had become a formidable reality whose serious consequences for literary and cultural history should not be underestimated.

## *The Intellectual Housewife*

If Tinayre's and Compain's romantic happy endings signaled the creation of a new narrative trajectory for the independent French woman, this path was intimately linked to the possibility of imagining a male partner who would embrace her struggle. Men were crucial to Belle Epoque literary feminism and to the reimagining of marriage in the women's press, where they authored many of the articles describing the new conjugal ideal.[39] Another way to understand the optimism of these writers, then, was through their faith in men who could be true partners and supporters.

This is, in fact, what separated Josanne from Pert's journalist protagonist Thérèse, whose suitor proves not to be up to the challenge of feminist marriage. It also explains Marbo's vehement response to Colette Yver's novel, which put little pressure on its male characters to rise to the challenge of meeting the modern woman's changing needs. Marbo's forceful editorial, playfully entitled "The Intellectual Housewife," or "La Femme Intellectuelle au Foyer" (a play on the French term for housewife "la femme au foyer"), reads both as a manifesto for Belle Epoque literary feminism and as a rearticulation of the *doxa* of *La Vie Heureuse* as it was expressed in the magazine's original mission statement. While the novel was about the viability of a marriage between two doctors, the essay addressed the effect of the expansion of women's roles upon the domestic sphere; it offered a justification for an intelligent, engaged wife, and a continuation of the work *Femina* described in its first issue as the "widening of the hearth (foyer)." Marbo argued that working outside the home only increased a woman's contribution to domestic life: "A woman who acquires a higher sense of life and of the moral strength of true workers, infinitely increases her value as a true woman. Her comfort with methodical reflection and her depth of knowledge make her more suited for day-to-day duties."[40]

Not every woman was cut out to be a housewife, Marbo argued, citing Emma Bovary as one example. Such women should have other options. Remarkably, in this context, the question of whether women should work was not the point of contention. At issue was whether a working woman could also be a good wife and homemaker—and there was much at stake for the *femme moderne* in finding an answer in the affirmative.

Marbo's article chastised Yver for what was seen as a *roman à thèse*, from the beginning hurtling towards the foregone conclusion that "woman can't balance a job in the sciences with her duties as a wife."[41] She contrasted Yver's unhappy couple with the vision of conjugal bliss promoted by *Femina* and *La Vie Heureuse*: that of marital collaboration. According to Marbo, a shared profession like that of Thérèse and Fernand was a promise of marital harmony (witness the happy Curie family) leading to the highest pleasures, as it prolonged "work in love and love in work" and neither suffered from this proximity. This aspect of Marbo's critique built off the already well-established ideal introduced in the magazines' series on exemplary celebrity *ménages*. A *Femina* article on "Ménages de savants" from 1904 had led off with none other than the Curies as an example.[42]

Marbo was visibly frustrated both by Yver's presentation of Thérèse as a miserable homemaker and by the suggestion that such a fault was somehow linked to her career. It doesn't actually take that much time to keep an ordered household, she argued, and if one is not good at such things this is certainly not a result of intellectual exertion or ambition. Thérèse and Fernand were simply a poor match. Finally, echoing Noël Delysle's treatise and Louise-Marie Compain's euphoric ending, Marbo's essay concludes with a fantasy of male symmetry in a not-so-distant future: "Soon the day will come," she promised, "when almost all men will want to find in their companions a bright, enlightened heart." Like

Compain, Tinayre and Pert, Marbo dreamt of a new man just over the horizon who would find a thinking, accomplished woman a welcome, desirable partner.

In her sobering response, Yver spoke exactly to this point. She did not deny female intellectual prowess or that there were women who were not cut out to be housewives. But she insisted on a definition of marriage based on female sacrifice. Could one imagine a woman doctor baking delicious *petits plats* for her husband, like Yver's humble Dina, who renounces her medical career to marry? "She would not have time," stated Yver. "And that is the essence of the whole novel."[43] Sacrifice, she wrote, might be a threat to female pride; but it was the only path to marital happiness, the only way to keep husbands happy.

Men, it seems, were the last frontier of Belle Epoque literary feminism, and it therefore made sense that the opinion survey following Yver's novel was directed at them. The ability to imagine men as part of the conversation was the difference between a happy ending and a tragic one, in feminist terms. The answers to *La Vie Heureuse*'s survey suggest that many men had no issue with working wives and mothers—at least according to the editors' executive summary. In contrast to other contexts, where a balance of opinion was carefully displayed, when it came to the possibility of balancing domestic and professional life in order to define modern marriage, *La Vie Heureuse* refused ambiguity. With excerpts from a dozen exemplary responses to their survey, the magazine claimed that by and large, their readers had recognized that "even the most elite work can be compatible with always watchful tenderness and the most humble attention to housework."[44]

## *Writing Beyond the Belle Epoque Ending*

Yver's novel was certainly not the only piece of fiction to inspire extensive commentary and debate; hers is but one example of the way in which *Femina* and *La Vie Heureuse* served as an extension of the discursive frame of Belle Epoque novels, a way for readers to "write beyond the ending," to take up Rachel Blau DuPlessis's now classic notion.[45] French readers, after all, had a long tradition of editorializing fictional texts after their publication: witness the debates surrounding Madame de Lafayette's *La Princesse de Clèves*, or the alternative versions of Françoise de Graffigny's *Lettres d'une péruvienne*, in which the heroine ends up happily married.[46] *Femina*'s own 1904 article "Les Associées" had been introduced as a corrective to a 1902 novel, *L'Associée*, which had launched many discussions on the topic of modern marriage. Acknowledging that novel's "pessimistic" ending, the article went on to propose an examination of famous couples as important counterpoints to the novel's message; these couples offered examples of what collaborative marriage could be, even if such a phenomenon was not yet widespread.[47] Nor was marital equality the only subject to elicit debate, although marriage in general did seem to dominate. In response to Daniel Lesueur's *La force du passé*, *Femina* surveyed Jeanne Marni, Anna de Noailles and Juliette Adam on the conjugal compatibility of those holding traditional Christian beliefs with freethinkers, before opening up a survey to readers at large on the ending of that novel.[48] In their literary criticism, then, the magazines presented a view of fiction as open and subject to interpretation.

Reading Belle Epoque novels through this dynamic, responsive, discursive network thus expands our sense of the fiction of this period, and just where it begins and ends. Without knowledge of the discussion elicited by her novel, it would be easy to read the fact that Yver was awarded the Prix Vie Heureuse for this novel teleologically: as a rejection of women's ambitious efforts at career by a prize committee made up of so many regular contributors and media darlings. But with this context in mind, one can read it instead as an endorsement of the *discussions* that Yver elicited through her compelling portrayal of the difficult choices facing women. Throughout the novel, Thérèse scrutinizes the women around her for answers: should she model herself on the high-achieving female mentor who never married but has an active romantic life or the friend from medical school who gave it all up to become a devoted wife and mother? These alternative female paths are so realistically and sensitively portrayed that the reader is kept guessing as to what Thérèse's own decision will be until the final pages of the novel.

Analogously, I would suggest, the significance of both Tinayre's and Compain's novels to the very identity of the *femme moderne* can be understood precisely in the tension between the title of Tinayre's novel and her happy ending—which is the same apparent contradiction between her original title, *Le coeur de Josanne*, and the one she ultimately chose, *La rebelle*. As Noël and Josanne make their way back to each other, he tenderly refers to her as "my dear rebel." She objects, explaining that she rebelled against moral injustice but not against love, and not against him. And yet, this is the title Tinayre ultimately gave her novel. If Tinayre showed her readers that it was possible to be both a rebel and a wife, then, her novel also vividly betrayed the fact that there was no widely accepted term, no single category for this kind of feminist stance outside of the women's press; new woman, eternal woman, liberated woman, rebel, citizen—her protagonist faced off against all of these labels, no single one fitting the bill.

Through Josanne's conflict, Tinayre dramatized the challenges of translating the complex and perhaps even contradictory stance of the *femme moderne* to a more general audience. In the next chapters, I will consider the relationship of the women's press and its particular feminism to a more general reading public, and examine more broadly the way the magazines and their innovations were received by "mainstream" readers. In other words, what happened to the impeccable *femme moderne* when she stepped out of her highly circumscribed editorial context with so many of her pressing questions so effectively raised yet not fully answered?

## CHAPTER 6
# JEAN LORRAIN'S WOMEN'S MAGAZINE
*Emma Bovary Meets Celebrity Culture*

AS Jean Lorrain's 1908 novel *Maison pour dames* opens, Madame Emma Farnier, a young newlywed from Avignon, thumbs through the pages of a women's photographic magazine, *Le Laurier d'Or*, only to discover that Florise d'Ellebreuse has won the grand prize in the publication's poetry contest. With this discovery, Emma's life is transformed. Florise d'Ellebreuse, it turns out, is the pseudonym that Emma herself had chosen when she hopefully (and surreptitiously) submitted her flowery and somewhat audacious, sensual poems to a *tournoi de poésie* sponsored by the glossy publication. Emma/Florise is immediately sent to Paris to be repackaged for rapid celebrity, and the novel gleefully recounts the moral downfall that accompanies her rise to fame.

*Le Laurier d'Or* was intended as a direct send-up of *Femina* and *La Vie Heureuse*, "those illustrated magazines," in Lorrain's words, "devoted fully to women's glory, that of the woman painter, the woman artist, the woman sculptor, the woman writer," to which it is explicitly compared.[1] Lorrain, a decadent writer better known for novels like *Histoire des masques* (1900) and *Monsieur de Phocas* (1901), as well as for his flamboyant homosexuality, rather improbably wrote for *Femina* in 1905 and 1906, contributing reports as well as the serialized novel *Ellen*. With the first installment the editors acknowledged that readers might be a little surprised to find this author "whose works thus far would not be welcome in just any hands" in the pages of *Femina*. But rest assured, they clarified, this would be the famous novelist's first work appropriate for young women.[2] *Maison pour dames* was published shortly after his death, and it is not clear whether he had intended it for a general public. In addition to naming *Femina* and *La Vie Heureuse* as the imaginary *Le Laurier d'Or*'s competitors and mocking the magazines' "poetry tournaments," Lorrain's biting roman à clef mixes reality with fiction in its depiction of the magazine's contents. The novel cites directly from articles that actually appeared in *Femina* and *La Vie Heureuse* and loosely disguises its favorite "authoresses" as well as numerous female Belle Epoque literary figures. Some, like Lucie Delarue-Mardrus, Séverine, Daniel Lesueur, Jeanne Marni and Gabrielle Réval, are named explicitly, others in thinly veiled disguise: Madame Myriam Hegland (Myriam Harry); la comtesse Hamarande (Anna de Noailles).

Lorrain's novel has been cited in recent studies of the women's press as a window onto their workings—a caricature, or satire, but with more than a grain of truth—as witnessed in its ripped-from-the-headlines qualities.[3] But Lorrain's novel is a fantasy that caricatures female desire and the *presse féminine*'s power to manipulate it: it resolves the very real threat of female intellectual parity suggested by the magazines by masking it as errant female desire, more easily coded negatively than female brains. Indeed, despite his familiarity with the content of the magazines, Lorrain's scathing satirical novel shows the difficulty an outsider might have in distinguishing between Belle Epoque literary feminism and other kinds of challenges to Belle Epoque gender norms. The novel presents a fundamental misreading of *Femina* and *La Vie Heureuse*, one which maps the new ambitions of the *femme moderne* onto an outmoded nineteenth-century narrative of ill-fated female desire—completely ignoring, then, the ways in which these publications deliberately set themselves apart.

## *Le Laurier d'Or*

The name given to Lorrain's heroine is no coincidence. It is not hard to imagine that Emma Bovary, a few generations later, would have been seduced by *Femina* and *La Vie Heureuse*, just as she fantasized about passionate romance she knew from best-selling novels. Like that of her namesake, Emma Farnier's naïve ambition is guided by the hope of an escape route from her marriage. Hardworking Emile, *fonctionnaire* par excellence, is repeatedly referred to by the less-than-awe-inspiring epithet "Farnier the mortgage officer." After a long four years, Emma is bored. Because she has no children, the narrator explains, "the idle, sentimental young woman had all the time to daydream" (2). These dreams are nourished by magazines like *Le Laurier d'Or*, whose seductive powers reach far beyond Emma Bovary's fairy tales from the convent or the magazines Flaubert had her devour: *La Corbeille* and *Le Sylphe des salons*. Emma Bovary was already constructed as a kind of ideal reader of the women's press, with all the time in the world to project her dreams into their tantalizing pages.[4] In contrast to the early prototypes that Emma B. read, however, *Le Laurier d'Or* portends to speak directly to Emma F.; and, delightfully, the lines of communication go both ways, so that she can send in her poems and become one of the celebrated, by dint of her own talent. Indeed, for this generation, women do not need to force their husbands into path-breaking surgeries in order to squeeze out some ancillary glory for themselves. This Emma's professional mistakes—and shame—will be all her own.

In her study of the postmodern city, Paula Geyh observes that if advertising is about "confrontations with mirror images that suspend one's consciousness and unconscious, and hence one's space of desire, between the fantasy of success and the reality of failure," then the postmodern innovation is the place of one's own potential celebrity in this space: "the desire for and illusion of the possible dissemination of this image of oneself."[5] As precursors to this phenomenon, *Femina*'s and *La Vie Heureuse*'s *concours, enquêtes* and *tournois* (see Fig. 6.1), influenced as they were by the advertising industry, exploited this new nexus of desire for female magazine readers by offering women a new kind of mirror through which to see themselves (and in the process coded both celebrity and writing as roles appropriate for women). Lorrain, on the other hand, ridicules his heroine's seduction by these precise forces. Emma Farnier's fantasy is much more specific than that of her predecessor, who dreamt vaguely of bliss, passion, ecstasy. She dreams instead of a particular brand of celebrity offered through "the top feminist journal of its day": "her name proclaimed from all corners of Paris, what am I saying, France, Europe, or even further away! And her picture published in the Review and certainly reproduced in other newspapers; the party given in her honor; the travel funds at her disposal; her volume of poetry finally published, for publishers would run after the top female poet of the year, if not of the century!" (7). Note that in this fantasy, literary glory is described as a corollary of celebrity, and not the other way around.

Like Flaubert's Emma, whose tragic disappointments can be anticipated through Flaubert's incisive prose long before her wedding night,

**Figure 6.1** Winners of a *Femina* poetry "tournament" (March 1, 1907).

this Emma's sparkling, naive dreams of a more glorious existence are quickly deflated—and with much less subtlety. In the process, Lorrain's narrative gives voice to the same anxiety expressed by Flaubert and a legion of his nineteenth-century contemporaries about the effect of urbanism on the bourgeois woman, who loses control when the city's sophisticated tastes unleash her desires. Hunger for celebrity maps onto those other feminine desires, and the consumerism of the newly accessible department store, or *grand magasin*—channeled for Madame Bovary through her broker Monsieur Lheureux (whose very name bespeaks her longed-for pleasures and the hedonistic indulgence of consumption)—is passed down through the magazine.[6]

Emma Farnier's unfeminine ambition finds its first victim in the fragile marriage bond: she must tell her husband, who, while privy to some of her poetic efforts, had been ignorant not only of her delusions of grandeur but of the outlet through which she had channeled them. After three nights of sexual favors, he allows her to accept her prize, and they head off to the brave new world of the Parisian literati—encouraged by the coincidence that the magazine's publisher Robert M. de Farenbourg is—behind his fancy pseudonym—none other than Emile's long-lost schoolmate. This presumed stand-in for Pierre Lafitte is another example of the dissolution of French tradition that Emma's achievement represents. Anyone, it seems, can climb to the highest social heights, if skilled in the new rules of the game.

Emma's exchange—conjugal sex for glory—only forewarns of the prostitutional stance in which she will soon find herself trapped. Indeed, the beautiful world of *Le Laurier d'Or* is revealed to be an illusion—nothing more than the construction of greedy snake-oil purveyors who manipulate images and concoct seductive prose in order to tug at the heartstrings of those too simple to know any better. The women around *Le Laurier d'Or* are perverse lesbians, the men sleazy sex fiends; no one cares about truth and beauty. The magazine world is unveiled as a cesspool of greed and filth.

Upon Emma's arrival in Paris, she is ushered to a photo shoot, where, perhaps not surprisingly, the most extensive window onto the magazine's work is offered by the dashing photographer Robert Evimore. Compared to Christ himself, with a strong "Nazarene resemblance" that is said to have determined his artistic career, Evimore's miracles are limited to the dazzling technology of photo alteration: he will superimpose the photograph he takes of Emma in Paris onto the more exotic landscapes of her Avignon hometown—with its medieval Palais des Papes and scenic promontories. This unfamiliar technological feat in itself gets the provincial couple's hearts beating faster. To give the wide-eyed couple an idea of what he's going for, Evimore then lays before them back issues of *Femina* and *La Vie Heureuse*, offering incisive commentary as he flips through their pages. He stops, for example, on the "Ménages de poètes" article we examined in Chapter 5, showing Emma and her bewildered husband the glorious celebrity couples modeling modern marriage. As he points to the Rostands, he urges, "read the caption, it's admirable" and proceeds to quote it directly: "Madame Edmond Rostand, exquisitely poetic, has made herself, now, the exquisite Muse of her husband." (Emma is delighted thinking she and Emile can pose as a couple before Evimore reminds her that those are *artist* couples, and "it's not the wife but the husband who makes the *ménage d'artistes*.") Evimore's lesson in the careful genius of combining text and image makes up the better part of Lorrain's chapter: frequently quoting directly from the magazines, he points out Daniel Lesueur surrounded by pigeons in Venice's Saint Mark's Plaza (*Femina*, March 1902), Gabrielle Réval with her adorable son (an image that both "charms and intrigues"), and the Poet Queen Carmen Sylva herself ("you'd think it was Catherine the Great"), before arriving at "the nec plus ultra of the genre": Lucie Delarue-Mardrus.

"Not only did Madame Lucie Mardrus have genius," Evimore explains breathlessly, showing Emma the pictures of the poetess in Tunisia, "but she was lucky enough to have for a husband an intellectual and a traveler doubling as the even rarer writer." He continues: "Not only did Madame Lucie Mardrus have the opportunity to travel around and visit the most beautiful country in the world, but her husband had the terrific idea of kodaking (*kodachquer*) her in the most unexpected sites and most captivating costumes" (55). He goes on to narrate those costumes, marveling at the accompanying captions as "masterpieces," which he reads aloud word for word, enraptured. If Lorrain, who devotes four entire pages of his novel to describing Delarue-Mardrus's appearances in the magazines, seems particularly irritated by the glorified presence of this particular muse, perhaps it was because his own novella, *Ellen*, was first introduced on a page of *Femina* that faced one featuring the poetess in oriental garb.[7]

By the end of this encounter, Emma and Emile—for he is simply a male version of her, this mediocre mortgage officer, the provincial husband gamely following his wife's bidding—are demoralized, their dreams quickly deflating. How could they compete with such figures? "Madame Farnier had never wandered through Kroumirie and the sands of the desert; Madame Farnier had never mounted a horse, in men's clothing, on the roads of North Africa" (59). Her energies sapped, Emma hardly protests when Evimore cuts off her sleeves and opens her collar to expose her neckline.

After this long discourse on the actual articles that appeared in *Femina* and *La Vie Heureuse*, Lorrain retreats deep into fictional territory, abandoning the provocative Belle Epoque narrative of new kinds of female visibility in favor of the older but persistent storyline. To her husband's alarm and incomprehension, Emma quickly drains her prize money in an effort to accommodate the sartorial demands of her new role, in the familiar trope of Bovaresque feminine desire channeled into shopping. Soon she is being courted by the seedy old Monsieur Agrado, and seduced by the painter Madame de Mauves, who covers her with baffling kisses that her innocent mind struggles (and fails!) to interpret. The newest "it-girl" of the publishing world, she cannot move without being ogled and is inundated with fan mail teeming with sexual innuendo. Gossip rags detail her unrealized sexual exploits as *faits accomplis*, while the poor young wife from Avignon is transformed into a full-fledged Sapphic demimondaine on the verge of that disease of the (nineteenth) century, hysteria.[8] Alarmed at her own naiveté, Emma laments, "I came to Paris, not to do prostitution, but rather, literature" (255); the parallel construction of the sentence betrays the public aspect of both activities that made them equivalent, at least for women. At the novel's end, Emma and Emile have fled home (although the family has already written to sever ties with these shame-ridden relatives)—bonded together now through their mutual shame. Hardly "poetess of the year" material, Emma is fully humbled when she returns to her existence as the chastened wife of the lowly mortgage broker. In the final scene, the journalist who has written an article for *Le Scandale* describing Emma's lesbian seductions is attacked by a posse of women artists and writers, his face bleeding from their violent scratches. The editor of *Le Laurier* watches smugly, having orchestrated this revenge on the rival journalist who had prevented him from expanding his lucrative enterprise on the back of this new celebrity.

Jean Lorrain inserts his women's magazine, then, into the narrative trajectory of so much French realist and naturalist fiction, taking Emma F. to her logical and inevitable conclusion, the errant bourgeois woman at the center of the late nineteenth-century narrative of decline. In the process, he invokes a litany of similarly unfortunate female heroines. Emma is explicitly compared to Dinah de la Baudraye of Balzac's 1837 *La muse du département*, also "diverted from a peaceful life by the mirage of fame."[9] Balzac's provincial bluestocking (herself a playful send-up of George Sand) tries to live up to the passion she evokes in her own poetry, written, of course, under a pseudonym, only to be chastened by the realities of Paris. Emma's much-anticipated arrival onto the Parisian social scene, with the uttering of her name passing in the crowd from "mouth to mouth," is also evocative of the entrance of Zola's notorious courtesan Nana in his novel of the same name. Along the way, of course, Lorrain has furthered that persistent nineteenth-century slippage between woman writer and prostitute.

Finally, as in Maupassant's 1884 short story "The Necklace" ("La parure"), whose antiheroine Mathilde Loisel is a close spiritual cousin of Madame Bovary, *Maison pour dames* invites readers to take pleasure in a cautionary tale about unbridled female ambition, bred of consumerist lust and the desire to imitate those more fortunate. In Maupassant's text, Mathilde (who is introduced as a charming young woman born "as if by an error of fate, into a family of workers") loses the necklace she had borrowed from a rich girlfriend in order to attend a ball; she spends the next ten years working to pay back debts incurred in replacing it, only to discover that the original had been fake.[10] It's too late, of course, for Mathilde, haggard and worn, to learn the lesson that modern life means a lack of distinction between real and fake riches—a lesson for which she herself served as an example in her glorious appearance at the ball. Just as the invitation that the earnest husband Monsieur Loisel brings home is not enough—his wife then needs a dress and jewelry to attend the ball—Emma F.'s prize earnings are quickly poured into the clothes and accessories she must purchase in order to take part in the world to which her poem has served as an invitation (and Maupassant's tale is perhaps evoked in Lorrain's penultimate chapter, "The Queen's Necklace," where Monsieur Agrado tempts Emma with dazzling jewels). As Mathilde and Emma Bovary before her, the provincial Madame Farnier is punished for attempting to climb beyond her God- and marriage-given lot, ruined but chastened by this unfortunate encounter with Paris and its temptations. Indeed, all three texts are Cinderella-stories gone awry: women longing to be lifted out of their mundane existences in order to become princesses, but denied happy endings. Lorrain's cruel yet lighthearted narrator, like Flaubert's and Maupassant's playfully sadistic ones, seems to take pleasure in bringing Emma down along with the women's press to which she had hinged her dreams of a better life.

The discomfort with women's upward social mobility reflected in Balzac, Flaubert and Maupassant's works maps onto a distinct unease in Jean Lorrain's writing with the expansion of women's intellectual opportunities. His novel reads the magazines via enduring nineteenth-century stereotypes through which women were either *courtisanes* or *ménagères*—harlots or housewives; the story follows Emma's attempted (and failed) conversion from the latter to the former, without destabilizing either side of the dichotomy. Interestingly, Lorrain associates *Le Laurier d'Or* with feminism, a term both *Femina* and *La Vie Heureuse* consciously avoided precisely because of its association with the rejection of conventional gender norms. If *Le Laurier* might be considered feminist, it was in the sense of that particular Belle Epoque brand of gender resistance so eloquently described in Mary Louise Roberts's *Disruptive Acts*: the bold, audacious behavior of certain Belle Epoque women meant to upend gender orthodoxy and allow women into brave new realms. Lorrain's novels remind us that the women he portrayed would likely have been considered feminists by many because of this behavior, but would have been just as likely to eschew the term, which was associated with a specific political stance. While many famous Belle Epoque women writers did in fact exploit the associations of modern femininity with sexual audacity in their novels, those women were not the darlings of *Femina* and *La Vie Heureuse*. Lorrain's depiction thus conflates two very different modes of challenging gender norms during the Belle Epoque, demonstrating how the audacious "New Woman" stereotype, then and now, occulted other forms of resistance and feminist expression. While *Femina* and *La Vie Heureuse* were consumed with celebrity, they steered carefully away from gossip or scandal. Indeed, they worked vigilantly to be the very image of propriety. And despite Lucie Delarue-Mardrus's frequent presence (which we know to have been somewhat anomalous), the rest of "Sapho 1900" was absent from these pages. The word *lesbian* would never be printed; illicit sexuality or (heaven forbid!) adultery never even suggested. Some of the most famous women writers of this generation (Rachilde, Colette, Renée Vivien) and some of the most prolific popular writers (Jane de la Vaudère) would never be found, let alone mentioned, in their pages because of the very audacity of their prose.[11]

Lorrain's novel brings into relief the extent to which the nuanced feminist stance of these magazines and the particular ideology they seemed to represent for thousands of French women was invisible to those not seeking it. Even someone who wrote for *Femina*, and who had read enough articles from both *Femina* and *La Vie Heureuse* to cite several of them directly in his novel, was unable (or unwilling) to recognize the other kinds of discussions taking place within these publications, or to distinguish between their straightlaced bourgeois feminism and the overtly "disruptive act" challenges to gender norms enacted in other venues, print and elsewhere. The conversation orchestrated by *Femina* and *La Vie Heureuse* was taking place between and among a substantial group of women and a select number of men; but those not part of the conversation seem to have been largely oblivious to it.

By misunderstanding the complexity (or internal contradictions) of Belle Epoque feminism in this way, Lorrain's novel reads the world of the women's press in much the same way that other misogynistic Belle Epoque critics read the surge of women's writing from the period. The world he describes, albeit satirically, mirrors Charles Maurras's 1905 commentary on the underworld of women writers as a secret city of lesbians: "where man only appears as an intruder or monster."[12] The democratization of female intellect was a source of deep anxiety for many male critics of the Belle Epoque, who feared not only that women were abandoning their wifely duties (women writers of this generation were often figured as lesbians or prostitutes), but that the influx of female-authored writing would soon eclipse their own share of the market.[13] It's worth noting in this context that of all the different kinds of women celebrated in *Femina* and *La Vie Heureuse*, Lorrain chose women writers as his object of ridicule. According to critic Octave Uzanne, by 1894, 1,211 women were members of the Société des gens de lettres; in an essay dated May 1903, the critic Jean Ernest-Charles sarcastically referred to "the five hundred and some odd women who published novels this month"—a figure intended to have shock value. The year 1908 in which Lorrain's novel was published may in fact have been a tipping point for French women writers: the point at which the woman writer became fully visible in all her success.[14] Following that year, numerous volumes were devoted to analyzing the phenomenon: literary critic Jean Bertaut wondered whether there was a crisis at hand or the first step of an evolution, whereas Jules Flat worried about distinguishing between the "crowded battalions" of women writers and those who had true talent.[15]

Lorrain's novel diffused the threat of the thinking woman by resurrecting the link between female creativity and moral corruption and then exacting fictional revenge. As Emma Farnier narrowly escapes from the nefarious hyper-sexualized underworld of Parisian journalism, his satire leaves her in much the same position in which Emma Bovary started, fifty years earlier: destined for a life of frustration. But much had changed in those fifty years, including, importantly, the availability of new screens upon which women could project their fantasies of upward mobility. His literary revenge does nothing to address the very real question of the emergence of large numbers of women writers—the ones far from scandal or secret sexual rituals. In light of this, it's particularly telling that Marbo's 1907 response to Yver's *Princesses de science*—"The Intellectual Housewife"—about whether educated, professional women could have successful marriages, closed with a meditation on none other than Emma Bovary herself. Women who were not cut out to be housewives should be able to become *"useful minds,"* claimed Marbo, echoing *Femina*'s own 1902 promise to guide women in that direction.[16] "Had she been capable of it, Madame Bovary would have been better off studying medicine," she wrote, imagining Emma as a doctor in her own right. In the narrative of the women's press, then, Emma Bovary's problem was not desire itself, but the absence of ways for women to direct ambitions that did not conform to their circumscribed domestic roles. *Femina* and *La Vie Heureuse* thus served as modes of ordering what might otherwise be disordered; sexual deviance was no longer a result of intellectual exertion or excesses of imagination, but rather, lack of available paths for women to direct those processes. Send Emma to medical school and her problems are averted. As for Emma Farnier? In another novelist's hands, she might have read some Tinayre and Compain and found a way to work through her literary success in order to update her marriage so as not to die of boredom: then she could fit right into the magazines' framework for the *femme moderne*, and perhaps even discover her own means of work-life balance.

Lorrain's novel traces the rise and fall of a fictional fifteen minutes of female literary glory. In the next chapter, we will see the real-life version of this story: what happens when an actual woman writer made famous by *Femina* and *La Vie Heureuse* falls prey to the whims of a fickle public just beyond her devoted female readership.

# CHAPTER 7
# A BELLE EPOQUE MEDIA STORM
*Marcelle Tinayre and the Legion of Honor*

ON January 19th, 1908, a Henriot cartoon in the "Semaine illustrée" section of the Parisian daily *Le Petit Journal* depicted an elegant woman in the distance, descending a well-appointed staircase.[1] Throngs of people swarm the street below her; one fellow has climbed up a lamppost to catch a glimpse and another hovers from a treetop. In the caption, a couple looking on discusses the spectacle. Asks one: "So what is it? Everyone is looking!" Replies the other: "It's the woman who did not want to be honored (*décorée*) in order to avoid being noticed."

As Parisian readers at the time well knew, the woman in question was none other than Marcelle Tinayre; the decoration at stake was that of the Legion of Honor, the award established by Napoleon to honor French patriotism. Less than two weeks earlier, Tinayre's name had been leaked as a presumptive nominee for the rank of chevalier.[2] She would not have been the first woman to receive the honor, nor the first woman writer—fellow novelist Daniel Lesueur had been decorated in 1900; but the award was primarily given to men, and controversy still brewed around Sarah Bernhardt's repeated exclusion from its ranks (she would not be decorated until 1914).[3] On January 7, following the announcement, the daily newspapers *La Liberté* and *La Patrie* featured interviews with Tinayre and the following day *Le Temps* published a letter from the author reflecting on her nomination. In these articles, Tinayre expressed amusement and surprise over her sudden glory: "A knight! Me, a knight! No, it's too funny," she mused to *La Patrie*, adding that she would not be the kind of masculine hero Napoleon had in mind when creating the honor. She couldn't possibly wear the red ribbon, she told the interviewers, referring to the medal that accompanies the honor—a cross-shaped badge suspended from a ribbon traditionally worn over the left breast—for doing so might lead people in the metro to notice her and misinterpret her identity. This decision, she reported, went against the advice of her seamstress, who thought it would look lovely against a black suit (*Le Temps*). The Legion of Honor, Tinayre insisted, was not something she would have ever solicited; indeed, when Aristide Briand—then minister of Public Instruction and Worship—had mentioned it to her at an earlier moment, she told him he could better please her with a strand of pearls (*La Liberté*). Further, the award might trouble her young son, "who doesn't want his mommy to be 'different from other ladies'" (*Le Temps*) or discourage her hard-working artist-husband, "whose boutonniere was still free of decoration" (*La Liberté*).

Over the next several days, nearly one hundred articles appeared in the Parisian press, far beyond the carefully circumscribed pages of *Femina* and *La Vie Heureuse*. In fact, Tinayre's comments were analyzed by publications across a wide spectrum of political affiliations, from the extreme right to the left-leaning; major dailies and gossip rags participated in the media storm in nearly equal measure[4]: it was a veritable media frenzy surrounding a scandal that became known as the *Affaire Tinayre*. The vast majority of voices opposed Tinayre's nomination, citing her mockery of French tradition and a hyperfeminized modesty that was deemed disingenuous, as the Henriot cartoon attests. Tinayre's words were scrutinized relentlessly, and her feminism, maternal obligations and career choice became journalistic fodder for essays, satires, letters, cartoons and polemics over the course of nearly two weeks. When the official list of honorees was finally released one week later, Tinayre's name was notably absent; her nomination had not been ratified.[5]

Tinayre's well-documented unraveling at the hands of the mass press reveals a troubling disconnect between the image of modern femininity promoted in *Femina* and *La Vie Heureuse* and ones accepted by the mainstream media. It demonstrates, once again, the extent to which the *femme moderne*'s carefully choreographed balance of femininity and feminism was difficult to assimilate beyond its meticulously constructed domain. The self-effacing remarks of a woman being celebrated for her intelligence and creativity—comments perfectly natural within the pages of the women's (semi-)glossies and consistent with their model of feminine achievement—were attacked as an absurd, disingenuous performance outside of them. Even more stunning in Tinayre's public bashing was the fact that this writer had herself been so savvy, as we have seen, in manipulating the image of herself circulated to readers.

A key element of this disconnect can be traced to the magazines' sophistication as a media outlet, reminding us that *Femina* and *La Vie Heureuse* were still innovative in developing their particular genre of the biographical feature story. The magazines' frequent multipage exposés on any given woman writer (as well as their biographical articles on other female role models), with their visually dramatic combination of photography, intimate looks inside the home, and "candid" personal commentary, created a sense of intimacy between the public female figure and her readers. While stories about famous men (and women) were regular features of other illustrated magazines, these figures were generally admired from a critical distance. *Femina* and *La Vie Heureuse* were unique in their efforts to collapse the boundary between idol and *lectrice*, always trying to make it look as if the reader was genuinely a part of the conversation. Tinayre's casual, personal comments were a product of this modern celebrity relationship, which Richard Schickel dubbed that of "intimate strangers" in his book on celebrity culture in twentieth-century America. But her offhand tone was strikingly dissonant with both the cultural practices of the daily press (where photos never appeared) and the sense of gravity surrounding the national honor. The Tinayre episode vividly demonstrates, then, how the complications of a nascent celebrity and media culture were intertwined with the fate of the *femme moderne*. What we have here is a perfect (media) storm, as anxiety and confusion about modern gender roles hit up against anxiety and confusion about modern celebrity.

## Marcelle Tinayre's Adventure

Tinayre's initial controversial remarks appeared on January 7 and 8, after her nomination was announced, in the letter (supposedly solicited) that she wrote to *Le Temps* and in interviews she promptly offered to *La Patrie* and *La Liberté*.[6] "It's true, I've been decorated. It's not my fault," began the letter addressed to the editor of *Le Temps*, published on the front page of the paper. Tinayre insisted that she did nothing to solicit the honor, an admission repeated in the other two publications.[7] She went on to reflect on what she described as an already uncomfortable relationship to celebrity, explaining that she had always been both "a little bit shy and a little bit prideful." Fame, she asserted, did not conjugate well with femininity, noting that while the writer might have pretenses to vanity, "the woman scoffs at the writer, and she is the one who has the last word." In the letter as well as in the two interviews, Tinayre explained that, despite her deep appreciation for and willingness to accept the honor, she had decided that she could not wear the "pretty ribbon and the pretty cross" in public.[8] She gave a series of reasons for this decision, all of which seemed to point to a discomfort with being thrust into a traditionally masculine role: the decoration would attract uncomfortable attention to her in public; Napoleon had intended it for male heroes; so many others had merited it, including her husband, but remained unadorned; it would upset her young son, whose antifeminist inclinations she admitted being troubled by (and thus cleverly acknowledged both her feminism and her willingness to live with its opponents).

In the context of *Femina* and *La Vie Heureuse*, Tinayre's conscientiously diffident comments to the Parisian dailies would likely have been received as a welcome feminization of the masculine role of authorship, a reminder that, though a writer, she was still womanly. But in the context of the mainstream press, destined towards a primarily male audience (or at least one where the male point of view served as the generic neutral) and unaccustomed to the register of discourse in which she was speaking, those same words appeared nothing short of preposterous. Not surprisingly, Tinayre's apparent irreverence provided an opening for a backlash against women writers, whose success and rising numbers had been posing an increasing threat to their male counterparts in the early years of the century. The conservative commentator Jean Ernest-Charles, who had brooded over the proliferation of women writers in a regular Saturday column, was among the most forceful to take the bait.[9] Following a strongly worded piece in the January 8 *Gil Blas* mocking Tinayre's modesty, on January 18, he devoted an entire issue of his journal *Le Censeur politique et littéraire* to the affair. Entitled "Madame Marcelle Tinayre's Adventure," it was a collection of approximately forty articles that had appeared in the previous ten days, setting the tone through Ernest-Charles's initial declaration: "There are too few occasions for laughter in the world."[10] Beyond a reason to laugh, Ernest-Charles promised the affair would offer insight into "contemporary mores," literary and otherwise. Ernest-Charles was particularly irritated by what he perceived as Tinayre's inappropriate garnering of publicity, which he saw as characteristic of women writers as a group (although he also admitted that they probably learned this from their male predecessors and peers). In an article entitled "Women of Letters" that appeared in the January 12 edition of the *Gil Blas*, he wrote: "Publicity! Publicity! Publicity! Women writers are publicity crazy!"[11] Without mentioning Tinayre's name explicitly, he mocked her supposed high manners throughout the piece, before launching into a tirade against women writers, who, he claimed, had overly benefited from attention granted them.[12] For Ernest-Charles, then, Tinayre's feminized persona and her carryings-on about her appearance were merely a ruse—part of a greater shared effort by women writers to hide their decidedly unconventional behavior (writing, making money) in conventionally feminine terms, for their own purely selfish motives. The contemporary woman writer, this argument suggested, was not the delicate woman she pretended to be, but rather, no better than the aggressive bluestockings of the nineteenth century, and thus hardly a true woman after all. Ernest-Charles's response put the woman writer in the same camp as other subversive female figures of the Belle Epoque—including feminists, suffragettes, cyclists, and all variations of the New Woman—who were perceived as abandoning conventional sex roles and thus threatening basic social structures.

Matching Ernest-Charles in vitriol for the *femme de lettres* was a piece by the writer Clément Vautel in the January 10 edition of *La Liberté*. Vautel picked up on the comments of Tinayre's young son that he wanted her to be like other mothers. Calling attention to the fact that, even without the red ribbon, the woman writer was already not a conventional mother, Vautel's piece showcased a notion that Tinayre and the women's press were working particularly hard to fight: that motherhood was incompatible with writing, and implied a lapse in maternal and wifely performance. Vautel thus imagined young Noël Tinayre describing what exactly those other mothers were doing that his was not:

I mean that they take care of their little boy and their husband, that they survey the kitchen, that they never go out alone, that they don't read old books, that they never have ink-stained fingers, that they don't lock themselves in their room all afternoon to do work, work always more work . . . These moms don't talk about complicated things, they don't have wrinkled brows; they are simple, patient, very sweet.

This imagined dialogue was followed by the admonition: "If Madame Tinayre is reasonable, she will stop writing immediately."[13]

Vautel's and Ernest-Charles's tirades are examples of a common consequence of public scandals in the media age, which can produce a rush of previously censored sentiment momentarily made acceptable by dint of the public figure's blunder. Just as the intense preoccupation with the New Woman that had dominated print culture of the previous decade was beginning to fade, Tinayre's comments clearly irritated nerves still sensitive about shifting gender roles; they tapped into fears that the women making their way into the public sphere were acting disingenuously, arriving at success through manipulation rather than merit, and thus subverting the very gender norms they often feigned to preserve.

Writers like Ernest-Charles and Vautel exploited the affair in an attempt to reignite these debates, hoping to prove, it seems, not unlike Jean Lorrain, that women were not meant to be writers after all. Their comments seem almost predictable in that context. But these were in fact the minority voices during those two weeks in January 1908. Indeed, despite the harsh criticism of Tinayre's behavior apparent in these examples, the majority of her critics took pains to demonstrate their appreciation of Tinayre's talent, and many went out of their way to defend women's right to hold the honor. Franc-Nohain spoke of her "incontestable talent"; *La Presse* described her as "a woman of talent" and *L'Autorité* recognized her "very lovely talent."[14] Reacting to Tinayre's statements that she did not think Napoleon would have approved of her nomination, numerous critics insisted that her award was fully consistent with Napoleon's wishes to honor accomplishments beyond the military.[15] Demonstrating proof of their belief in honoring women, if not this particular woman, many critics offered suggestions of female honorees to replace Tinayre; they included Sarah Bernhardt and the women writers Mademoiselle Dufau and Georges de Peyrebrune.[16] *L'Éclair* invited previously decorated female honorees to comment on the scandal. Among them was the first *femme de lettres* to be decorated, Daniel Lesueur, who insisted that the only appropriate response to the honor was her "silent gratitude."[17] Lesueur's astutely circumspect comment suggests that the controversy around Tinayre did not so much regard honoring a woman for her writing as it was concerned with the way in which she received it—the image of accomplished woman that she projected. Thus, while it is tempting to read the media outrage and the sheer quantity of responses to Tinayre's comments as affirmation of wider French discomfort with women's advances in the public sphere, and as proof of the public's continued denigration of the woman writer, this interpretation misses the import of the Tinayre affair.[18] While certainly the negative associations of the woman writer and the New Woman persisted and were stirred up by these events, what the media frenzy reveals most pointedly about Belle Epoque society is that most of the public was attempting to move away from the rigid gender roles of the past, and yet not quite able to imagine what a professional woman writer should look like or what her public role should be. It was a moment of ambivalence, if not confusion—one that, ironically, so many women novelists themselves were engaged in working through, as we have seen. Most crucially, the question that rose dramatically to the surface was no longer *whether* a woman should hold the honor, but rather *how* she should go about doing so.

One of the issues that the public responded to most vociferously was Tinayre's initial declaration that she would not wear the red ribbon, so as not to be noticed by the corner grocer—despite her seamstress's urging to put it on her *tailleur noir*.[19] Among dozens of others parsing these comments, Franc-Nohain, a frequent contributor to *Femina* and *La Vie Heureuse*, mocked Tinayre's seeming preoccupation with the challenge of wearing the "the star of the brave" on a chest that, "fortunately!" in her words, didn't resemble that of a soldier, as a frivolous concern that betrayed a lack of respect for Napoleonic tradition ("and with what a tone, what a smile," he insisted). But while the press relentlessly mocked Tinayre's emphasis on fashion and appearance, her sartorial challenge was the stage on which a much larger debate was playing out over the place of conventional femininity in the public sphere (one not unlike recent scrutiny of both Hillary Clinton's and Sarah Palin's wardrobes, or those of Rachida Dati and Cécile Duflot on the other side of the Atlantic).

In Tinayre's case, the challenge was actually rooted in the basic, practical problem that Franc-Nohain was so quick to dismiss: how *does* a decorated woman writer wear the medal? Citing her comment that she would have preferred a chain of pearls, Emile Faguet remarked in the January 9 issue of *Le Gaulois* that she deserved the jewelry *and* the medal. "The necklace is for the charming woman; the ribbon is for the artist. When one is both one and the other, one must accept the two decorations. [ . . . ] Why else do you have shoulders and also genius?" This was one real aspect of Tinayre's dilemma: how to bear her shoulders and wear the ribbon. If decorated men regularly wore theirs upon their lapel, was a woman expected to do the same even when inhabiting more traditional roles? One possible solution was concocted by none other than *Femina* in 1904, when Julia Bartet became the first actress to receive the honor. In celebration, *Femina* raised 1800 francs from subscribers in order to present her with a diamond-encrusted version of the cross that traditionally accompanied the medal, and honored Bartet with a gala affair. Tinayre herself seemed to refer to this indirectly when she told Delaunay in a published interview, "I think I've found a way out of the problem. Here it is: it's to have a tasteful jeweler make a tiny diamond cross that I will put on as a brooch."[20] Such an object, one imagines, could be worn in multiple circumstances, while remaining subtle enough (and assimilable to other kinds of female ornamentation) not to attract undue attention. Despite its clear relevance to the Tinayre scandal, no other reference to *Femina*'s honoring of Bartet appeared in the general press, a fact which serves as another striking proof of the disconnect between the women's magazines and their peer publications during this time.

Rather than a red herring or a way to distract from the "real" gender equality question at hand, the preoccupation with clothing was quite fundamental, as it signaled the challenge of *imagining* this public figure and thus allowing her into the collective social imaginary. This was precisely the work in which *Femina* and *La Vie Heureuse* were engaged: their pages were an explicit effort to offer a model of what a successful modern woman should *look* like. But Tinayre's comments suddenly made visible for a broader reading public the jumble of contradictions upon which that image of female success was based; we can thus recognize, in the reaction, the extent to which this model was tightly circumscribed by the controlled framework of the women's press and the rigid parameters that Belle Epoque literary feminism had set for itself. Much of the ink spilled in response to Tinayre's remarks was devoted simply to repeating what she had said and quoting other papers quoting her. While Tinayre's charming tone was entirely familiar to her *chères lectrices*, the very act of reframing her words outside of their original context (her own letter and interviews) served as commentary in itself; the only editorializing needed in some cases was an added italics or exclamation point ("a string of pearls!").[21] Tinayre's well-established public image amongst her readership was thus revealed to be just that: a construction intended for, and embraced by, a very limited audience.

## Modesty, a Feminine Virtue?

Tinayre later clarified her original refusal to wear the ribbon in *L'Écho de Paris*, saying: "I will wear the ribbon with pride in circumstances that seem to me appropriate and suitable, but not on the street," and elaborated to *L'Intransigeant* her horror of being hounded by curious onlookers.[22] But this clarification hardly satisfied readers. Like the Henriot cartoon, which called attention to the contradiction between Tinayre's willingness to speak to the press and her avowed refusal of public recognition, a January 9 article in *L'Aurore* entitled "Modesty, a Feminine Virtue," read: "Madame Tinayre, who is discreet, thus confides to thirty-eight million French people and all the citizens of the world that she will not wear her decoration at all."[23] Discretion, or modesty, was indeed key to Tinayre's self-presentation, as she offered herself up as a talented and hardworking writer blind to her own success. But this insistence on feminine modesty, of all traits, seemed fundamentally incompatible with the obligations of celebrity: how could one appear in widely circulating publications, exposing one's private life for general consumption, and claim this quality—while also claiming a desire to avoid unwanted attention? On top of this inherent contradiction, French tradition added another level of pressure, as it had always privileged a firm line between public and private life. The seemingly disproportionate response to Tinayre's remarks, then, stemmed at least in part from deep discomfort with this new and largely unfamiliar aspect of celebrity culture, further exacerbated by Tinayre being a woman and thus meant to be an exemplar of discretion herself. Even as she insisted on her traditional feminine values, Tinayre's comments horrified readers who saw this insistence—by virtue of its public framework—as both unfeminine and anathema to the rules of French propriety.[24]

*Femina* and *La Vie Heureuse*, on the other hand, attempted to resolve the internal contradiction of the discreet female public figure through a systematic conflation of those traditionally separate public and private spheres. As we saw in the feature stories discussed in Chapter 2, Tinayre and her colleagues' public personae—the images of them circulated to the thousands of readers of *Femina* and *La Vie Heureuse*—often relied on the assimilation of the woman writer with her domestic domain. Reading the features on Tinayre, one has the impression that she never left the house and would never want to do so.[25] After all, the modest woman writer does not parade around flaunting her talents; rather, she can only be admired if one catches a glimpse of her within her own home. Her very public image within the magazines thus served to reinforce the idea that she had never left the private sphere, collapsing in that sense their opposition. The extensive photographic documentation of women writers in their domestic interiors helped tremendously to maintain this illusion: readers became familiar with Tinayre in her own home, and could picture her next to her husband, playing with her children (Fig. 7.1). Tinayre's comments to *Le Temps*, *La Patrie* and *La Liberté* following news of her nomination must also be considered, therefore, in the context of this familiar, familial image she had developed in the women's press. When, in the mainstream publications, she ever-so-charmingly offered a glimpse into the colorful domestic world she shared with a precocious son, doting husband and opinionated seamstress, she was referencing well-documented biographical details that would have been deemed highly relevant in the pages of *Femina* and *La Vie Heureuse*.[26]

Moreover, Tinayre's remarks about not wanting to be noticed are actually not as inconsistent as they might first appear: there is a difference between the public nature of appearing in a magazine and the public nature of appearing on the street. While she had no problem revealing her intimate details to the press, she did not want that intimacy with strangers on a personal level (a challenge celebrities and their fans have been wrestling with ever since). But this distinction was still quite new in 1908. Tinayre herself had not yet quite worked out the precise balance between her public and private roles, perhaps because *Femina* and *La Vie Heureuse* actually only offered a media solution; they had not yet offered a way for women to assimilate public and private roles outside of their pages—in other words, in the real world, on the street, in ordinary life.

Tinayre gave voice to one aspect of this lingering tension explicitly, if playfully, in her letter to *Le Temps*, when she spoke of the battle between the woman and writer: "The writer might perhaps be tempted towards vanity, but the woman could care less about the writer, and

**Figure 7.1** Marcelle Tinayre pictured at home with her family in a *Femina* feature story (October 1, 1904).

she's the one who has the last word. It's the writer who is decorated, but it's the woman who has to wear the decoration![27] In this context, the term writer, or *écrivain* (and thus the public aspect of her identity) was not at all neutral, but rather remained very much a masculine identity, placed in tense opposition to the woman whose identity he shared. Tinayre's comments in effect underline the dearth (or absence) of public space that *Femina* and *La Vie Heureuse* had ultimately allotted for their version of the *femme écrivain*, as she was revealed to be nothing more than a journalistic construction, a contradiction in terms. The public persona crafted in the women's press could, paradoxically, only be imagined in the private sphere, or in a perfectly circumscribed public forum—such as a reception honoring her. To appear in the metro or on the street—that is, in daily life—as a celebrated *écrivain* would somehow be an affront to her carefully maintained femininity.

Picking up on this conflict in the January 9 edition of the *Gil Blas*, Michel Psichari parsed Tinayre's comment, writing of the "heroic combat" in Tinayre's mind between the *écrivain* and the *femme* in a dialogue that astutely staged the competing interests over the way the woman writer might want to be seen:

THE WRITER: Decorated! . . . Thus, the star of the brave will shine on my chest!

THE WOMAN: You're joking? Never, never will I consent to wear the red ribbon: I'll be taken for a bluestocking!

THE WRITER: Is that possible?

THE WOMAN: In the metro, when people see me, they'll think: it's a woman who must be a nun who took care of victims of the plague.

THE WRITER: Not at all! They'll think: it's the famous author of *La maison du péché*, the most admirable of novels, the most poignant, the most marvelous, the most sublime . . .

THE WOMAN: Be quiet! It's not proper to say everything out loud, even things that are true, especially what you're saying.

THE WRITER: So you're forbidding me to put the medal of honor on my corsage?

THE WOMAN: Yes!

THE WRITER: Will you at least let me make that decision public?

THE WOMAN: Of course. And could you at the same time reconcile my legitimate pride as a woman of letters with my simple feminine modesty—without looking like you're doing so!

Psichari's satire cleverly explains the paradox at the heart of Tinayre's struggle. If a celebrity has often been defined as "someone who is famous for being famous," Tinayre became famous for ostensibly not wanting to be famous—or rather, for trying very hard to look like she did not want to be famous.[28] Psichari unpacks the multiple conflicting impulses of the Belle Epoque woman and writer that effectively render a respectable public image impossible. The *femme* was trapped now in her beautifully appointed home, unable to maintain her established persona as *écrivain* beyond the private sphere without somehow tainting it or being mocked for wanting to protect it. *Femina* and *La Vie Heureuse* had found a way to envision a modern female ideal balancing femininity and feminism; what they failed to imagine was how the female *celebrity*—the actual human being who existed beyond their pages—could step out of their pages and onto the boulevard.

Tinayre's excessive professions of modesty, I would suggest, were the result of a feminist double-bind crucial to understanding the gendered nature of celebrity in Belle Epoque France. Unlike her male peers, who routinely lobbied for nominations to the Legion of Honor and then wore their ribbons with pride, thereby acknowledging their acceptance of well-earned public attention, Tinayre believed in her right as a woman to hold the honor but knew that admitting so would be considered unfeminine.

Pride, as the Psichari dialogue so vividly demonstrates, was a masculine characteristic in the Belle Epoque, whose only feminine corollary was modesty. By so publicly acting out her modesty, however, Tinayre revealed her desire for the very attention she declared neither to want nor deserve. Men had the right to celebrity in the Belle Epoque, and their process of claiming it went unquestioned; women's fame, on the other hand, was only acceptable to the extent to which they appeared not to have orchestrated or desired it. By taking such public pains to appear unconcerned about her fame, Tinayre revealed to the French public just how acutely preoccupied with it she truly was, thus serving herself up to be devoured by the very print culture she sought to control.

One of the great ironies of the Tinayre affair is that the person most aware of this double standard may have been Tinayre herself, and that her awareness was likely what motivated her remarks.[29] Tinayre was a sometime journalist herself (a fact she reminds readers of in both her letter to *Le Temps* and her interviews with *La Patrie* and *La Liberté*, explaining her willingness to speak as an act of compassion for her fellow writers). She left several clues of the extent to which she was keenly aware of the power of the women's press and the roles it required its female subjects to assume. She appears to have been an active player in constructing her public identity in the pages of *Femina* and *La Vie Heureuse* as a talented yet modest ultrafeminine figure. In a *Femina* feature story, she is quoted as telling the interviewer: "Tell them that I love my children, that I'm a good mother—even if I don't know how to wash up a child or teach them to read." This comment put Tinayre in the same paradoxical position as did her comments about her nomination—she insisted on her modesty, but that very insistence calls the modesty itself into question. On the one hand, Tinayre is all the more admirable in her childrearing for her modesty in describing her lack of skill. On the other, she is revealed to be aggressively trying to control the way in which she is depicted.

## *Femininity and Feminism*

Tinayre's blunder in so unrelentingly insisting on her modesty forced the tacit acknowledgment that femininity could be used as a strategy; it gave way to a larger conversation about the relationship between feminism and femininity that demonstrated just how alien *Femina* and *La Vie Heureuse*'s *femme moderne* was to some mainstream readers. In his tongue-in-cheek address to her, Emile Faguet, who had written a highly favorable review of *La rebelle* in 1905, urged Tinayre to wear the ribbon, while accusing her of confusing femininity with feminism.[30] "You think you're a feminist," he declared in a strikingly perceptive conclusion. "You're not a feminist: you are a woman, and very much a woman. In this regard, you don't want to resemble men, and a red ribbon seems to be an anomaly." Faguet's comments point to why Tinayre's behavior seemed so inscrutable: as with the *écrivain*, the identity of feminist, according to his logic, was in tension with that of woman. The public associated a woman winning the Legion of Honor—and therefore assuming the stature of the *écrivain*—with feminism, and expected femininity to recede to the background. Belle Epoque literary feminism, however, allowed these seemingly opposing values to be reconciled; yet it did so in ways not always transparent to those unfamiliar with its workings.

The editors of *Femina* and *La Vie Heureuse* energetically provided a narrative—both textual and visual—to make the unfamiliar assimilable, explaining to readers again and again with the help of visually seductive evidence that it *was* possible to be both feminine and feminist. The 1904 photo spread of Tinayre herself in *La Vie Heureuse* (Fig. 2.18) serves as one of the most compelling examples: Tinayre sits at her desk, poised between daughter and manuscript, while the caption describes her ability to have it all: "Between the started manuscript and the child to whom she gives her hand, Madame Tinayre—even while composing wonderful books—has maintained the very spirit of feminine life—a tender heart, love for little ones, the taste for decorating her home." To modern readers, the caption seems almost redundant, narrating a picture that appears to speak for itself. The Tinayre affair makes clear, however, that every drop of evidence and guidance was crucial to making this new model of femininity believable. All this discursive work *was* in fact necessary to show that public achievements did not disallow traditional family structures, and that feminism could also be feminine.

Notably, a few female critics understood precisely what Tinayre was doing. Berthe Delaunay applauded Tinayre for making feminism more palatable, explicitly articulating the *doxa* of the women's press and challenging the opposition of "feminist" and "feminine" that informed Faguet's comments: "If Madame Marcelle Tinayre is a writer with great talent and striking intelligence who loudly claims the title feminist, she also knows how to remain womanly and motherly, and how to make feminism—which some inconsiderate viragos have alienated reasonable folks from—lovely."

The actress Régine Martial was similarly perceptive: "Women writers don't want to look like fossils. In order to affirm their femininity, one of them has exaggerated this gesture to such an extreme that it became puerile." Reminding readers of Tinayre's reference to Blaise Pascal in remarks to *Le Matin* well before the controversy, Martial added: "After her nomination, Madame Tinayre must have said to herself: if I say serious things I am going to annoy everyone."[31] She saw Tinayre's behavior as a consequence of modern life, noting that George Sand (by then widely recognized as a great writer)—had she lived fifty years later—might have felt the need to do some "modern pirouettes" and ended up in a similar predicament. "She started playing hula hoops with the cross of the Legion of Honor," wrote Martial, and with this playful image seemed to anticipate the contemporary references to "jumping through hoops" and "juggling acts" as a way of signaling the complex negotiations of the working mother. Martial ultimately blamed the moment, saying it was the fault of her "era" rather than her intelligence. In other words, Martial recognized that in this brave new media world, all sorts of dangers lurked for the famous woman.

On January 13, the Conseil de l'Ordre failed to ratify Tinayre's nomination in a highly unusual rejection of the minister's recommendations. A few commentaries followed in the coming days, after which the scandal largely went the way of media frenzies—into silent oblivion. There was little outcry from the women's press—no mention in the *Journal des femmes* after its initial acclaim for Tinayre, and a decidedly measured piece in *La Française*. *Femina*, on the other hand, rose to the occasion.

**Figure 7.2** Marcelle Tinayre, "whom we believed for a week to be a chevalier of the Legion of Honor." Frontispiece to *Femina* (February 1, 1908).

In her first cover appearance, Tinayre appears sitting inside her home; she leans gently into the book that she is reading, her arm resting on a table modestly decorated with a flower-filled vase (Fig. 7.2). The caption reads: "Madame Marcelle Tinayre, whom we believed for a week to be a chevalier of the Legion of Honor." The paragraph beneath summarizes the affair: "Our eminent collaborator, the much-lauded author of *La rançon*, *La maison du péché* and *La rebelle* and so many other witty and pleasing sketches, was on the list of nominees for the most recent Legion of Honor. Everyone was thrilled for an honor so well earned, when we learned that the news had been premature. It should only be a postponement." There is no mention of the scandal beyond these words. Inside, a caption beneath another demure photo describes its subject: "The eminent writer, who prides herself on being as much a woman as an artist, loves flowers, which she enjoys arranging in vases herself."

# CONCLUSION
## *Imagining the* Académicienne

AND so, we might ask (in that "if a tree falls in a forest" kind of way), did the *femme moderne* really exist? Was there any reality to this high-achieving, elegant role model beyond the pages of the magazines? And just what sort of reality was it?

The Tinayre affair pointed to one of the key benchmarks by which the woman author's talents could be affirmed: through literary consecration, a French tradition nearly as old as authorship itself. And while the Legion of Honor represented one way of being made official, compared to other French academies, it was a young institution with a broad, evolving mandate—and a postrevolutionary one. The Académie française, however, dated back to the monarchy, and carried with it the elite credentials that the magazines, despite their embrace of certain modern values, unabashedly admired. Some of *Femina* and *La Vie Heureuse*'s most frequent contributors were among the "Immortals" of the Academy, and their bylines in the most prominent publications were set off by the graceful epitaph "of the Académie française." Women's election to the Academy would mean intellectual parity at the highest level.

Following the Tinayre affair, the question of women's "academization," as it was phrased, resurfaced both in the pages of *Femina* and in the generalist press in multiple ways that help us to further think through, by way of conclusion, the parameters of Belle Epoque literary feminism. Between 1908 and 1909, eight of the forty seats of the Academy of Letters were open and needed to be filled through new elections, bringing right up to the surface a question that had been percolating for several years: the possibility of including women, especially given the rising numbers of possible female candidates.[1] *Femina*'s handling of the debate around women and the Academy brings into focus the unique nature of its feminist strategies, whose results came not necessarily from achieving concrete goals but from changing the way readers thought about women's achievement. At the same time, the particular anxiety among some members of the literary *Tout Paris* in relation to opening the Academy to women sheds light on some of the ideological limits of Belle Epoque literary feminism.

In January of 1909 *Femina* announced a new contest: readers were invited to elect forty women, past and present, to represent an ideal "Academy of Women"—a structure that was often suggested as an alternative to female academization. (Similar surveys had been conducted in 1902, by *Femina* as well as by the *Journal des débats* and the *Annales politiques et littéraires*, although they were not mentioned in this context.) To launch this survey, the magazine included a remarkable double-page photo spread of the contenders, in a feat of bold photoshopping *avant la lettre*. Entitled "Sur le pont des arts," it featured fifty-nine famous women writers past and present crowded together on the bridge leading to the Academy, with a legend on the bottom that matched photographic image with the identity of each woman (Fig. C.1). Visibly indomitable through their sheer numbers, these were the teeming battalions so often invoked in other contexts in reference to women writers' recent successes.[2] Editor Simone d'Ax, who signed the piece, promised to reward the readers whose suggestions came closest to matching those of the majority with various sorts of prizes. "And now, *chères lectrices*," she cheerily invited, "compare the merits of our sisters of yesteryear and today, and send us your list. *Courage* and good luck!"[3]

Of course, by 1909 a female academy did exist, in the jury of the Prix Vie Heureuse that had been meeting regularly since 1904 (see Chapter 1).[4] Caroline de Broutelles had launched this contest in part to respond to the fact that women would not be awarded the Prix Goncourt; Joris-Karl Huysmans had admitted as much, with respect to his friend Myriam Harry, whose *La conquête de Jérusalem* had seemed a likely contender. She went on to be the first winner of the Prix Vie Heureuse.[5] Its jury was an exclusively female version of the *Tout Paris*, including all the usual suspects associated with both magazines: Anna de Noailles, Marcelle Tinayre, Lucie Delarue-Mardrus, Daniel Lesueur, Séverine.[6] Their meetings in lavish establishments, and the results of their deliberations, were reported in the pages of *La Vie Heureuse*. Yet despite the prize's lasting legacy in the much-coveted Prix Femina and its link to such a powerful coterie of famous women, the Prix Vie Heureuse did not carry much in the way of initial cultural capital.[7] Its existence is hardly even mentioned in the discussions that took place in 1909 around academization, even though so many women interviewed were members of its prize committee.

Within a few days of *Femina*'s survey, reactions began to appear in various newspapers, including *L'Écho de Paris*, *Le Temps* and *La Liberté*.[8] The pieces from *Le Temps* and *L'Écho de Paris* were decidedly less than enthusiastic. Both articles were framed by what was apparently a frequent commentary: if the Academy was really just a kind of salon, then how could it be that it had no women? The *Le Temps* article affirmed, however, that women were fully present in spirit and influence, and would gain nothing from actual membership. Franc-Nohain's piece in *L'Écho de Paris* was far more skeptical, as he decried the dissolution of gender differences that would surely follow women's competition for this ultimate accomplishment.[9] Despite his affirmation of women's talent, Franc-Nohain insisted on that talent remaining "feminine," hoping that women would continue to write "women's literature." Above all, he urged that they avoid the kinds of battles that would surely ensue if they had to compete directly with men.

Thus, while the editors of *Femina* repeatedly applauded and celebrated the outpouring of women's writing that they believed was directly linked to their publication, these pieces remind us that just beyond the magazine's parameters, the phenomenon was met on slightly different terms. In September 1907, for example, the newest of Pierre Lafitte's publications, *Je sais tout*, had published a feature on the recent emergence of women writers entitled "Five Thousand Women Writers!" The article's mixed message is apparent from the outset: "We are witnessing today the invasion of women in the domains of novels and poetry," the caption announced, attributing this success to *Femina*, but employing the military terms so often used to describe the threat that this success posed to that of their male peers. While the article appeared to celebrate women's newfound literary achievement, its statistics betrayed a certain anxiety: in twenty years, women would attain seventy-five percent of fiction writing, a prediction offset by the assurance that men would still control the sciences, history and philosophy, and that—rest assured—this increase had had absolutely

**Figure C.1** "The March to the Academy." The announcement of a contest to elect fictional *académiciennes* in *Femina* (January 1, 1909).

# L'ACADÉMIE

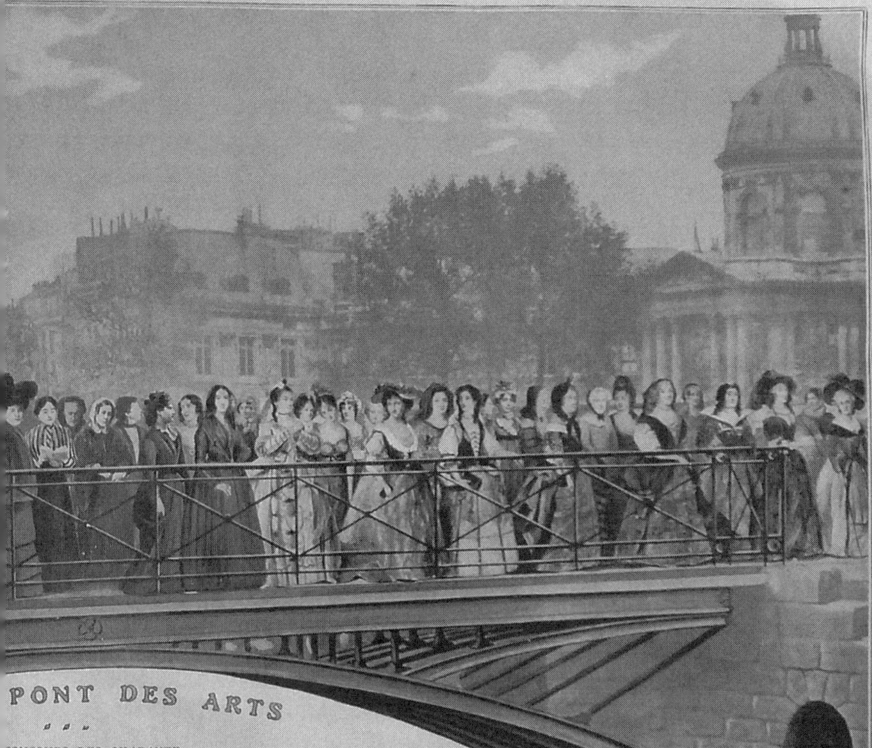

## PONT DES ARTS

### CONCOURS DES QUARANTE

onversa-
t pas de
pole qui
cadémie
es exclut
que nous
ux-Arts
mes de
asses A

es Arts,
dignes

les qua-

rante femmes qui, à leur avis, pourraient composer une académie féminine idéale.
Pour ce concours, qui sera clos le 15 février et dont les résultats paraîtront dans
notre numéro du 15 mars, nous procéderons, pour décerner les récompenses, comme de
coutume : c'est-à-dire que nous établirons une liste idéale d'après les réponses de nos
lectrices et que les gagnantes seront celles dont la liste se rapprochera le plus de la
liste idéale ainsi établie.
  La concurrente classée première recevra un objet d'art d'une valeur de deux cents
francs; les seconde et troisième un objet d'art d'une valeur de cent et soixante-quinze francs.
De plus dix souvenirs seront décernés aux dix concurrentes qui se classeront après les
trois premières.
  Et maintenant, chères lectrices, comparez les mérites des œuvres de nos sœurs
d'autrefois et d'aujourd'hui que vous reconnaîtrez sur notre page et envoyez-moi votre
liste. Donc courage et bonne chance !

SIMONE D'AX.

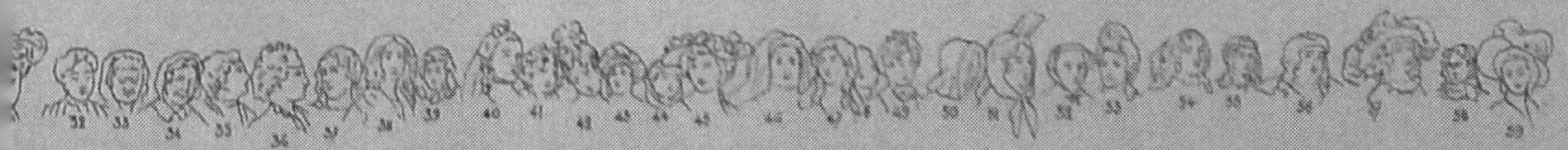

no effect on the number of female users of the Bibliothèque nationale. The primitive imagery that accompanied the article was equally telling: on the front page sits a man at his desk, plume in hand, surrounded by female icons of varying but increasing sizes that are meant to stand for the gradual increase in percentage of women writers (Fig. C.2). A tiny woman at a relatively empty desk on the left represents the miniscule place the *femme écrivain* took up twenty years earlier—the male writer in the center would hardly notice her; but on the right, the new woman writer's desk—papered over like his own—edges up against his elbow. A few pages later, in another remarkable act of Lafittian photoshopping (noted in the caption as the product of "complex photographic techniques that will not escape our readers' notice"), a hall of "the most famous women writers" is depicted, with each celebrity holding a stack that represents the number of books she has written (Fig. C.3). The room is filled with these towering piles, in a "friendly disorder" that is in distinct tension with the women's elegant attire and the grandeur of the room itself. If part of the energy of both *Femina* and *La Vie Heureuse* was directed toward showing the compatibility of

**Figure C.2** "Five Thousand Women Writers!" *Je sais tout* (September 15, 1907).

female authorship with both traditional domestic roles and an upper-bourgeois or aristocratic lifestyle, these images show something substantially different: the women's books literally taking over a beautifully appointed interior, and no babies anywhere in sight.[10]

Not everyone, it seems, was ready to welcome the woman writer's success unequivocally, in particular to the extent that it threatened the place that male writers were left to occupy. The *Je sais tout* piece ends with the assumption that women would soon enter the Académie française. And while this was presented as inevitable rather than terrible, women's "triumphal" arrival at that "last citadel" was described as forcing men to struggle in order to hold on to the few literary places from which they had not yet been "dislodged." In a magazine printed by the same publishing house, directed by many of the same journalists, this piece suggests that Belle Epoque literary feminism may have succeeded not simply beyond anyone's expectations, but beyond certain supporters' comfort zones.

The discussions taking place in these publications point to the questions that *Femina* was precisely *not* asking, and thus the way in which it guided readers to a certain kind of thinking. The pieces in *Le Temps* and *L'Écho de Paris* contemplated *whether* women should be "academized" in some way; for *Femina* the question was no longer whether, but rather *how*. *La Liberté*, on the other hand, shared *Femina*'s point of departure. On January 10, 1909, ten days after the announcement of *Femina*'s contest, it published its own survey asking famous writers (including Tinayre herself) whether a female academy should be created or whether the Académie française should be open to women writers.[11] Like *Femina*, then, it started from the assumption that change was necessary. The writers interviewed were split, leading Hélène Avryl to summarize their conclusions in a February *Femina* article as follows: "Women should have access to the Académie française; and if that is decidedly impossible, then the founding of an academy of women becomes necessary." Everyone, she concluded, seemed to agree on one thing: "Ceci ou cela, mais quelque chose" (this or that, but something).[12] The status quo was simply no longer an option.

In the months that followed, *Femina* managed, remarkably, to realize both parts of Avryl's equation within its pages: the editors imagined a separate female academy as well as women's "academization" among their male peers. In April, when the magazine published the final results of their survey—for which they received an impressive 6,700 responses—

**Figure C.3** "The Most Famous Women Writers" holding the number of books they have written. *Je sais tout* (September 15, 1907).

## Cinq mille femmes de lettres!

FRANÇAISES CONTEMPORAINES

Clichés Manuel, Boissonnas et Taponier, Reutlinger, Braun, Pouchet, Lallie, Hermann, Otto, Jognet, etc.

(6 vol.). — 11. M$^{me}$ Marie-Anne de Bovet (25 vol.). — 12. H$^{me}$ Jean Pommerol (11 vol.). — 13. M$^{me}$ Daniel Lesueur

they included another dramatically doctored image (Fig. C.4). This time, cropped portraits of the elected women were pasted into the halls of the famed dome where members held their meetings. There, Marcelle Tinayre, Anna de Noailles, Colette Yver and Lucie Delarue-Mardrus faced George Sand, Madame de Lafayette, Madame de Sévigné and Madame de Scudéry.[13] If the *immortels* were not going to relent in what was widely seen as simple force of habit, *Femina* would overcome them through photographic technology.

A few months later, *Femina* published a speech that Fernand Vandérem imagined giving for Anna de Noailles, if she were to be elected. The choice of Noailles was no coincidence. In a manner akin to Tinayre's double-bind,

**Figure C.4** "A Female Academy," *Femina* (April 15, 1909). The forty members elected by *Femina*'s readers were, from left to right: Madame Edmond Rostand, Lucie Delarue-Mardrus, Marcelle Tinayre, Anna de Noailles, Gérard d'Houville, Gabrielle Réval, Madame Catulle Mendès, Jean Bertheroy, Jane Dieulafoy, L. F. F. Goyau, Judith Gautier, Myriam Harry, Marie Curie, J. Marni, Gyp, Claude Ferval, Madame Alphonse Daudet, Séverine, Hélène Picard, Georges de Peyrebrune, duchesse de Rohan; Daniel Lesueur, Juliette Adam, duchesse d'Uzès douairière; comtesse de Ségur, Madame de Genlis, Madame Emile de Girardin, Marceline Desbordes-Valmore, Madame de Staël, Madame Julie de Lespinasse, George Sand, Madame Récamier, Françoise-Marguérite de Grignan, Madame Deshoulière, Madame de Maintenon, duchesse de Montpensier, comtesse de La Fayette, Madame Necker, Madame de Scudéry, Madame de Sévigné.

in 1907 the glamorous and much-adored countess was urged to submit a letter of candidacy for one of the open seats, but modestly refused, hoping, in vain, that she would be elected nonetheless.[14] Although never made an *académicienne*, she was decorated as a commander of the Legion of Honor in 1931, which, as we know, required no such official declaration of intent. Modeled on the "reception" speeches for newly elected members, which were regularly published in full in major newspapers, Vandérem's "Réception" for Noailles was introduced as an extension of ongoing conversations about women's academization that had been taking place at "dinners, soirées and five-o'clocks" since the first set of elections the previous spring.[15] During this time, it had apparently become common to improvise the speeches that might be offered to future "*immortelles*," and his was deemed so compelling that he was invited to publish it.

Vandérem's playful exercise, cautiously framed with "all the reservations such unofficial hypotheticals include," soon became a series. The fake welcoming speech for Marcelle Tinayre, published in *Femina* two months later, highlights the contingent, mitigating reality of the women's press—one which could celebrate women in ways French society as a whole was not yet prepared to do. Referencing the Legion of Honor affair at the outset, Vandérem acknowledged its role in the author's passage from "average notoriety to enormous popularity" in record-breaking speed, as well as the important role that fame could play in election to the Academy (making literary esteem, just as Lorrain had described it, a corollary of celebrity, rather than the other way around). The essay's references to current events underline the peculiar nature of Vandérem's exercise, which was not simply about applauding unrecognized achievement. Rather, Vandérem situated Tinayre's election to the Academy within a contemporary and *real* social space—one in which women writers were *already* famous and celebrated and regularly decorated for their skills—rather than some imagined utopic future in which such a thing might become possible. The only thing standing in the way of Tinayre's election, in this context, was the almost arbitrary fact that the Académie française did not actually allow women members; as Hélène Avryl had put it in February of that same year, the situation was "insoluble" only because of three centuries of stubbornness. There was no law preventing women's academization, she sighed, just an old tradition, *rien qu'une tradition*.[16]

Vandérem's column, on the other hand, did not make this point. Only the conditional grammar of the subtitle (first introduced in the Noailles piece) reminded readers that this speech was not Tinayre's actual welcome: "Vandérem imagines today that Madame Marcelle Tinayre has been elected to the Académie française [ . . . ] and he responds, hypothetically, to the speech that she would have given."[17] Again one cannot help but stumble over the gendered hypotheticals, as the male editor gives an imaginary response to an imaginary speech by a woman accepting an imaginary honor. The man is still left bestowing the honor, the celebrated woman's voice—even the imagined one—elided in this scenario. She has no choice (hypothetically) but to demur from the background. And yet, with this series, *Femina* had found a way to mask women's absence from the academy—and even rectify it—without overtly criticizing it.

In November of 1910, Marie Curie—much admired in *Femina* and *La Vie Heureuse*—declared her candidacy for the Academy of Sciences. Still awaiting these results, the Academy of Letters finally announced the opening of an official debate about electing women to join their ranks. In the meantime, *L'Intransigeant* published an extensive survey to determine which women writers should be the first elected. In responding, it seems many of those interviewed were stumped by a theoretical obstacle: what would the *académicienne* wear? Once again, the challenge of imagining what the modern woman should *look* like came to the fore, this time explicitly presenting itself as an obstacle to her achievements. Unlike the Legion of Honor, which simply required an accessory, participation in the Academy required the donning of full regalia, the gender specificity of which was often remarked upon in the debate: the famous "green habit" consisted of a black coat and tails embroidered with green and gold, and a black feathered hat. The member would also receive a personalized ceremonial sword.

In their first issue of the new year in January 1911, *Femina* set about addressing this very problem: they invited the most prominent designers to imagine outfits for the women voted most likely to be elected: Myriam Harry, Daniel Lesueur, Anna de Noailles, Madame Edmond Rostand, Gérard d'Houville, Jane Catulle Mendès and Marcelle Tinayre—and then invited those women to comment on the choices (Fig. C.5). While most of the women joined lightheartedly into the discussion, Tinayre

**Figure C.5** Designs for women writers Daniel Lesueur, Marcelle Tinayre and Rosemonde Rostand to wear if they were elected to the Académie Française. *Femina* (January 1, 1911).

(*"prudente!"*) had learned her lesson: "You shouldn't count your chickens before they're hatched, or dress the *académicienne* before she's elected," she balked, clearly wary of making the same mistake twice. But she was in safe territory within these particular pages. This sort of questioning was precisely the work of *Femina*: to present the fantasy of what the French woman could become in terms that were wholly real; to fully realize the *femme moderne* according to women's own desires, whatever "the actual state of morals." Indeed, we might say that this was the very essence of Belle Epoque literary feminism as a strategy: the subtle insinuation of a future so real, so familiar, so possible, that it would be difficult to believe that it was *not* actually true.

## *A Belle Epoque?*

In her companion pieces to *Femina*'s 1909 discussions about a women's academy (as we saw in Chapter 1), Hélène Avryl was almost giddy with the notion that the publication was about to achieve a "femino-literary victory," a term she used twice, in the second instance explicitly distinguishing such a victory from feminism ("heaven forbid!"). The time is right, she mused, for the injustices inflicted on women writers over time to be reversed, and for artistic merit to be founded upon equality, whose ultimate proof would be admission to the Académie française. It was a future that she described vividly and joyfully.

What Avryl did not see was that the femino-literary victory brought about by *Femina* had already been achieved, for it was not quite the one she envisioned. Between the kind of idealism Avryl was expressing and the full resolution of many of the very issues at stake in *Femina* there was in fact a tremendous gap. This gap, I would argue, is precisely the reason why the question of whether there was a Belle Epoque for women has remained so slippery.

While suffrage was certainly not a central or direct concern of the magazines, it was a subject that increasingly found its way into their pages. The sense that this issue was being addressed, even if by others, was part of the optimistic context in which other discussions were taking place. And yet, it would not be achieved for French women until 1944, with their first occasion to vote coming in 1945.

The ratification of a more equal legal definition of marriage, which had seemed on the cusp of happening in 1904, was similarly farfetched.

Article 213 of the Civil Code would not be altered until 1938, gender hierarchies not excised until 1970 to reflect a more equal status quo.[18]

Finally, election of women to the Académie française, which seemed so imminent in 1909 and constituted an achievement in which both *Femina* and *La Vie Heureuse* were actually directly implicated—that of women's literary consecration—would not happen for an astonishing seventy years, until 1980, when Marguerite Yourcenar was elected. Of the 718 members throughout history, only six have been women to date.

This gap between fantasy and reality, I would argue, has made it difficult to measure women's progress during the Belle Epoque. "The French lag" or *décalage*, as it has been described with respect to suffrage in particular, refers not simply to the time lapse, but to the discrepancy between a cultural mindset seemingly prepared for change and the enactment of actual institutional and legal reforms.[19] It may also be the reason why we have been slow to recognize the crucial feminist engagement of these publications. But this gap should not prevent us from identifying the significance of *Femina* and *La Vie Heureuse*'s dreaming, and the dramatic ideological shift that these kinds of dreams represented. The magazines are a reminder to look beyond traditional historical markers of change (legal, institutional) in order to recognize other kinds of signs of social progress, evidence that individuals or communities were very much living and thinking in ways not yet officially reflected or recorded.

I want to turn back to the fictional network surrounding *Femina* and *La Vie Heureuse* for a moment, to gain some purchase on how this ideological shift was experienced. In both Marcelle Tinayre's *La rebelle* and Louise-Marie Compain's *L'un vers l'autre*, an older unmarried woman comforts and encourages her protégée, pointing towards the promise of a more welcoming future ahead. Tinayre's Mademoiselle Bon feels compassion for Josanne, in this "transitional time period" in which women are forced into contradictory and conflicting positions. Similarly, the director of Laure's school in Compain's novel explains that she and her peers have sacrificed love and marriage in the interest of nurturing young women towards better, more fulfilling paths. "We are a generation of sacrifice: incomplete beings, non-viable, who are preparing for the birth of more perfect, happier creatures," she announces. Like the archaeopteryx, the strange animal that preceded birds on the evolutionary chain, the women of this period are "transitional beings, not loveable in themselves, perhaps, but beautiful for what they herald."[20] This sentiment is also expressed through Thérèse, Camille Pert's modern woman, who describes the suffering of the current generation. Compain's heroine Laure, on the other hand, is described not as one of these bizarre figures but rather, "already the perfect bird," ahead of her time.

*Femina* and *La Vie Heureuse*, I want to suggest, were also manifestations of this perfect bird ahead of its time: depicting not so much an awkward transition but the beautiful realization of a process that, in reality, had only just begun. As such, they mirrored the optimism of Tinayre's and Compain's feminist fables, whose happy endings give an indication of the sense of possibility associated with the *femme moderne*. The novels themselves offer numerous windows into the vehicles of this progress: from the career paths in the publishing world that Josanne frequented, to the education that Laure's female colleagues were shaping for young women, to their roles as educators. This spirit of energy and progress associated with modern femininity was the benchmark of *Femina* and *La Vie Heureuse*, and their accumulation of visual evidence only added to the sense of certainty that there would be no more archaeopteryx, that the perfect creature had arrived.

Through their journalistic manipulations—photographic and textual—*Femina* and *La Vie Heureuse* allowed women to imagine themselves with achievements they would not be able to take for granted for decades. A visual index of this progress can be discerned in the difference between the 1902 image of an imaginary female academy from *Femina* (Fig. 1.5), where the forty female nominees are pictured in side-by-side portraits, and the doctored image from 1909 (Fig. C.4), where the women were cut and pasted into the halls of the Academy itself. This was precisely the distance that the editors of *Femina* had traveled in seven short years, spurred by thousands of enthusiastic responses from their readers. Whereas in 1902 they could recognize the women capable of intellectual achievement, in 1907 they could boldly situate these same women in the halls of the academy. It is not irrelevant, either, that the difference between these two images also corresponds to advances in photographic technology. The accomplishments of Belle Epoque literary feminism were very much tied to the magazines' work at the forefront of journalistic innovation, which dramatically expanded the possibilities for imagining women's success.

*Femina* and *La Vie Heureuse*, then, took control over a narrative of female progress that was charged with fear and negativity and transformed it into a gorgeous success story (and therein, incidentally, lies the lesson for today). While it is difficult to measure the influence of this kind of shift in expectations, we can see rather clearly the ways that the magazines quickly and substantially changed the conversation. In 1910 Vandérem, writing under the pseudonym "Janine," a young woman he impersonated in regularly published correspondence, had already joined an ongoing conversation about women's changing roles that stemmed from controversy surrounding Tinayre's suppressed Legion of Honor nomination. Addressing those who still appeared uncertain as to whether women writers should be allowed to receive the honor, Janine argued that women should certainly be rewarded for outstanding literary achievement and went on to address a related issue: how to ensure that one's future husband would be prepared for such an eventuality, unlikely though it might be. "Since the Legion of Honor problem is not yet really one of those that gets negotiated in an engagement," Janine explained in her usual tongue-in-cheek style, "my future husband is lacking preparation on the subject." Yet Janine imagined that, upon reflection, her new spouse would become properly and perhaps even overly enthused, reaching out to whatever connections he might have in order to secure his wife's honor. "At least that's how I imagine the kind of young man I would like, a modern young man, in accordance with our liberated times (*selon notre libre époque*)."[21] Vandérem's playful musings in the voice of this young woman illustrate the subtle, yet deeply powerful, work that both magazines did on the level of hearts and minds—as well as the extent to which men often participated in them, modeling a certain kind of modern outlook (while maintaining strategic power over its rapidly extending parameters). In the discussion surrounding the Académie française, men repeatedly invoked this strategy of pushing women towards new successes by raising their sense of their own potential. In the words of academician Emile Faguet—one of the first to come out in favor of allowing *académiciennes*—if women writers were not yet intellectual equals to men, it would still be good to tell them that they were, "since that is perhaps the way in which it will happen."[22] Belle Epoque literary feminism recognized that women's achievement corresponded directly to the expectations set out for it; on the other hand, the men associated with this movement also, sometimes, held tightly to their control over those expectations.

Through these simple shifts, crucial changes in gender roles were forced into motion. The novels that we have examined offer further evidence that people were already living in different ways, with new horizons before them. And thus, even though Marcelle Tinayre was not nominated to the Legion of Honor, and even though the Academy would not elect a woman for seventy years, and even though French marriage would not be redefined as partnership for decades, in the alternate reality of these magazines, a new generation of educated women was already busily integrating professional aspirations with expanded domestic and marital ones, finding itself that much closer at least to the *possibility* of having it all.

## *Posterity and the* Femme Moderne

The modern women of the Belle Epoque saw themselves as living in a time of transition, moving steadily towards a brighter future when their struggles would be resolved. But, as we know, the course of French history spun in an unexpected direction, stopping the trajectory imagined by *Femina* and *La Vie Heureuse* in its tracks and leaving that next generation in entirely different territory. In 1916, as the Great War lurched into its final years, Hachette bought out Pierre Lafitte's publications, and *Femina* and *La Vie Heureuse* merged.[23] Because of the historical circumstances, this new version was sober and less sure-footed. During the war, gender roles had been radically redefined, and Belle Epoque literary feminism, linked as it was to an aristocratic world that had more or less disappeared, had lost its identity. Gone with it was the chipper editorial voice urging women to read—and write!—in a certain way. Numerous new publications appeared on the scene, and *Femina et La Vie Heureuse Réunis* took its place in what was an entirely different marketplace, no longer in the avant-garde of imagining the modern woman, nor an exclusive or dominant voice. Eventually, the title reverted to *Femina*, which had been diluted to a simple fashion magazine catering to a wealthy, upper-class audience.

Within a few years, the celebratory modern woman that *Femina* and *La Vie Heureuse* had worked so hard to create was supplanted by the heart-stopping postwar version of the *femme moderne*: rebellious younger sister to the New Woman, this willful, sexualized figure—fueled by the media—was associated with sexual freedoms and independence, constituting a direct threat to tradition and family.[24] When we look back now on the 1900s, we tend to remember the women who link up more directly with this audacious postwar figure—Colette, Gyp, Rachilde—or we try to squeeze some of the lesser-knowns—Marcelle Tinayre, Myriam Harry—into the shape of the New Woman. (For those truly in the know, Anna de Noailles stands out as a gifted poet, bridging the romantic and modern, but a rarity for her time.) By November 1954, when *Elle* magazine (in a piece that Roland Barthes famously mythologized) devoted several pages to what was seen as the dramatic new phenomenon of French women writers ("Women Writers Make Their Presence Known!"), it was as if Belle Epoque literary feminism had never happened (Fig. C.6).[25] What is fascinating is not so much that the *Elle* article celebrated contemporary women writers' balance of novels and children—expressly, as the article notes, in distinction to the bluestocking of the nineteenth century—but that they were *still* celebrating it. Beyond this, the similarities between *Elle*'s presentation of the *femme de lettres* and that of *Femina* and *La Vie Heureuse* are striking, even as the Belle Epoque versions far outpace *Elle* 1954 in terms of creativity and visual innovation. Like *Femina*'s "Sur le pont des arts" retouched photograph, *Elle* depicts a crowd of women, imposing by their sheer numbers—displaying, then, the same impulse to supply some kind of visual breadth to this information, to literally flesh out the statistics. In the accompanying article, well-known literary critic Robert Kemp offers a sweeping history of French women writers, and then rattles off a list of literary awards for which the current writers are often in the running—including the Femina, with absolutely no sense that the prize might be related to this history.[26] He wonders why women, who have achieved in so many professional realms, have not made it as writers, by and large, despite the "wide open doors" before them. No mention is made of the Académie française, which will welcome Kemp himself within a brief two years, while Marguerite Yourcenar—upon whom he heaps praise—will wait nearly another thirty.

Lost, of course, in this narrative is the vibrant literary community that had radically changed what it meant to be a woman writer in France in the early 1900s; and the link between this community and a powerful

**Figure C.6** "Seventy Novelists, Three Hundred Novels: Women Writers Make Their Presence Known!" *Elle* magazine (November 22, 1954).

# les Femmes de Lettres s'imposent →

sont des romancières consacrées, beaucoup sont en course pour les prix littéraires. Le critique Robert Kemp vous en parle p. 64.

8. CLAUDE MARTINE (femme de Cecil Saint-Laurent, 1 roman) : « Arthur et Olympe s'entendent ».

9. MARGUERITE DE FELCOURT (2 enfants, 1 livre) : « Les Saints Enfants ».

10. SUZANNE ROUVIER (2 enfants, 2 romans) : « La Rue de l'Oued ».

11. MARGUERITE CAILLEUX (3 enfants, 1 roman, a publié dans ELLE des extraits de son « Mariage vécu ») : « A chacun sa chance ».

12. JACQUELINE LENOIR (2 filles, 1 roman) : « Le Tour de France par deux enfants ».

13. NATHALIE SARRAUTE (3 filles, 2 romans) : « Martereau ».

14. JACQUELINE SAVERIA (1 roman) : « Ni saints ni saufs ».

15. MARGUERITE YOURCENAR (5 romans) : « Les Mémoires d'Hadrien ».

16. ELISE JOUHANDEAU (2 romans qui sont les deux tomes de sa vie romancée) : « L'Altesse des hasards ».

17. ELISABETH TREVOL (1 roman) : « Mon amour ».

18. MARIANNE ANDRAU (bien connue des lectrices de ELLE, 1 fille, 5 romans) : « Les Mains du manchot ».

19. CELIA BERTIN (Prix Renaudot, 5 romans) : « Contre-Champ ».

20. MARINA GREY (1 fils, 1 roman) : « Rendez-vous à cinq heures ».

21. ARLETTE GREBEL (3 enfants, 1 roman) : « Où vas-tu, papillon ? ».

22. CATHERINE ARLEY (comédienne, 1 roman) : « Tu vas mourir ».

23. SORANA GURIAN (2 romans) : « Les Amours impitoyables ».

24. MAYOTTE CAPECIA (3 enfants, 2 romans) : « La Négresse blanche ».

25. SIMONE FABIEN (3 enfants, 1 roman) : « Tu seras un homme ».

26. JEAN PORTAIL (3 romans) : « La Femme enchaînée ».

27. JACQUELINE MARENIS (7 romans) : « Les Bonheurs perdus ».

28. MARCELLE MAURETTE (2 romans, 14 pièces) : « La Vie privée de Mme de Pompadour ».

29. DANIEL GRAY (bien connue des lectrices de ELLE, 45 romans) : « Lui ».

30. MADELEINE ALLEINS (2 enfants, 3 romans) : « L'Etrangère dans les portes ».

31. HELENE PARMELIN (2 enfants, 2 romans) : « Noir sur blanc ».

32. VIVETTE PERRET (2 enfants, 2 romans) : « La Treuse ».

33. ANNA LORME (2 enfants, 1 roman) : « A peine sont-ils plantés ».

34. NICOLE DUTREIL (2 fils, 4 romans) : « La Poudre d'or ».

35. ADDY FREDERIQUE (1 roman) : « Avantage à Puno ».

36. FRANÇOISE SAGAN (bien connue des lectrices de ELLE, 1 roman) : « Bonjour Tristesse ».

37. BEATRIX BECK (Prix Goncourt, 1 fille, 4 romans) : « Des accommodements avec le ciel ».

38. CLAIRE SAINTE-SOLINE (1 fille, 13 romans) : « Mademoiselle Olga ».

(Suite page suivante.)

media outlet reaching thousands of women readers every month, urging them to see themselves differently. The Belle Epoque *femme moderne* lies outside of our traditional narratives of French feminist, literary and cultural history, evidence of a divergent path: a creature fully imagined, yet never fully realized. The women's magazines that invented her have been similarly eclipsed in histories of the press and photography, dismissed in passing as simple fashion magazines, despite their very specific and unique contributions to media history.[27] And yet, Belle Epoque literary feminism and the construction of the *femme moderne* constitute just a fragment of the many stories preserved in these publications. *Femina* and *La Vie Heureuse* remain rich with research possibilities for better understanding how this vibrant era imagined itself, while offering myriad potential challenges to the way we situate the Belle Epoque in broader French history.

# REFERENCE MATTER

# NOTES

*Introduction*

1. On the perceived dangers of female intellect, see Rachel Mesch, *The Hysteric's Revenge: French Women Writers at the Fin de Siècle* (Nashville: Vanderbilt University Press, 2006), 14–21.

2. For more on the Camille Sée laws implemented by Jules Ferry and their influence, see Françoise Mayeur, *L'Éducation des filles en France au XIXe siècle* (Paris: Hachette, 1979); Rebecca Rogers, *From the Salon to the Schoolroom: Educating Bourgeois Girls in Nineteenth-Century France* (University Park: Penn State University Press, 2005).

3. On the question of whether the Belle Epoque was favorable to women, see Diana Holmes and Carrie Tarr, eds., *A Belle Epoque? Women in French Society and Culture, 1890–1914* (New York: Berghahn Books, 2006); Susan K. Foley, *Women in France Since 1789: The Meanings of Difference* (New York: Palgrave Macmillan, 2004); James F. McMillan, *France and Women, 1789–1914: Gender, Society and Politics* (New York: Routledge, 2000); Christopher E. Forth and Elinor Accampo, eds., *Confronting Modernity in Fin-de-Siècle France: Bodies, Minds and Gender* (New York: Palgrave Macmillan, 2010).

4. Clarétie, Hervieu, Prévost and Adam were critically acclaimed writers. Clarétie, Hervieu and Prévost were members of the Académie Française. Edmond Rostand, elected to the Académie Française in 1901, was a playwright and poet best known for *Cyrano de Bergerac* (1897) and *Les Romanesques* (1894), which was the basis for the Broadway hit *The Fantasticks*. His wife Rosemonde was an accomplished poet as well. Decadent writer Catulle Mendès was briefly married to Judith Gautier before marrying Jeanne Nette, who became known as Jane Catulle-Mendès and was a prolific poet. Writer Alphonse Daudet, father of Léon and Lucien, was married to Julia, also a writer. Jane and Marcel Dieulafoy traveled through the Middle East together, with Jane documenting their discoveries. When her husband was deployed to the front during the Franco-Prussian war, she followed, in a soldier's uniform. With governmental permission, she continued to dress in men's garb from then on.

5. On the social world of Belle Epoque literary Paris, see Anne Martin-Fugier, *Salons de la IIIe République* (Paris: Perrin, 2003); Géraldi Leroy and Julie Bertrand-Sabiani, *La Vie littéraire à la Belle Epoque* (Paris: Presses universitaires de France, 1998), 29–53. On the important role of the salon for women in earlier centuries, see Elizabeth C. Goldsmith and Dena Goodman, *Going Public: Women and Publishing in Early Modern*

*France* (Ithaca: Cornell University Press, 1995), 1–9; Steven D. Kale, *French Salons: High Society and Sociability from the Old Regime to the Revolution of 1848* (Baltimore: Johns Hopkins University Press, 2004); Joan B. Landes, *Women and the Public Sphere in the Age of the French Revolution* (Ithaca: Cornell University Press, 1988).

6. J.-H. Rosny, *Mémoires de la vie littéraire* (Paris: G. Crès et Cie, 1927).

7. "Les Fêtes du Prix Vie Heureuse," *La Vie Heureuse*, April 1, 1907.

8. Many democratizing forces characterized the emergence of mass culture in France. See Lisa Tiersten, *Marianne in the Market: Envisioning Consumer Society in Fin-de-Siècle France* (Berkeley: University of California Press, 2001), 207–19; 126–28; 228; Rosalind Williams, *Dream Worlds: Mass Consumption in Late Nineteenth-Century France* (Berkeley: University of California Press, 1982), 154–209.

9. On the department store, see Rachel Bowlby, *Just Looking: Consumer Culture in Dreising, Gissing and Zola* (New York: Methuen, 1985). On the relationship between magazines and department stores in British culture, see Ellen Gruber Garvey, *The Adman in the Parlor: Magazines and the Gendering of Consumer Culture, 1880s to 1910s* (New York: Oxford University Press, 1996) 3–4.

10. *Femina*, February 1, 1901, 2. Most issues of *Femina* were approximately twenty to thirty pages; however, the pagination was continuous throughout a single year. Most pages of *La Vie Heureuse* do not include page numbers, so I have included them only when indicated.

11. Historian Karen Offen's pioneering work on late nineteenth-century French feminism has been crucial to demonstrating the diverse nature of its causes and identifications, as well for situating it within cultural, literary and social trends. I am grateful to her for sharing part of her work in progress, Debating the Woman Question, which brilliantly lays out the multiple strands of early Third Republic feminist claims and their relationship to one another. Several articles opened up this field of study and examined the multiple expressions of late nineteenth-century French feminist activism, as well as its expression in literature. See Offen, "Depopulation, Nationalism and Feminism in Fin-de-siècle France," *American Historical Review* 89, no. 3 (June 1984): 648–76; "Defining Feminism: A Comparative Historical Perspective," *Signs: Journal of Women in Culture and Society* 14, no.1 (1988): 119–57; "On the French Origin of the Words *Feminism* and *Feminist*," *Feminist Issues* 8, no. 2 (Fall 1988): 45–51.

12. I am continuing in this sense the work begun by Mary Louise Roberts in expanding our understanding of Belle Epoque feminism through her study of the New Woman, as well as Lenard Berlanstein's important work situating *Femina* in Belle Epoque feminist history. Roberts, *Disruptive Acts: The New Woman in Fin-de-Siècle France* (Chicago: University of Chicago Press, 2002); Berlanstein, "Selling Modern Femininity: *Femina*, a Forgotten Feminist Publishing Success in Belle Epoque France," *French Historical Studies* 30, no. 4 (Fall 2007): 623–49.

13. Habermas's notion of the literary public sphere, often invoked in early modern scholarship on the salon, is another way of demarcating this space. Jürgen Habermas, *The Structural Transformation of the Public Sphere: An Inquiry into a Category of Bourgeois Society*, translated by Thomas Burger, with the assistance of Frederick Lawrence (Cambridge: MIT Press, 1989), 29–30.

14. I am following in this sense Janet Wolff's suggestion with respect to the well-studied question of female *flânerie* that we demote the public/private binarism, which

tends to locate men and women in separate, gendered places. See her chapter "Gender and the Haunting of Cities: Or, the Retirement of the *Flâneur,*" in *AngloModern: Painting and Modernity in Britain and the United States* (Ithaca: Cornell University Press, 2003), 68–85. Wolff's essay is a coda to her original article, "The Invisible *Flâneuse*: Women and the Literature of Modernity," in *Feminine Sentences: Essays on Women and Culture* (Berkeley: University of California Press, 1990), 34–50, and the many responses it inspired. On nineteenth-century women writers, journalists and *flânerie*, see Catherine Nesci's fascinating study, *Le flâneur et les flâneuses: Les femmes et la ville à l'époque romantique* (Grenoble: ELLUG, 2007).

15. Berlanstein demonstrates the ways that female celebrities in the second half of the nineteenth century legitimized certain kinds of roles in "Historicizing and Gendering Celebrity Culture: Famous Women in Nineteenth-Century France," *Journal of Women's History* 16, no. 4 (2004): 65–91.

16. Berlanstein writes: "*Femina* participated in the same bold endeavor to which Durand had committed her newspaper, spreading a feminist message while changing the image of feminism, making it compatible with femininity. The difference was that for Durand, femininity was a tactic to strengthen the appeal of feminism, whereas femininity was at the core of *Femina* as a commercial enterprise" ("Selling Modern Femininity," 625). For the debate between these two scholars, see Cosnier, *Les Dames de Femina*, 285–303, and Berlanstein's review of Cosnier in *H-France* 9, no. 134 (November 2009): 566. Cosnier refuses to recognize *Femina* as feminist, in large part because of the overall conservatism of its message. However, she seems to be relying on a modern definition of feminism rather than considering the extent to which the magazine may have challenged Belle Epoque gender norms and attempted to expand women's roles, even within certain circumscribed parameters. Colette Cosnier, *Les Dames de* Femina: *Un féminisme mystifié* (Rennes: Presses Universitaires de Rennes, 2009).

17. Parts of the feminist ideology expressed by *La Fronde* were quite resonant with the emphasis on conventional femininity found in *Femina* and *La Vie Heureuse*. In 1898, Daniel Lesueur wrote about the importance of "charm, seduction and beauty" (Karen Offen, "The Birth of Feminism," Debating the Woman Question in Modern France, 16th–20th Centuries [in progress]) and in 1903 Marguerite Durand famously wrote that "feminism owes a great deal to my blonde hair" (Mary Louise Roberts, *Disruptive Acts*, 49).

18. There was very little overlap among the general staff writers for *La Fronde* and *Femina* and *La Vie Heureuse*. However, several high-profile women writers published in all of these publications: Gyp, Séverine, Marcelle Tinayre, Daniel Lesueur.

19. Jules Barbey d'Aurevilly, *Les bas-bleus* (Paris: Société Générale de librairie catholique, 1878); Several fin-de-siècle plays portrayed thinking women in a negative light, including Paul Hervieu, *Les Tenailles* (Paris: Lemerre, 1896) and Maurice Donnay, *L'Affranchie* (Paris: Olendorff, 1898). Albert Cim dedicated his novel *Bas-bleus* (Paris: A. Savine, 1891) to Barbey and Pierre-Joseph Proudhon, writing that both "so eloquently celebrated women who stay home and so vigorously lashed out at those women—of the pen, the club, or the street, who only aspire to become public." For more on the iconography of the female intellectual in the nineteenth century, see Janis Bergman-Colter, *The Woman of Ideas in French Art, 1830–1848* (New Haven: Yale University Press, 1995).

20. Among the causes taken up in the 1890s were venereal disease, infant mortality, prostitution, and abject poverty.

21. Lafitte founded *La Vie au grand air*, which is widely considered the first photographic magazine, in 1898. He would go on to launch *Musica* in 1902 and *Je sais tout* in 1905. A vivid history of *Femina* in its earlier years can be found in Paul Pottier and Louis Vauxcelles, "La presse d'aujourd'hui: *Femina*," *Gil Blas*, April 30, 1904; and Philippe Baudorre, *Barbusse: Le pourfendeur de la Grande Guerre* (Paris: Flammarion, 1995), 74–104.

22. L'Heureux was not the original editor-in-chief, but was brought in by July 1901. He promptly fired many of the female journalists who had worked for women's fashion magazines, and relied instead on a close creative team of newspaper men (Pottier and Vauxcelles, "La presse d'aujourd'hui"). Barbusse was close with Lafitte during the early years of *Femina* and was a crucial member of his creative team, eventually helping to launch and direct *Je sais tout*. The two had a falling out in 1910, when Barbusse began working for rival publications. Barbusse then resigned from the Maison Lafitte and was hired by Hachette to edit *La Vie Heureuse* (Baudorre, *Barbusse*), 74–83.

23. According to Pottier and Vauxcelles, Lafitte was inspired by *Ladies Magazine*, *Ladies' Field*, *The Boudoir* and *Ladies Pictorial*. The British women's press was far more extensive and diverse, although not as visually innovative. For a history of British women's magazines, see Margaret Beetham, *A Magazine of Her Own? Domesticity and Desire in the Woman's Magazine, 1800–1914* (New York: Routledge, 1996). There is little written on French women's magazines of the Third Republic, and no complete history of such. On French women's magazines in the first half of the nineteenth century, see Evelyne Sullerot, *Histoire de la presse féminine en France, des origines à 1848* (Paris: A. Colin, 1963) and Annemarie Kleinert's informative and comprehensive *Le journal des dames et des modes, ou la conquête de l'Europe féminine* (1797–1839). (Stuttgart: Jan Thorbecke Verlag, 2001). For a general overview of literary journals during the Belle Epoque, see Elisabeth Parinet, "L'édition littéraire: 1890–1914," in *Histoire de l'édition française*, Roger Chartier and Henri-Jean Martin, eds., vol. 4, *Le livre concurrencé, 1900–1940* (Paris: Promodis, 1986), 148–87. Both *Femina* and *La Vie Heureuse* are notably absent from Françoise Blum, "Revues féminines, revues féministes," in Jacqueline Pluet-Despatin, Jean-Yves Mollier, and Michel Leymarie, eds., *La belle époque des revues, 1880–1914* (Caen: Éditions de l'IMEC, 2002): 211–22; they are also absent from the more popular work by Vincent Soulier, *Presse féminine: la puissance frivole* (Paris: l'Archipel, 2008), which leaps from *La Fronde* to *Marie Claire*.

24. On Lafitte's use of photography in *La Vie au grand air*, see Kevin Moore, *Jacques Henri Lartigue: The Invention of an Artist* (Princeton: Princeton University Press, 2004), 72–82. No study of the specificity of *Femina* and *La Vie Heureuse*'s photographic innovations or their contextualization in the history of photography and the press has been undertaken to date. On the development of the genre of celebrity interview in the late nineteenth century, see Elizabeth Emery's fascinating study, *Photojournalism and the Origins of the French Writer House Museum (1881–1914): Privacy, Publicity and Personality* (Burlington, VT: Ashgate, 2012), 11–80. On the interrelated history of photography and the press, see Thierry Gervais and Gaelle Morel, *La photographie: Histoire, techniques, art, presse* (Paris: Larousse, 2008); Thierry Gervais, "L'Illustration photographique: Naissance du spectacle de l'information, 1843–1914" (PhD dissertation, École des hautes études en sciences sociales, 2007); Gilles Feyel, *La presse en France des origines à 1944* (Paris: Ellipses, 1999).

25. In a 1907 speech for Lafitte, Daniel Lesueur applauded *Femina* for being dramatically different from preexisting women's magazines, which she described as stale and boring, doomed from the start to "pitiful mediocrity." Daniel Lesueur, "Toast à *Femina*," *Femina*, February 15, 1907, 75.

26. These were Adolphe Brisson's words in a speech celebrating Lafitte's nomination to the Legion of Honor. "Le banquet Pierre Lafitte," *Femina*, February 1, 1907, 55.

27. *Femina*, February 1, 1901, 2.

28. While substantially more expensive than a regular newspaper, whose illustrated supplements might be free, this price was in line with other illustrated magazines: *La Mode Pratique* cost 25 centimes, but there were higher prices, up to 75 centimes, if one purchased the illustrated supplement; Yvonne Sarcey's *Journal de l'Université des Annales*, an illustrated magazine connected to *Les annales politiques et littéraires*, cost 60 centimes in 1908; in 1916, *Le Monde Illustré* cost 60 centimes.

29. Maurice de Thoren was a graphic artist best known for his painting *Tea on the Seine*, which appeared in *L'Illustré soleil du Dimanche* in August 1900.

30. Georges Prade, "Une femme peut-elle conduire une automobile?" *Femina*, February 1, 1901, 7.

31. On the bicycle and the New Woman, see Siân Reynolds, "Albertine's Bicycle: or, Women and French Identity During the Belle Epoque," *Literature and History* 10 (Spring 2001): 28–41; Christopher Thompson and Fiona Ratkoff, "Un troisième sexe? Les bourgeoises et la bicyclette dans la France fin de siècle," *Le Mouvement social* 192 (July–September 2000): 9–39.

32. Berlanstein, "Selling Modern Femininity," 626.

33. Pottier and Vauxcelles, "La presse d'aujourd'hui."

34. According to Berlanstein, "The periodical's sales were comparable to or larger than those of the newspapers that gave Lafitte his start as a journalist, *La Presse* (66,000) and *L'Écho de Paris* (134,000), and quite a bit larger than those of *Le Temps* (66,000), *Le Gaulois* (20,000), and *Le Figaro* (46,000), all thought to be influential in their day." "Selling Modern Femininity," 626.

35. Pottier and Vauxcelles, "La Presse d'aujourd'hui," quoted in Cosnier, 21.

36. Baudorre, *Barbusse*, 95–96.

37. Max Rivière, "La Maison des magazines," *Femina*, April 15, 1907, 172–76. As Cosnier notes, an earlier "garden party" in 1904 had attracted 10,000 visitors, including many famous artists, writers and celebrities. Cosnier, *Les Dames de* Femina, 21.

38. While *Femina* has been the object of two recent studies, *La Vie Heureuse* has received limited scholarly treatment. Notable exceptions are Margot Irvine, "The Role of Women's Magazines in the Creation of the Prix Vie Heureuse," in *Francophone Women's Magazines: Inside and Outside France*, ed. Annabelle Cone and Dawn Marley (New Orleans: University Press of the South, 2010), 23–31; Sylvie Ducas, "Le Prix Femina: la consécration littéraire au féminin," *Recherches féministes* 16, no. 1 (2009): 43–95; Guillaume Pinson, "La femme masculinisée dans la presse mondaine de la Belle Epoque," *CLIO: Histoire, femmes et sociétés* 30 (2009): 211–29.

39. *La Vie Heureuse* was launched at the same moment as its sister publication, *Le Conseil des Femmes*. Both were advertised as companions to *La Mode Pratique*. *Le Conseil des Femmes* was entirely different in format, and contained no photographs or advertisements. It was a much denser journal, for a more targeted audience, and was billed

as being for bourgeois women who were required to earn a living, without wanting to change their lifestyle or milieu. Unfortunately, we know little about *La Vie Heureuse*'s editorial staff. Most of the features did not include a byline, unless a famous writer had contributed. It is likely that many of the editors were men, but as with *Femina*, increasing numbers of women did contribute as time went on.

40. *La Vie Heureuse*, October 1, 1902, 2.

41. *Femina*, December 15, 1903.

42. Camille Pert, *Leur Egale* (Paris: H. Simonis Empis, 1899), 283.

43. See Roberts, *Disruptive Acts*; Diana Holmes and Carrie Tarr's introductory essay, "New Woman, New Republic?" in Holmes and Tarr, *A Belle Epoque?* (New York: Berghahn Books, 2006), 11–22; Debora L. Silverman, "The 'New Woman,' Feminism, and the Decorative Arts in Fin-de-Siècle France," in *Eroticism and the Body Politic*, ed. Lynn Hunt (Baltimore: Johns Hopkins University Press, 1991), 144–63; Jennifer Waelti-Walters, *Feminist Novelists of the Belle Epoque: Love as a Lifestyle* (Bloomington: Indiana University Press, 1990), 174–81. Michelle Perrot, "The New Eve and the Old Adam: Changes in French Women's Condition at the Turn of the Century," trans. Helen Harden-Chenut, in *Behind the Lines: Gender and the Two World Wars*, ed. Margaret R. Higonnet et al. (New Haven, CT: Yale University Press, 1987), 51–60.

44. Roberts distinguishes between the stereotype of the New Woman and new women—real historical figures who engaged in behavior that challenged traditional gender norms (*Disruptive Acts*, 21).

45. For more on Belle Epoque feminism and its variants, see, in addition to the Offen articles cited above, Charles Sowerwine, "Revising the Sexual Contract: Women's Citizenship and Republicanism in France, 1789–1944," in Christopher E. Forth and Elinor Accampo, *Confronting Modernity in Fin-de-Siècle France* (New York: Palgrave Macmillan, 2010), 19–42; Màire Cross, "1890–1914: A 'Belle Epoque' for Feminism?" in Holmes and Tarr, *A Belle Epoque?* (New York: Berghahn Books, 2006), 23–36; Florence Rochefort, "The French Feminist Movement and Republicanism, 1868–1914," in *Women's Emancipation Movements in the Nineteenth Century: A European Perspective*, ed. Sylvia Paletschek and Bianka Pietrow-Ennker (Stanford: Stanford University Press, 2004), 77–101; Joan W. Scott, *Only Paradoxes to Offer: French Feminists and the Rights of Man* (Cambridge: Harvard University Press, 1997), 90–124; Elinor Accampo, Rachel Fuchs, and Mary Lynn Stewart, eds., *Gender and the Politics of Social Reform in France, 1870–1914* (Baltimore: Johns Hopkins University Press, 1995).

46. Roberts argues that these two figures represent different kinds of resistance to gender norms (*Disruptive Acts*, 8). Holmes and Tarr, on the other hand, question the usefulness of separating two figures that overlap in so many important ways. Most Belle Epoque feminists, they argue, would also have been considered New Women ("New Republic, New Women?" *A Belle Epoque?*, 20–21).

47. This image, which brings together so many elements of the stereotype surrounding the New Woman, can be found in Debora Silverman, *Art Nouveau in Fin-de-Siècle France: Politics, Psychology, Style* (Berkeley: University of California Press, 1989), 68, and Roberts, *Disruptive Acts*, 24.

48. Ruth E. Iskin's study of women in Belle Epoque poster art offers numerous examples of independent women portrayed in a positive light, and thus contrary to

other images of the New Woman. I would characterize the images she examines as examples not of the New Woman, but rather versions of the *femme moderne*—an alternative, positively coded figure of modern femininity. Her examples also point to the role consumer culture played in promoting modern women, who were more likely to respond to positive images of themselves. See her "Popularising New Women in Belle Epoque Advertising Posters," in Holmes and Tarr, *A Belle Epoque?*, 95–112.

49. In her introduction to a volume on international manifestations of the New Woman, Linda Nochlin describes all images of the New Woman as expressing: "rebellion against oppressive notions of the 'womanly,' understood to be a life devoted to subordinating one's own needs and desires to those of men, family and children." This is precisely what distinguishes *Femina*'s and *La Vie Heureuse*'s rebellion, which does not recognize such devotion as oppressive. Linda Nochlin, "Foreword: Representing the New Woman—Complexity and Contradiction," in *The New Woman International: Representations in Photography and Film from the 1870s Through the 1960s*, ed. Elizabeth Otto and Vanessa Rocco (Ann Arbor: University of Michigan Press, 2011), vii–xi.

50. In their essay "New Republic, New Women?" Holmes and Tarr describe Marcelle Tinayre, who both wrote for and frequently appeared in *Femina* and *La Vie Heureuse*, as a "public New Woman," and her novel *La rebelle* as a novel about a New Woman (20). However, as we shall see in Chapter 5, this description ignores the novel's protagonist's own rejection of that terminology.

51. In 1896, Georges Mouret's *Revue Encyclopédique* published a long piece called "La Femme Moderne par elle-même," in which they asked notable women writers and artists to give a sense of their "intellectual personality," as part of their recognition that women were going through a period of transition towards new social functions. "La Femme Moderne par elle-même," *La Revue encyclopédique* November 18, 1896, 842–85. This was preceded by an essay by Jules Bois, "La Femme Nouvelle," which demonstrates the fluidity of the terms at the time. See Offen's discussion of his essay in *Debating the Woman Question*.

52. Marie-Anne Bovet, "Femmes Editrices," *La Vie Heureuse*, September 15, 1910, 229. This feminism is ideologically resonant with what was called familial or relational feminism at the turn of the century, similarly predicated upon equality in difference. The difference between relational feminism and Belle Epoque literary feminism is largely related to their form of expression and the apolitical nature of the latter. For more on relational feminism, see Offen, "Depopulation," 656–58. Florence Rochefort's understanding of fin-de-siècle feminism as an offshoot of republican utopianism is similarly relevant. Rochefort describes utopian republicans as challenging traditional republican ideology that viewed women exclusively as wives and mothers of future citizens ("The French Feminist Movement and Republicanism, 1868–1914," 77–101). Both of these scholars are describing overtly political stances, in contradistinction to what I am identifying as feminist here.

53. André Chaignon, "Une Excursion à la Mer de Glace," *Femina*, Sept. 1, 1903, 647–48.

54. A similar image appeared in the German magazine *Illustrierte Frauenzeitung* in 1910. The difference in message with *Femina* is worth noting. The caption for the latter, under the title "Feminism on a High Scale," described the woman in the image as proof that women are not subject to vertigo—despite popular conceptions. The ac-

companying German text, on the other hand, emphasized the dangers of doing such a thing in women's clothing and allowed that only "vertigo-free ladies" should consider such a task. The editors thus conveyed "a sense of danger pertaining to the female body and its clothing." Despina Stratigakos, "Female Firsts: Media Representations of Pioneering and Adventurous Women in the Early Twentieth Century." In *The New Woman International*, eds. Elizabeth Otto and Vanessa Rocco (2011), 64–65.

55. Mona Ozouf's controversial *Women's Words: Essay on French Singularity*, trans. Jane Marie Todd (Chicago: University of Chicago Press, 1997) described French feminism as having "a tranquility, a moderation, even a timidity about it" in opposition to American trends (xi). Without entering the debate on American versus French feminism or even validating that opposition (see Eric Fassin's excellent deconstruction of the opposition in "The Purloined Gender: American Feminism in a French Mirror," *French Historical Studies* 22, no. 1 [1999]: 113–38), my book historicizes some of Ozouf's claims about the enduring role of femininity in the French feminist tradition. Responses to Ozouf's book can be found in "Femmes: Une singularité française?" *Le Débat*, no. 87 (November-December 1995): 117–46. See also Offen's review, "Weighing Women's Words," *The European Legacy* 5, no.5 (2000): 737–41. Ideas about the role of femininity in France have trickled down to more popular analyses. In a recent *New York Times* article about enduring gender inequalities in France, for example, Katrin Beinhold wrote that "French women appear to worry about being feminine, not feminist." Beinhold, "Where Having It All Doesn't Mean Equality," *The New York Times*, October 11, 2010.

56. Joan Scott's important book *Only Paradoxes to Offer* addresses precisely this tension, arguing that French feminism has struggled with the paradox of women needing to protest a lack of rights predicated on their difference by calling attention to that very difference: "To the extent that it acted for 'women,' feminism produced the 'sexual difference' it sought to eliminate" (3).

57. This is my objection to Cosnier's conclusions regarding *Femina*: she dismisses these kinds of concerns as in tension with the magazine's feminism, whereas in fact they are central to its feminism.

58. Jean Mistler, *La Librairie Hachette de 1826 à nos jours* (Paris: Hachette, 1964) 333; Claude Bellanger et al., eds., *Histoire générale de la presse française, tome 3: De 1871 à 1940* (Paris: PUF, 1972) 382; Elisabeth Parinet, "L'edition litteraire, 1890–1914," 206.

59. Rochefort, "The French Feminist Movement and Republicanism, 1868–1914," 100.

60. On July 18, 2012, Housing Minister Céline Duflot was heckled on the floor of the Assemblé nationale because of the blue dress she was wearing. Daphnee Denis, "Sun Rises, Female French Minister Gets Heckled by Colleagues, Sun Sets," Slate.com blog posted July 19, 2012, http://www.slate.com/blogs/xx_factor/2012/07/19/cecile duflot and the floral dress just another day in the french parliament.html (accessed 1/7/13).

*Chapter 1*

1. In historicizing the advertising industry in France, Marjorie Beale argues that the early industry of *publicité* was defined by its efforts to establish itself within French high cultural traditions. Beale, *The Modernist Enterprise: French Elites and the Threat of Modernity, 1900–1940* (Stanford: Stanford University Press, 1999), 5. See also Marie-Emmanuelle Cheyssel, *La publicité: Naissance d'une profession* (Paris: CNRS Éditions, 1998); Marc Martin, *Trois siècles de publicité en France* (Paris: Éditions Odile Jacob,

1992); Michael B. Miller, *The Bon Marché: Bourgeois Culture and the Department Store, 1896–1920* (Princeton: Princeton University Press, 1981).

2. According to the advertisement, Cinderella "has come back to life in books read with interest, in the theater, and through the exquisite bounty that her fairy godmother's goodwill granted her." *Femina*, March 15, 1902. The ad may have been referencing the Cinderella ballet, numerous versions of which were produced and performed throughout the nineteenth century and the Belle Epoque; the early French film version of Cinderella in 1899; and Jules Massenet's opéra-comique produced in 1899. The seventeenth-century Perrault tale also remained popular in illustrated editions throughout the nineteenth century.

3. Zola's novel, *Au Bonheur des dames*, was published in the *Gil Blas* newspaper in 1882 and by Charpentier in 1883. It is usually translated in English as *The Ladies' Paradise*.

4. This is to be compared to other thoroughly researched democratizing forces in the late nineteenth century: the democratization of luxury, of taste and of art; in the former two cases women have been particularly recognized as playing a crucial role. See Tiersten, *Marianne in the Market*, 207–19; 126–28; 228; on the relationship between consumption and femininity, see Rachel Bowlby, *Just Looking*, 18–34.

5. *La Vie Heureuse*, October 1, 1902.

6. See, for example, Leo Braudy's *The Frenzy of Renown: Fame and Its History* (New York: Vintage Books, 1997), which considers the history of famous achievers, starting with Alexander the Great. Berlanstein synthesizes the extensive work on celebrity and its significance for French history in his "Historicizing and Gendering Celebrity Culture: Famous Women in Nineteenth-Century France," *Journal of Women's History* 16, no. 4 (2004): 65–91. See also Graeme Turner, *Understanding Celebrity* (London: Sage, 2004), 1–28, for an overview of recent criticism on celebrity.

7. Berlanstein, "Historicizing and Gendering Celebrity," 82 and Vanessa Schwartz, *Spectacular Realities: Early Mass Culture in Fin-de-Siècle Paris* (Berkeley: University of California Press, 1999). Schwartz's important work demonstrates how early mass culture and the mass press created a newly democratized culture in which "individuals from different classes were expected to derive pleasure from the same sights and experiences" (16).

8. See Richard Dyer, *Stars* (London: British Film Institute, 1979; cf. 2nd ed., 1998).

9. *Femina*, February 1, 1901, 2.

10. As Marjorie Ferguson writes of twentieth-century women's magazines: "the individual woman is a member not so much of society as a whole but of her society, the world of women." Ferguson, *Forever Feminine: Women's Magazines and the Cult of Femininity* (Aldershot, UK: Gower, 1985), 6.

11. Schwartz, *Spectacular Realities*, 202.

12. Prévost would be elected to the Académie française in 1909, and was a central figure in the Parisian *monde littéraire* so closely linked to the magazines. *Femina* had published his *Lettres à Françoise mariée*, fictional letters to his niece in which he offered counsel on life, love and marriage.

13. Prévost, "Lettres à la Lectrice," *Femina*, April 15, 1908, 169.

14. Berlanstein, "Selling Modern Feminity," 626 and "Ready for Progress? Opinion Surveys on Women's Roles and Opportunities in Belle Epoque France," *French Politics, Culture & Society* 27, no.1 (Spring 2009):1–22. The streets mentioned in the citation are

suggestive of generic provincial thoroughfares: the place du Martroi is in Orléans and the cours Gambetta in Lyon; there is a rue des Ursulines in Paris but also Bordeaux.

15. Ferguson notes how part of the reinforcement of women's magazines comes from their being a "source of positive evaluation," and that they "consciously set out to foster a woman's sense of her own worth," in part through preaching "the ideal of a woman's power of self-determination" (184–85).

16. Ferguson argues that "women's magazines collectively comprise a social institution which serves to foster and maintain a cult of femininity" (184). See also Cynthia Carter and Linda Steiner, eds., *Critical Readings: Media and Gender* (Maidenhead, UK: Open University Press, 2004).

17. Tiersten describes how "commercial taste experts [distinguished] the frivolity and irrationality of the merely fashionable Parisienne from the rational and artistic qualities of the chic consumer of taste" (121–22).

18. *La Vie Heureuse*, October 1, 1902, ii.

19. *Femina*, February 1901.

20. Gruber Garvey, 4.

21. See Gruber Garvey's discussion of the definition of "magazine" in *The Adman in the Parlor*, 3.

22. In his history of advertising in America, Roland Marchand argues that modern advertising was defined in the 1920s by the shift from depicting products themselves to showcasing their benefits. While in the beginning of the century advertisers focused on circulating brand names and images, later advertisers focused on the "reason-why" approach, appealing more directly to consumers as individuals. Marchand's work, however, overlooks the symbiotic relationship between modern magazines and their advertisements. I would argue that magazines like *Femina* and *La Vie Heureuse* bring to light an intermediary step: while the advertisements mostly depicted the products themselves, those products were juxtaposed with the images figured in the pages within the magazine, which implicitly depicted the benefits of those same products. See Marchand, *Advertising the American Dream: Making Way for Modernity, 1920–1940* (Berkeley: University of California Press, 1985), 10.

23. The Liane corset was likely a reference to Liane de Pougy, the famous courtesan whose 1901 bestselling novel *Idylle saphique* detailed her relationship with Natalie Clifford Barney. Corsets from Claverie were often named for famous women. It is likely that the Myriem corset advertised in 1911 was named for the writer Myriam Harry.

24. *Femina*, April 15, 1902, 125.

25. As Gruber Garvey has shown, British magazines beginning in the 1890s regularly relied on advertising contests both to draw in readers and to secure advertising revenue. Through these contests, readers "were encouraged to transfer that sense of participating in the community of the magazine through their actions as consumers" (6).

26. On the development of the journalistic *enquête* in the nineteenth century, linked as it was to sociology and positivism, see Dominique Kalifa, "Enquête et culture de l'enquête au XIXe siècle," *Romantisme 149* (September 2010) 3–23. Berlanstein has studied *Femina*'s opinion surveys in order to "explore how readers were conceptualizing women's place in society" ("Ready for Progress?" 2). His highly instructive essay is focused on Belle Epoque women's self-assessment, rather than tracing the relationship between the magazine and its readers.

27. Berlanstein, "Ready for Progress?" 5.

28. Smilis, "Les femmes et les elections," *Femina*, May 15, 1906, 214–15; "Non! La femme ne doit pas voter!" *Femina*, September 15, 1906, 405–6.

29. "Un Tournoi de poésie," *Femina*, February 1, 1903, 423.

30. This is also another place to mark the difference from the female reader as consumer constructed by British women's magazines. As Gruber Garvey has demonstrated, British women were frequently invited to participate in writing contests linked to advertisements, but these contests distinguished clearly between the kind of creative play they demanded and the "real" work of authorship and authority (166–83).

31. "Les Prix Femina," *Femina*, (February 1, 1904, 470.

32. Irvine's article, "Re-Reading Early Prize Winners: The 1904 Prix Goncourt and Prix Vie Heureuse," in *Re-Reading/La Relecture: Essays in Honour of Graham Falconer*, ed. Rachel Falconer and Andrew Oliver (Newcastle: Cambridge Scholars Press, 2011), 153–66, offers a very helpful early history of the Prix Goncourt and the Prix Vie Heureuse, and their relationship to one another. On the history of women's efforts to enter the Académie Française, see Christian Gury, *Académiciennes* (Paris: Éditions Kimé, 1996).

33. According to correspondence between Margot Irvine and independent scholar Philippe Rodriguez, Broutelles had ties to Goncourt jurists Gaston Chéreau, Justin Rosny (who was involved romantically with her sister) and Paul Margueritte.

34. Jacques de Nouvion, "Les Femmes et le Prix Goncourt," *Femina*, Nov. 15, 1904, 410–11. Irvine, "Re-Reading Early Prize Winners," 157–58.

35. An article in *Le Gaulois* noted that the Goncourt jury could never award a woman when four qualified men were also contenders (Dec. 4, 1904). An article in *La Fronde* quoted Joris-Karl Huysmans as saying that the jury could not set such a precedent as to award a woman their prize (Feb. 1, 1905). See Irvine, "Re-Reading Early Prize Winners," 157.

36. Harry's *La Conquête de Jérusalem* has a male protagonist and was compared to the colonial novels of her male peers, especially Pierre Lôti, while Frapié's novel "takes the form of a *journal intime*, a genre more often associated with women's writing than with men's." Irvine, "Re-Reading Early Prize Winners," 5–13.

37. This conclusion can be found in a pamphlet published by Hachette in 1906 describing the Vie Heureuse prize. It also includes biographies and photos of the members of its jury and descriptions of the prize's first meetings. This document can be consulted in the IMEC archives. A later, updated version of it can be found in the Bibliothèque historique de la Ville de Paris.

38. Berlanstein attributes the prize's origins to the Prix Vie Heureuse. Sylvie Ducas, on the other hand, acknowledges the synergy between the two magazines in her excellent and informative article, "Le Prix Femina: La consécration littéraire au féminin."

39. Irvine discusses the history surrounding the establishment of a female academy in Une Académie de femmes? *@nalyses* 3, no. 2 (Spring–Summer 2008), http://www.revue-analyses.org/index.php?id=1134 (accessed November 29, 2012).

40. The article describing *Femina*'s original poetry tournament announced in the subtitle that the prizes would be judged exclusively by women.

41. Marcel L'Heureux, "Une Académie Féminine peut-elle passer du rêve à la réalité?" *Femina*, October 15, 1902, 316–17.

42. "Les Prix Femina," *Femina*, November 1, 1905, 510.
43. "Les Prix Femina," *Femina*, December 15, 1904, 470.
44. "Autour du 'Prix Vie Heureuse': Un nouveau concours offert à nos lectrices," *La Vie Heureuse*, August 1, 1906.
45. André Gide was excluded from entry in 1909 because he was already an established author. See Ducas, "Le Prix Femina," 62.
46. Hélène Avryl, "Notre concours des quarante: Une académie de femmes," *Femina*, April 15, 1909, 206.
47. Jean Bertheroy, "Le Prix Vie Heureuse pour 1904," *La Vie Heureuse*, March 1, 1905.
48. "Les Prix Femina," *Femina*, December 15, 1904, 470.
49. Lucie Delarue-Mardrus, "L'âme des livres," *Femina*, April 15, 1908, 172.
50. Maurice Laval, "Enquête sur la littérature féminine, *Femina*, May 15, 1906, 217.
51. *La Vie Heureuse*'s slightly different pitch may have been linked to its affiliation with another Hachette publication, *Le Conseil des femmes*, which they described on their cover as "the indispensable complement to *La Vie Heureuse*." This other publication was far more austere (no photographs) and was aimed at professional women.

## Chapter 2

1. Marie d'Ourlac, "George Sand," *Femina*, October 15, 1901, 332–33.
2. This term was inherited from the English, who began using it to describe female intellectuals in the eighteenth century.
3. I am referring here to the visual stereotype of the New Woman in France and not the "new women," actual women challenging Belle Epoque gender norms that Roberts discusses in *Disruptive Acts*.
4. D'Ourlac consciously set her biography in a separate space: "It's a joy to talk about this woman of genius, as if in the margins of the encyclopedia entries devoted to her." The notion of women's history in the margins will of course become critical to feminist historiography later in the twentieth century. D'Ourlac's description of Sand can also be understood as a kind of "resurrection biography," which supplies a matriarchal prehistory along the lines of what Janet Beizer describes in *Thinking Through the Mothers: Reimagining Women's Biographies* (Ithaca: Cornell University Press, 2009). In this case, what are resurrected are the feminine and especially maternal aspects of that history that Sand's formidable intellect threatened to eclipse.
5. "It was in tandem with such visual technologies of mass reproduction as lithography, offset printing, photographs, stereographs, and the cinema that—costumed in bloomers, drop-waisted skirts, or trousers—New Womanhood went global." Elizabeth Otto and Vanessa Rocco, "Introduction: Imagining and Embodying New Womanhood," in *The New Woman International: Representations in Photography and Film from the 1870s to the 1960s*, ed. Elizabeth Otto and Vanessa Rocco (Ann Arbor: University of Michigan Press, 2011), 3.
6. On the role of photography in modern celebrity, see Peter Hamilton and Roger Hargreaves, *The Beautiful and the Damned: The Creation of Identity in Nineteenth-Century Photography* (Exhibition Catalog. London: Lund Humphries, 2001).
7. Alison and Helmut Gernsheim describe the At Home photography of the 1870s and 80s as a precursor to reportage portraiture. They note that Felix Tournachon and

Paul Nadar introduced the first photo interview, of the chemist M. E. Chevreul in 1886 in *Le Journal Illustré*. With the exception of Sarah Bernhardt, the images they cite are of famous men, and they focused on the individual rather than the home. See their *A Concise History of Photography* (New York: Grosset & Dunlap, 1965), 129. On Dornac's portraits see Emery, *Photojournalism and the Origins of the French Writer House Museum*, 67–76; Emery, "Dornac's 'At Home' Photographs: Relics of History," in *Proceedings of the Western Society for French History*, 36 (2008). http://hdl.handle.net/2027/spo.0642292.0036.016. Last accessed 1/7/13. Dornac gained renewed attention in 2008 when nearly two hundred of his photographs were rediscovered and auctioned off, including images of Baudelaire, Zola and Mallarmé. See Souren Melikien, "Dornac: Unmasking a Photographer of Parisian Society," *The New York Times*, May 2, 2008.

8. "Nearly all celebrity photographs until the late 1880s represented just the torso, the exterior trappings of celebrity." Emery, *Photojournalism*, 67.

9. "Adolphe Brisson's volume *Portraits intimes* (1894–1901), was comprised of portraits and interviews, thus providing a window into the home life of contemporaries as did works such as *Pointes sèches: Physiognomies littéraires* (1898), *Paris intime* (1899), or *L'Envers de la gloire* (c. 1904). Books like Charles Buet's *Médaillons et camées* (1885), Maurice Guillmot's *Villégiatures d'artistes* (1897), or Paul Acker's *Petites confessions: visites et portraits* (1903) similarly conveyed the impression of visiting famous people at home. [ . . . ] Other series of French articles published in the periodical press [ . . . ] similarly played into the public's hunger for first-hand information about the private lives of public figures. They included "Une heure chez . . . " in the *Revue Illustrée* and "Nos Contemporains chez eux" in *Le Monde Illustré*." Emery, *Photojournalism*, 51.

10. By the 1890s, there were more than 1,400 professional photographers in Paris (Emery, *Photojournalism*, 63). See also Michel Frizot, ed., *A New History of Photography* (New York: Köneman, 1989), 123.

11. Roberts, *Disruptive Acts*, 106.

12. "Madame Séverine," *Femina*, October 1, 1902, 295.

13. Jane Dieulafoy, "Comment j'ai écrit 'Parysatis,' par Madame Jane Dieulafoy." *Femina*, August 15, 1902, 247.

14. This image can be contrasted with Dornac's portrait of Dieulafoy, his only version of a woman writer at her desk. The purpose of Dornac's image seems to be to show the extent of Dieulafoy's masculinity—her dark man's suit matches the weightiness of the desk at which she sits. *Femina*, on the other hand, chose to depict Dieulafoy *not* at her desk, recontextualizing her, perhaps, to offset her already strong associations with masculinity.

15. Maurice Level, "Enquête sur la littérature féminine," *Femina*, May 15, 1906, 217.

16. The use of photography elaborates on the *visite au grand écrivain* genre earlier in the century. See Olivier Nora, "La Visite au grand écrivain," in *Les lieux de mémoire*, ed. Pierre Nora (Paris: Gallimard, 1997), 2:131–56.

17. For more on what these images of men at their desks revealed and many wonderful examples of these images, see Emery, *Photojournalism*, 62–76.

18. "La Femme Moderne par elle-même," *La Revue Encyclopédique*, 1896, 842–85.

19. Very little has been written about Lesueur. On reading her novels as feminist romances, see Diana Holmes, "Daniel Lesueur and the Feminist Romance," in *A Belle Epoque?* eds. Holmes and Tarr, 197–210.

20. This photograph was actually not taken in Zola's home but rather in a studio, against a fake backdrop whose edges can be discerned in the background.

21. Mary Léopold-Lacour, "Daniel Lesueur," *Femina*, March 1, 1902, 74.

22. This pose is familiar from impressionist painting as well. See, for example, Degas' 1879 portrait of Duranty.

23. "Madame Alphonse Daudet," *Femina*, January 15, 1903, 415–16.

24. "Le Dialogue des Bêtes par Mme Gauthiers-Villars," *La Vie Heureuse*, May 1904.

25. On clutter in High Victorian décor, see Alastair Duncan, *Art Nouveau* (New York: Thames and Hudson, 1994), 8.

26. Willa Silverman, *The Notorious Life of Gyp: Right-Wing Anarchist in Fin-de-Siècle France* (New York: Oxford University Press, 1995); Roberts, *Disruptive Acts*, 152–64.

27. Maurice Guillemot, "Gyp," *Femina*, November 15, 1902, 343–45.

28. Abbéma was a widely recognized and accomplished painter of the Belle Epoque, who would be named Chevalier de la Légion d'Honneur in 1906. *Femina* often included her prints in the magazine as bonus excerpts.

29. The first art nouveau works were produced between 1893 and 1895 in London, Brussels and Paris. On the aesthetics and tradition of art nouveau, see Gabriel Weisberg, *Art Nouveau Bing: Paris Style 1900* (New York: Harry Abrams, 1986); Victor Arwas, *Art Nouveau: The French Aesthetic* (London: Andreas Papadakus, 2002).

30. Debora Silverman, *Art Nouveau*, 158. In contrast to art nouveau movements of other European countries, France's art nouveau movement did not pit itself against national tradition by trying to bring art to the people; rather than fully democratize art, it sought to extend art's hierarchy while making available to the masses the refined taste of the elite. See Rosalind Williams's discussion of this ambivalence in her chapter "Decorative Arts Reform and Democratic Consumption," *Dream Worlds*, 154–209.

31. Situating the New Woman in the context of French anxiety about depopulation and changes in divorce law, Silverman has summarized: "The femme nouvelle, a middle-class woman seeking independence and education rather than marriage and life at home, thus made her claims in a context where maternity and family were issues fraught with special political and national significance" (67).

32. For more on Noailles' biography, see Elisabeth Higonnet-Dugua, *Anna de Noailles, cœur innombrable: Biographie, correspondence* (Paris: Michel de Maule, 1989); François Broche, *Anna de Noailles, un mystère en pleine lumière* (Paris: Laffont, 1989); Patricia Ferlin, *Femmes d'encrier* (Paris: C. de Bartillat, 1995). On her poetry, see Catherine Perry, *Persephone Unbound: Dionysian Aesthetics in the Work of Anna de Noailles* (Lewisburg, PA: Bucknell University Press, 2003). A reading of her novel *Le visage émerveillé* can be found in Mesch, *The Hysteric's Revenge*, 158–69.

33. It's not clear whether Noailles rejected art nouveau furniture or the harsher lines of the movement's initial products. According to Silverman, "By the 1900 exhibition, a significant shift had occurred: the terms *art nouveau* and *modern style* were used to identify architectural forms and meanings antithetical to those they had signified in 1899" (5).

34. The precise nature of the literary criticism offered in both *La Vie Heureuse* and *Femina* is beyond the purview of this book, but certainly merits further discussion. Generally speaking, Noailles is read in the context of late nineteenth-century "lyrisme féminin."

35. See Debora Silverman, *Art Nouveau in Fin-de-Siècle France*, 154–59.

36. Quoted in Silverman, 157.

37. *La Vie Heureuse*, October 1902.

38. See Vanessa Schwartz's fascinating analysis of the Musée Grévin in *Spectacular Realities*, Chapter 3.

39. This title curiously references the satirical series Les Hommes d'Aujourd'hui that appeared in the French press beginning in the 1870s.

40. Art nouveau artisan René Lalique and others created "a new mythological creature, half-woman, half-dragonfly [...] Everywhere floated strange sea creatures [...] for designers seemed hypnotized by the mysteries of submarine life." Williams, *Dream Worlds*, 174.

41. Silverman has recently demonstrated the link between the undulating lines of art nouveau and Congo motifs of the vine and the elephantine. See her "Art of Darkness: African Lineages of Belgian Modernism, Part I," *West 86th* 18, no. 2 (Fall–Winter 2011): 139–81.

42. Art nouveau was suited perfectly to this task, as it offered gates or frameworks that could easily be added to existing structures, providing a simple way to update their look.

43. Baronne A. de Rothschild, "Une femme poète appréciée par une femme de lettres," *La Vie Heureuse*, October 1, 1902, 10.

44. For example, a review of Tinayre's *La Maison du péché* in *Femina* from January 1903 indicated that it was not "un livre pour les jeunes filles."

45. Mary Léopold Lacour, "Madame Gabrielle Réval," *Femina*, October 1, 1903, 685. On Réval's writing, see Juliette Rogers's chapter on women's education novels in her *Career Stories: Belle Époque Novels of Professional Development* (University Park: Penn State University Press, 2007), 80–111.

46. "La plus jeune des femmes de lettres: Gérard d'Houville et L'inconstante," *La Vie Heureuse*, May 1903.

47. Roland Barthes, "Novels and Children," in *Mythologies*, trans. Annette Lavers (1957; reprint, New York: Noonday Press, 1972), 50.

48. Robert Kemp, "Depuis Colette, plus de *bas bleus*," *Elle*, November 22, 1954, 62–65.

49. "En Visite Chez Marcelle Tinayre," *La Vie Heureuse*, June 1903.

50. Henri Duvernois, "Oeuvres de Femmes," *Femina*, April 15, 1905.

51. Best known for her 1904 novel *La Maison du péché*, Tinayre was one of two women to sit for the baccalaureat in 1899; her novel *Hellé* received the Prix de l'Académie that same year. The most extensive biographical information about her can be found in Alain Quella-Villéger, *Belles et rebelles: Le roman vrai des Chasteau-Tinayre* (Bordeaux: Aubéron, 2000). See also Mélanie Collado, *Colette, Lucie Delarue-Mardrus, Marcelle Tinayre: Emancipation et Résignation* (Paris: L'Harmattan, 2003); Mesch, *The Hysteric's Revenge*, 81–99.

52. "En Visite chez Marcelle Tinayre," *La Vie Heureuse*, March 1903.

53. In fact, when I showed this image to a group of students in 2011, they immediately saw its resemblance to an American Express ad in which Tina Fey sits under her desk surrounded by a mess of papers while her baby daughter occupies her desk chair. While the AmEx ad called attention to the joyous chaos of having both career and family, *La Vie Heureuse* was determined to portray this dual role as entirely balanced and unchaotic.

## Chapter 3

1. In using the term *Orient*, I am referring to a constructed notion of the East rather than an actual geographical entity, with Edward Said's groundbreaking critique of European orientalism in mind. See Said, *Orientalism* (New York: Vintage Books, 1978). On the French fascination with the Orient during the late nineteenth century and Belle Epoque in particular, see Esin Atil, Charles Newton and Sarah Searight, *Voyages and Visions: Nineteenth-Century European Images of the Middle East from the Victoria and Albert Museum* (Washington, DC: Smithsonian Institution Traveling Exhibition Service; Seattle, WA: University of Washington Press, 1995); Jill Beaulieau and Mary Roberts, eds., *Orientalism's Interlocutors: Painting, Architecture, Photography* (Durham, NC: Duke University Press, 2002); Ali Behdad, "Orientalist Desire: Desire of the Orient," *French Forum* 15, no. 1 (January 1990): 37–51; Reina Lewis, *Gendering Orientalism: Race, Femininity, and Representation* (New York: Routledge, 1996); Linda Nochlin, "The Imaginary Orient," chap. 7 in *The Politics of Vision: Essays on Nineteenth-Century Art and Society* (New York: Harper and Row, 1989); Mahmut Mutman and Meyda Yegenoglu, eds., *Orientalism and Cultural Differences* (Santa Cruz: Center for Cultural Studies, University of California, 1992).

2. Harry was the daughter of William Shapira, an antiquities seller who was accused of selling fake biblical documents and later committed suicide. Those documents are now thought to have been authentic and possibly part of the Dead Sea Scrolls. Her family was one of the first residents of the house later inhabited by the artist Anna Ticho, which now houses a café and museum. See Roger Pierrot, "Myriam Harry et Jérusalem," *Hebrew University Studies in Literature and the Arts* 18 (1990): 49–57; David Mendelson, "Les écrits Eretz-Israéliens de langue française de 1880 à 1948," in *Ecrits français d'Israël de 1880 à nos jours*, ed. David Mendelson and Michael Elial (Paris: Lettres Modernes, 1989), 13–47.

3. *La conquête de Jérusalem* tells the story of Siona, loosely based on Harry's life. It was followed by, among others, *La petite fille de Jérusalem* (1914); *Siona à Berlin* (1918); *Siona à Paris* (1919); *La tendre cantique de Siona* (1922). For more on Myriam Harry's biography see Cécile Chombard Gaudin, *Une Orientale à Paris: Voyages littéraires de Myriam Harry* (Paris: Maisonneuve et Larose, 2005).

4. See Irvine, "Re-Reading Early Prize Winners," 3–5.

5. More information on Lucie Delarue-Mardrus can be found in Hélène Plat, *Lucie Delarue-Mardrus: Une femme de lettres des années folles* (Paris: Grasset, 1994); Mélanie Collado, *Colette, Lucie Delarue-Mardrus, Marcelle Tinayre: emancipation et resignation* (Paris: l'Harmattan, 2003); Myriam Harry, *Mon Amie Lucie Delarue-Mardrus* (Paris: Ariane, 1946). There is also a very informative website maintained by Patricia Izquiérdo, Anne-Marie van Bockstaele and the Association des Amis de Lucie Delarue-Mardrus, http://www.amisldm.org.

6. Writer André Billy famously used the expression "Sapho 1900" to describe the lesbian artistic community of Belle Epoque France in *L'Epoque 1900* (Paris: Editions Jules Tallandier, 1951). Delarue-Mardrus had relationships with Natalie Clifford Barney and Renée Vivien, whose portrait of Petrus and his wife in her 1904 autobiographical novel *Une femme m'apparut* is said to be based on Delarue-Mardrus and her husband.

7. For an early but informative essay on the relationship between art nouveau and the Orient, see Clay Lancaster, "Oriental Contributions to Art Nouveau," *The Art Bulletin* 34, no. 4 (December 1952): 297–310.

8. Both Bernhardt and Mérode have been recognized as early models of celebrity. Emily Apter has described Mérode's legacy as a "stereotype compiled in large measure from the Orientalist performances of famous actresses: Sarah Bernhardt's Cleopatra, Sibyl Sanderson's Thaïs, Rose Caron's Salammbô, Madame Héglon's Delila, Loïe Fuller's pseudo-Eastern veil dance, Sada Yacco's Salome." Apter, *Continental Drift: From National Characters to Virtual Subjects* (Chicago: University of Chicago Press, 1999), 142. For the most complete collection of images of Mérode, see Michael Garval's fascinating study, *Cléo de Mérode and the Rise of Modern Celebrity Culture* (Surrey, UK: Ashgate, 2012).

9. By *feminist*, Apter appears to mean challenging gender norms rather than affiliated with the feminist movement. *Continental Drift*, 131.

10. In her brilliant analysis of the veil in nineteenth-century Paris, Marni Kessler describes French women's appropriation of the Muslim veil as "a visual symptom of a colonial convergence that took information about the East and displaced it, albeit in a limited way, onto the French woman." Kessler, *Sheer Presence: The Veil in Manet's Paris* (Minneapolis: University of Minnesota Press, 2006), 140.

11. "Madame Myriam Harry," *La Vie Heureuse*, April 1904.

12. On the notion of strategic mimicry in a colonial context, see Homi Bhabha, "Of Mimicry and Man: The Ambivalence of Colonial Culture," in *The Location of Culture* (New York: Routledge, 1994), 85–92.

13. Judith Gautier, "Une fête chinoise chez Pierre Lôti," *Femina*, June 15, 1903, 567–69.

14. *Femina* cover, September 15, 1905.

15. These images are even more startling in our day given the controversies surrounding the wearing of Muslim headgear in French society.

16. "Princesses, Grandes Dames, Bourgeoises," *La Vie Heureuse*, April 1, 1903.

17. On the equation of the Orient with femininity, see Kessler, *Sheer Presence*, 166n. Derek Gregory describes the colonizing nature of European photography of Egypt during the nineteenth century as part of a project of "unveiling" the Orient, through which the tourist is positioned in the masculine position as "spectator-voyeur, consumer-collector and sovereign-subject." See his "Emperors of the Gaze: Photographic Practices and Productions of Space in Egypt, 1839–1914," in *Picturing Place: Photography and the Geographical Imagination*, ed. Joan Schwartz and James Ryan (London: I.B. Tauris, 2003), 195–225.

18. "Un Ménage d'artistes," *La Vie Heureuse*, September 1907.

19. Nochlin points out the crucial displacement of any Western presence in Orientalist art, arguing that Western elements are elided in order to reinforce the mystery of the Orient and the authenticity of the work. See "The Imaginary Orient," in *The Politics of Vision*, 37–38. See also Kessler's reading of this in relationship to the veil in Manet's Paris, 132–38.

20. "Madame Myriam Harry," *La Vie Heureuse*, April 1904.

21. Lucie Delarue-Mardrus, *Mes mémoires* (Paris: Gallimard, 1938), 151.

22. "Poésies de femmes," *Femina*, March 1, 1905, 101.

23. "Poésies de Mme Lucie Delarue-Mardrus," *Femina*, October 1, 1905, 446.

24. Cf. Cosnier, *Les Dames de Femina. Un féminisme mystifié* (Rennes: Université de Rennes, 2009), 76.

25. "Les Cowgirls," *Femina*, October 1, 1906, 448.

26. Jean Lorrain cites this photo series at length in *Maison pour dames*, as we will see in Chapter 7.

27. On cross-dressing and orientalism, see Marjorie Garber, "The Chic of Araby: Transvestism and the Erotics of Cultural Appropriation," in *Vested Interests: Cross-Dressing and Cultural Anxiety* (New York: Routledge, 1992), 304–52.

28. "Madame Delarue-Mardrus aux pays Arabes," *La Vie Heureuse*, September 1905.

29. Delarue-Mardrus published eleven collections of poetry and at least forty-seven novels and novellas in her lifetime. There is very little criticism of her work in English, though a growing body in French. For analysis of Delarue-Mardrus's best-selling novel, *Marie, fille-mère*, see Mesch, *The Hysteric's Revenge*, 99–118. A special issue of the journal *Inverses* dedicated to Delarue-Mardrus was published in 2008. A more complete bibliography can be found on the website of the Association des Amis de Lucie Delarue-Mardrus, http://www.amisldm.org/bibliographie/critique/.

*Chapter 4*

1. Daniel Lesueur, "Toast à *Femina*," February 15, 1907, 75.

2. On the question of female agency in turn-of-the-century photography, see Abigail Solomon-Godeau, "The Legs of the Countess," *October* 39 (Winter 1986): 65–108.

3. Myriam Harry, *Mon amie Lucie Delarue-Mardrus* (Paris: Ariane, 1946); Lucie Delarue-Mardrus, *Mes mémoires* (Paris: Gallimard, 1938).

4. The fact that *La Vie Heureuse* rarely included bylines makes it difficult to attribute much of its commentary.

5. Jacques de Nouvion, "Madame Marcelle Tinayre," *Femina*, October 1, 1904, 348.

6. Marcelle Tinayre, *La rebelle* (1905; repr., Paris: Calmann-Lévy, 1906), 37.

7. This has led some to assume that *Le Monde Féminin* was meant to be *La Fronde*, but there are several markers that point more clearly to *Femina* and *La Vie Heureuse*, including the presence of men on the editorial staff, the emphasis on fashion and domestic concerns, and the description of their readers.

8. Camille Pert, *Leur égale* (Paris: Simonis Empis, 1899), 283.

9. Lucie Delarue-Mardrus, "L'âme des livres," *Femina*, April 15, 1908, 172.

10. Lucie Delarue-Mardrus, "Les Adversaires," *Femina*, November 1908, 498.

11. On the relationship between female intellect, reading and hysteria, see Rachel Mesch, *The Hysteric's Revenge*, 14–21; Evelyne Ender, *Sexing the Mind: Nineteenth-Century Fictions of Hysteria* (Ithaca, NY: Cornell University Press, 1995); Janet Beizer, *Ventriloquized Bodies: Narratives of Hysteria in Nineteenth-Century France* (Ithaca, NY: Cornell University Press, 1994).

12. Delarue-Mardrus, "Les Adversaires," 498.

13. Cover of *Femina*, August 15, 1910.

14. Lucie Delarue-Mardrus, "En Normandie," *Femina*, August 15, 1910, 444.

15. "According to the terms of the magazine, Lucie Delarue-Mardrus is not a 'real woman'—her female lovers aren't secret and she is not a mother, but what absolves her is her position-taking: as if from the moment that she said she wasn't a feminist, you could forgive her for everything else, even for being a lesbian." Cosnier, *Les Dames de Femina*, 76.

16. Most of the prominent Belle Epoque women writers who were not regular stars of the magazine—Colette, Natalie Barney, Liane de Pougy, Rachilde—also eschewed feminism.

17. Jean Lorrain seems closer to explaining Delarue-Mardrus's success in his send-up of the magazines, to be explored in Chapter 7: "This young man with the cigarette hanging from his mouth, a fist at his waist, sporting musky leather and corduroy, is still Madame Lucie Mardrus. How could the public resist such a suggestive feat of drag?" Lorrain, *Maison pour dames*, 56.

18. Myriam Harry, *Mon amie Lucie Delarue-Mardrus*, 43–44.

19. Delarue-Mardrus, "En Normandie," *Femina*, August 15, 1910, 444.

*Chapter 5*
This chapter is based on my article "A New Man for the New Woman? Men, Marriage and Feminism in the Belle Epoque," *Historical Reflections/Réflexions Historiques* 38, no. 3 (Winter 2012): 85–106.

1. Colette Yver, *Princesses de science* (Paris: Calmann-Lévy, 1907), 11.

2. Camille Marbo, "La femme intellectuelle au foyer," *La Vie Heureuse*, August 1907.

3. More extensive analysis of Tinayre's and Compain's novels and the role of men in exploring marriage reform in *Femina* and *La Vie Heureuse* can be found in my article "A New Man for the New Woman?," 85–106.

4. Georges Art, "La Crise du mariage," *La Revue bleue*, Sept. 25, 1897. See Jean Elisabeth Pedersen, *Legislating the French Family: Feminism, Theater, and Republican Politics, 1870–1920* (New Brunswick, NJ: Rutgers University Press, 2003), 42–74. By the end of the nineteenth-century, marriage was no longer simply a financial arrangement between fathers and husbands in France; as *mariages d'inclination* increased, marriage was conceived as a relationship based on love and ensuring the couple's satisfaction. Michelle Plott, "The Rules of the Game: Respectability, Sexuality and the *Femme Mondaine* in Late Nineteenth-Century Paris," *French Historical Studies* 25, no. 3 (2002): 531–36.

5. Pedersen, 13–41; Theresa McBride, "Divorce and the Republican Family," in *Gender and the Politics of Social Reform in France, 1870–1914*, ed. Elinor Accampo, Rachel Fuchs and Mary Lynn Stewart (Baltimore: Johns Hopkins University Press, 1995).

6. The divorce debates were revived in the summer of 1900 following the Second International Congress of Feminine Work and Institutions. See Edward Berenson, *The Trial of Madame Caillaux* (Berkeley: University of California Press, 1992), 153–54. Pedersen explores divorce plays in detail, including Emile Augier's 1876 *Madame Cavarlet*; Paul Hervieu's 1895 *Les Tenailles*; and Paul Bourget's 1908 *Un Divorce*. See Pedersen, 13–102.

7. "L'Associée," *Femina*, January 15, 1903, 408.

8. According to Màire Cross, the Civil Code was seen as "the greatest injustice to women in France in the nineteenth century." Cross, "1890–1914," 28.

9. "Faut-il rajeunir le code?" *La Vie Heureuse*, April 1, 1904, 65–66.

10. "In modifying it, one sometimes restores it to a state worse than its original construction." Ibid., 66.

11. Article 213 reads: "The husband owes protection to his wife. The wife owes obedience to her husband." On the familial laws of the civil code, see Berenson's helpful summary, *The Trial*, 107–9.

12. Henri Duvernois, "Le Mot 'amour' et le code civil," *Femina*, April 15, 1905, 181.

13. The May 1, 1905 edition of *Femina* contained two Henriot cartoons that referenced these proposed reforms. The first shows a woman reading what looks like a newspaper to her friend. The caption reads: "Very good, the new code ... but it should have required the husband not only to love his wife, but to adore his mother-in-law." The second cartoon features a dialogue between a middle-aged man and woman: "The new code requires the husband to love his wife." "... If you don't mind ... does it say up to what age?"

14. This article begins with the admonition that "Eh bien, oui, on *doit* se marier!" (Well, yes, one *must* get married!) Jeanne Brémontier and Franc-Nohain, "A quel âge doit-on se marier?" *Femina*, December 15, 1905, 578.

15. See for example, the story on Myriam Harry and her husband Emile Perrault by Charles Genaux, "Ménages d'artistes," *La Vie Heureuse*, September 1907; Jules Huret, "Ménages de savants," *Femina*, March 1, 1904; "Un ménage d'artistes: M et Mme Paul Adam," *La Vie Heureuse*, January 1905.

16. "Ménages de poètes," *Femina*, June 15, 1904. This is an interesting expansion of the woman as "artist of the self." In her key domestic role, she and her husband can now make art of themselves together.

17. The grammatical discrepancy of this last sentence calls attention to the particular linguistic idiom of the magazines, notable for a precious, affected style often difficult to translate. "Le cœur des femmes, connait-il des raisons nouvelles?" *La Vie Heureuse*, October, 1901.

18. See for example, M. de G., "Une Associée de demain," *Femina*, June 1, 1907, 243, and M. D'Auray, "Les Associées," *Femina*, January 15, 1903, 408.

19. Marcel Prévost, *Lettres à Françoise mariée* (Paris: Librairie Félix Juvan, 1908), 36.

20. Because of its heroine's job as a schoolteacher, Compain's novel has most often been treated in the context of girls' education. Jennifer Waelti-Walters and Steven Hause, eds., *Feminisms of the Belle: A Historical and Literary Anthology* (Lincoln: University of Nebraska Press, 1994), 92–93; Waelti-Walters, *Feminist Novelists of the Belle Epoque*, 126–37; Juliette Rogers, "Educating the Heroine: Turn-of-the-Century Feminism and the French Women's Educational Novels," *Women's Studies* 23 (1994): 321–34. Rogers reads both *La rebelle* and *L'un vers l'autre* separately as "novels of female professional development," focusing typologically on the ways that they differ from the male bildungsroman structure (*Career Stories*, 99–111; 163–73).

21. Emile Zola, "Le roman expérimental," in *Oeuvres complètes*. On the influence of Zola and naturalism on turn-of-the-century women writers, see "Virility and the Intellectual Woman, or Can a Woman Be a Naturalist?" in Mesch, *The Hysteric's Revenge*, 81–118.

22. Compain's later involvement with the organized feminist movement should not prevent us from considering her work in the context of Belle Epoque literary feminism. Her later works continue to reflect a struggle to define modern femininity and the balance between love and career. For more on Compain, see Mesch, "Louise-Marie Compain," *Dictionnaire des femmes créatrices*, ed. Antoinette Fouque, Mireille Calle-Gruber, and Béatrice Didier (Paris: Edition des Femmes, forthcoming).

23. Compain's great-niece is the feminist sociologist Evelyne Sullerot. This biographical information comes from a telephone interview I conducted with Sullerot in October 2008.

24. Jacques de Nouvion, "Mme Marcelle Tinayre," *Femina*, October 1, 1904, 348–49.

25. On the absence of a French marriage plot in nineteenth-century French fiction, see Masha Belenky and Rachel Mesch, "Introduction," in "State of the Union: Marriage in Nineteenth-Century France," ed. Belenky and Mesch, special issue, *Dix-Neuf: The Journal of the Société de dix-neuviémistes* 10, no. 1 (November 2008): 1–6.

26. Louise-Marie Compain, *L'un vers l'autre* (Paris: P-V Stock, Editeurs, 1903), 28–29.

27. Marcelle Tinayre, *La rebelle* (Paris: Calmann-Lévy, 1905), 13.

28. At the outset of the novel, Josanne is still married to her sickly husband, whom she married young in a loveless union, but is raising a son conceived with her lover. Noël, however, does not seem to be bothered by Josanne's previous marriage.

29. For Noel, this means accepting Josanne's son, which happens after he is nearly lost to illness. For Henri, on the other hand, this means rejecting his parents' patriarchal model of marriage, which left his mother powerless over her own property.

30. The recognition of men supporting this alternative feminist ideal supports Karen Offen's recent argument that "male feminism was, in fact a 'genre' that developed substantially during the Third Republic." See her "Is the 'Woman Question' Really the 'Man Problem'?" in *Confronting Modernity in Fin-de-Siècle France*, ed. Christopher E. Forth and Elinor Accampo (New York: Palgrave Macmillan, 2010), 40–62.

31. On the importance of Nietzsche's thought to women novelists challenging Belle Epoque gender hierarchies, see Venita Datta, "Superwomen or Slaves? Women Writers, Male Critics and the Reception of Nietzsche in Belle-Epoque France," *Historical Reflections/Réflexions Historiques* 33, no. 3 (Fall 2007): 421–47.

32. M. D'Auray, "Les Associées," *Femina*, January 15, 1903, 408.

33. See, for example, Henri Duvernois, "Une interview de Marcelle Tinayre," *Femina*, April 15, 1906, 169. The subtitle reads: "Marcelle Tinayre, author of the sensational novel *La rebelle*, shares with *Femina* readers the ideas that motivated the book."

34. "Les Associées," *Femina*, 407.

35. Emile Berringer, "Les livres et les écrivains," *L'illustration*, March 17, 1906, 170. An article in *Femina* asked Tinayre to justify some of those choices. Henri Duvernois, "Une interview de Marcelle Tinayre," *Femina*, April 15, 1906, 169. In 1909, *Femina* editor Fernand Vandérem applauded Tinayre for not having any "suffragette" instincts in her fiction writing. See his "Réceptions: Marcelle Tinayre," *Femina*, December 15, 1909, 675.

36. In her classic study, Nancy Armstrong argued for historicizing the British novel and demonstrated the ways in which eighteenth- and nineteenth-century novels "helped redefine what men were supposed to desire in women and what women, in turn, were supposed to desire to be." Tinayre's and Compain's novels are similarly significant to both cultural and literary history. See her *Desire and Domestic Fiction: A Political History of the Novel* (New York: Oxford University Press, 1987), 251.

37. Janet Beizer describes the necessary expulsion of subversive female sexuality in nineteenth-century French literature as "the process whereby the disabling of the hystericized female body paradoxically becomes an enabling force for the discourse that produces it" (*Ventriloquized Bodies*, 249).

38. It is no coincidence that Thérèse's ideal of marriage matches the one that would be described in *Femina* and *La Vie Heureuse*. She describes her alternative marriage as: "not the cowardly and traiterous servitude of slave to master . . . but a magnificent

and admirable partnership between two hearts and desires . . . the indissoluble union of friends, lovers, siblings" (146).

39. Articles and essays on the topic were signed alternately by men and women and both famous men and women were quoted as voices of authority; the writers Paul Hervieu, Eugène Brieux and Marcel Prévost served on the extraparliamentary committee working towards reforming the Code in the interest of gender equality.

40. Camille Marbo, "La Femme intellectuelle au foyer," *La Vie Heureuse*, August 1907.

41. Susan Suleiman defines the *roman à these*, or ideological novel, as seeking "through the vehicle of fiction, to persuade their readers of the 'correctness' of a particular way of interpreting the world." Suleiman, *Authoritarian Fictions: The Ideological Novel as a Literary Genre* (New York: Columbia University Press, 1983), 1.

42. Jules Huret, "Ménages de savants," *Femina*, March 1, 1904, 77.

43. Colette Yver, "Réponse de Colette Yver à Mme Camille Marbo," *La Vie Heureuse*, October 1907.

44. "Réponses à notre enquête, Epouseriez-vous une femme qui travaille," *La Vie Heureuse*, November 1907.

45. Rachel Blau DuPlessis, *Writing Beyond the Ending* (Bloomington: Indiana University Press, 1985).

46. On rewritings of Lafayette's *La Princesse de Clèves*, see Nicholas D. Paige, *The Ancien Régime of the Novel* (Philadelphia, University of Pennsylvania Press, 2011), 37–57; Julia Douthwaite, *Exotic Women: Literary Heroines and Cultural Strategies in Ancien Régime France* (Philadelphia: University of Pennsylvania Press, 1992), 126.

47. The article "Les Associées," for instance, explicitly offers examples of famous couples that counter widespread perception of "l'état actuel des moeurs." *Femina*, January 1, 1903, 407.

48. Henri Duvernois, "*La force du passé* par Daniel Lesueur," *Femina*, July 1, 1905, 316.

*Chapter 6*

1. Jean Lorrain, *Maison pour dames* (Paris: Ollendorff, 1908), 45.

2. Jean Lorrain, "Ellen," *Femina*, October 1, 1905.

3. Cosnier begins her study of *Femina* with a summary of the novel: "It's a precious document to the extent that it describes a very specific milieu," 16; see also 15–20; Irvine notes "What his book chiefly points out is the lack of connection between the lives of the readers of *Femina* and *La Vie Heureuse* [ . . . ] and the exotic lives of the women they wanted to read about." Irvine, "The Role of Women's Magazines in the Creation of the Prix Vie Heureuse," 28.

4. Annemarie Kleinert helpfully compares Flaubert's *La Corbeille* to the actual magazine in *"Le Journal des Dames et des Modes,"* 118–22.

5. Paula Geyh, *Cities, Citizens and Technologies: Urban Life and Postmodernity* (New York: Routledge, 2009), 56.

6. Lisa Tiersten writes: "Emma Bovary's predicament prefigures not only the convergence of middle-class femininity with consumerism, but also the widely felt anxiety about the relationships between individual will and social responsibility in modern market society that made the female consumer so controversial a figure during the early Third Republic." *Marianne in the Market*, 11.

7. See *Femina*, October 1, 1905.

8. Hysteria was often known as *la maladie du siècle*, a twist on the *mal du siècle* that had plagued romantic writers earlier in the century.

9. See Margaret Cohen's reading of this novel in *The Sentimental Education of the Novel* (Princeton: Princeton University Press, 1999), 165–85; Honoré de Balzac, *La muse du département* (1843) in *L'illustre Gaudissart et la muse du département*, ed. Bernard Guyon (Paris: Garnier Frères, 1970), 189.

10. Guy de Maupassant, "La parure," *Le Gaulois*, February 17, 1884.

11. Colette appeared before her divorce from Willy. Jane de la Vaudère (author of numerous salacious medical novels) appears in *La Vie Heureuse* in November 1903 as the author of verse to accompany a musical interlude included in the magazine.

12. Charles Maurras, "Le romantisme féminin," in *L'avenir de l'intelligence* (Paris: Albert Fontemoing, Editeur, 1905), 249.

13. In *The Hysteric's Revenge*, I argued that the fear of female sexuality so often associated with nineteenth-century France actually masked a deeper anxiety surrounding female intellect. On reactions of male critics to the increased numbers of women writing, see 9–16.

14. Patricia Izquiérdo, "La réception des écrits de femme: les années décisives 1908–1909," in *Masculin/féminin et presse au XIXè siècle* (Actes du colloque, Sainte Etienne: Publications de l'Université de Saint Etienne, 2013).

15. Jean Ernest-Charles, "Les 'Bas-bleus' et la littérature feminine," in *Les Samedis littéraires*, 5 vols. (Paris: Sansot, 1905), 2:231; Jean Bertaut, *La littérature féminine d'aujourd'hui* (Paris: Librairie des Annales Politiques et Littéraires, 1909); Jules Flat, *Nos femmes de lettres* (Paris: Perrin, 1909).

16. Camille Marbo, "La Femme Intellectuelle au foyer," *La Vie Heureuse*, August 1907.

*Chapter 7*

This chapter is based on my article, "A Belle Epoque Media Storm: Gender, Celebrity and the Marcelle Tinayre Affair," *French Historical Studies* 35, no. 1 (Winter 2012): 93–121.

1. Henriot, *Le petit journal*, Jan. 19, 1908. Gabrielle Houbre describes this image in "L'honneur perdu de Marcelle Tinayre: l'affaire de la Légion d'honneur ratée (1908)," in *Les ratés de la littérature*, ed. Jean-Jacques Lefrère, Michel Pierssens and Jean-Didier Wagneur (Tusson, Fr.: Du Lérot, 1999), 89–101. Houbre's impeccably researched piece was the first scholarly article to reconstitute the details of the scandal following Tinayre's nomination to the Legion of Honor.

2. The ranks for the Legion of Honor are knight (chevalier), officer, commander, grand officer and grand cross.

3. Although the first actress was awarded the Legion of Honor in 1904, Bernhardt did not become a chevalier until 1914, and was promoted to officer in 1921. Roberts, *Disruptive Acts*, 325n.35. For more on the controversies surrounding Bernhardt's public image, see Berlanstein, *Daughters of Eve*, 209–36. On the first women to receive the honor, see Haryett Fontanges, *La Légion d'honneur et les femmes décorées, étude d'histoire et de sociologie féminine* (Paris: Alliance Cooperative du Livre, 1905).

4. Houbre provides a helpful breakdown of the range of political affiliations and scale in the publications that responded to the affair: "from the extreme-right to the nationalist right (*La Libre Parole, L'Autorité, La Patrie, L'Écho de Paris, L'Éclair, La Presse, L'intransigeant, Le Gaulois*) to the leftist-republican and extreme leftist (*L'Aurore,*

*Le Radical, La Petite République, L'Humanité, Le Rappel, L'Action, Messidor*) by way of more moderate dailies without a clear political bent (*La Liberté, Le Temps, Le Figaro, Le Matin, Le Journal, Le Petit Journal, Le Petit Parisien*) without forgetting the *Gil Blas*, the Parisian gossip newspaper" ("L'honneur perdu," 94).

5. Tinayre did not, then, refuse the Legion of Honor, although she was almost immediately remembered as having done so (Quella-Villéger, *Belles et rebelles*, 278). Numerous sources continue to describe her this way, largely because French Wikipedia contains this misinformation.

6. Controversy brewed about the context for Tinayre's initial letter. In a letter published January 9, 1908 in *L'Écho de Paris*, Tinayre insisted that the editor Adrien Hébrard had invited her to write to *Le Temps*.

7. The January 11 edition of the *Messidor* charged that Tinayre had written a letter to Briand asking to be considered for the honor.

8. Marcelle Tinayre, "La croix de Madame Tinayre," *Le Temps*, January 9, 1908.

9. Houbre describes Jean Ernest-Charles as "a lawyer who was a specialist in literary trials, and who had published political works before turning to literary criticism" (Houbre, "L'honneur perdu," 94). See Ernest-Charles, *La littérature française d'aujourd'hui* (Paris: Perrin et Cie, 1902); Also see "Livre de femmes," *Les Samedis littéraires* (Paris: Sansot, 1905) 1:85–93.

10. Jean Ernest-Charles, ed., *Le Censeur*, January 18, 1908, 65–94. Houbre notes that he excluded some of the articles most favorable to Tinayre, including Paul Lagardère's piece in the January 10 *Le Petit Parisien*.

11. Jean Ernest-Charles, "Femmes de lettres," *Gil Blas*, January 12, 1908.

12. "They always want to attract attention for themselves. All they know how to do is make up stories so that people will admire them more." Ernest-Charles, "Femmes de Lettres."

13. Clément Vautel, "Note parisienne," *La Liberté*, January 10, 1908.

14. Franc-Nohain, "La mode nouvelle," *La Liberté*, January 8, 1908; "Madame Tinayre et ses amis," *La Presse*, January 9, 1908; Guy de Cassagnac, "Causons chiffons!" *L'Autorité*, January 11, 1908.

15. Emile Faguet, "Vous le porterez!" *Le Gaulois*, January 9, 1908.

16. "Pour Sarah Bernhardt," *Gil Blas*, January 9, 1908; "La Croix de Mme Tinayre," *Gil Blas*, January 8, 1908; "Pour Georges de Peyrebrune," *Gil Blas*, January 10, 1908.

17. "L'opinion des femmes décorées," *L'Éclair*, January 9, 1908.

18. Houbre reads the affair as an example of media producing an event ("journalistic strategies produced, indeed created, 'the event' of the missed Legion of Honor") but also as expressing "the tenacious misogyny and antifeminism of the Belle Epoque" ("L'honneur perdu," 101).

19. Tinayre initially told *La Liberté*: "You know, I won't wear the decoration. I don't really want to be noticed by the [. . .] corner grocer." René de Valfori, "Conversation avec Mme Tinayre," *La Liberté*, January 7, 1908.

20. *Gil Blas*, January 10, 1908.

21. Emmanuel Arène, "La croix du jour," *Le Figaro*, January 11, 1908.

22. Tinayre, "Les Explications de Mme Tinayre," *L'Écho de Paris*, January 9, 1908; Tinayre, "Je ne l'ai pas refusée, nous dit Marcelle Tinayre," *L'Intransigeant*, January 10, 1908.

23. "La modestie, vertu féminine," *L'Aurore*, January 9, 1908.

24. The regular features on visits to celebrity homes that had become popular in the periodical press by the 1890s certainly collapsed some of these boundaries. But in these stories, part of the thrill was the sort of detective work required of the journalist. The famous person might answer questions in an interview, but the tone was still one of distance and hierarchy. See Emery's *Photojournalism*, 47–80.

25. The features of Myriam Harry and Lucie Delarue-Mardrus on their travels are of another variety, of course. They showed the woman writer as a kind of performer, like the actress, outside of the bounds of bourgeois existence.

26. Tinayre actually had three children, but she only mentions one in the letter. A fourth died in childhood in 1896.

27. Marcelle Tinayre, *Le Temps*, January 8, 1908.

28. Berlanstein describes this formulation as a paraphrasing of Daniel Boorstin's famous description of a celebrity as someone who is "well-known for his well-knownness." See Berlanstein, "Historicizing and Gendering Celebrity Culture," 66, and Boorstin, *The Image: A Guide to Pseudo-events in America* (New York: Vintage, 1961), 57.

29. The paradoxical nature of Tinayre's predicament merits comparison with Joan Scott's description of the contradictions inherent to French feminism, whereby women had to argue at once that sexual difference was irrelevant to citizenship, but in order to act on behalf of women had to insist on their sexual difference. In addition to being caught in a similar feminist double-bind, Tinayre's story highlights the "internal tensions and incompatibilities" of Belle Epoque feminism to which Scott encourages attentiveness. *Only Paradoxes to Offer*, 16.

30. Emile Faguet, "La rebelle," *Revue Latine*, 1905, quoted in Eugène Martin-Mamy, *Marcelle Tinayre* (Paris: E. Sansot, 1909), 39.

31. Régine Martial, *Gil Blas*, January 18, 1908.

## Conclusion

1. In 1908 Jean Richepin, Henri Poincaré and Francis Charmes were elected; they were joined in 1909 by Marcel Prévost, Jean Aicard, Eugène Brieux, René Doumic and Raymond Poincaré. This was not the first time the question of electing women had been raised. For a complete history, see Christian Gury's excellent study, *Les Académiciennes* (Paris: Éditions Kimé, 1996).

2. Paul Flat refers to the "crowded battalions" of women writers in *Nos femmes de lettres* (Paris: Perrin, 1909), ii; Jules Bertaut describes the "battalion" of women writers as "a sort of mass marching in one unified spirit toward victory!" in *La littérature féminine d'aujourd'hui* (Paris: Librairie des annales politiques et littéraires, 1909), 11.

3. Simone d'Ax, "Sur le pont des arts," *Femina*, January 1, 1909, 16–17.

4. As Sylvie Ducas notes, the prize committee was rarely referred to as an Academy, but rather as a company, assembly or committee ("Le Prix Femina," 63).

5. Irvine describes the prize as a joint product of *Femina* and *La Vie Heureuse* that "helped to consecrate and legitimize writing by women at the turn of the century," in "The Role of Women's Magazines in the Creation of the *Prix Vie Heureuse*," 21.

6. The original jury was composed of Juliette Adam, Arvède Barine, Thérèse Bentzon, Jean Bertheroy, Pierre de Coulevain, Julia Daudet, Lucie Delarue-Mardrus, Jane Dieulafoy, Claude Ferval, Judith Gautier, Lucie Félix-Faure-Goyau, Daniel

Lesueur, Jeanne Marni, Anna de Noailles, Jane Catulle Mendès, Georges de Peyrebrune, Poradowska, Gabrielle Réval, Séverine, Marcelle Tinayre and Caroline de Broutelles as permanent secretary. See "Le Prix Vie Heureuse," *La Vie Heureuse*, February 1905.

7. On the initial disregard for the prize, see Irvine, "Une Académie de femmes?"

8. Hélène Avryl, "Les femmes et l'Académie," *Femina*, February 15, 1909, 95; Avryl, "Une Académie de femmes," *Femina*, April 15, 1909, 206.

9. Franc-Nohain, "Choses et autres," *L'Écho de Paris*, January 15, 1909, 1; "L'Académie et les femmes," *Le Temps*, January 20, 1909, 1.

10. A final full-page image features an enormous open book, which a crowd of male and female hands appear to be clamoring for. While the caption attributes these hands to readers, in context they are suggestive of a struggle between authors themselves, men and women battling over their right to the book at the center.

11. François de Tessan, "Académiciennes?" *La Liberté*, January 10, 1909, 1. In this piece he announced a forthcoming series of letters from women on the topic. See also January 15 and February 1, 1909.

12. Avryl, "Les femmes et l'Académie," *Femina*, February 15, 1909.

13. George Sand had famously refused election to the Academy, a fact often noted. But, as François de Tessan had noted in *La Liberté*, "times have changed." De Tessan, "Académiciennes?" *La Liberté*, January 10, 1909, 1.

14. Gury, *Les Académiciennes*, 110–11.

15. Fernand Vandérem, "Réceptions: La comtesse M. de Noailles," *Femina*, October 15, 1909, 561.

16. Hélène Avryl, "Les Femmes et l'Académie," *Femina*, February 15, 1909.

17. Fernand Vandérem, "Réceptions: Madame Marcelle Tinayre," *Femina*, December 15, 1909, 645.

18. Article 213 of the Civil Code, which described husbands giving protection in exchange for wives' obedience, was changed in 1938, but until 1970 still referred to the husband as "head of the family" and stipulated the circumstances under which the wife could make familial decisions. In 1972, it was revised so that "the spouses together control the material and moral direction of the family."

19. See Karen Offen, "Women, Citizenship and Suffrage with a French Twist, 1789–1993," in *Suffrage and Beyond: International Feminist Perspectives*, ed. Melanie Nolan and Catherine Daley (Auckland, NZ: Auckland University Press, 1994), 151.

20. Compain, *L'un vers l'autre*, 250.

21. Janine, "Remarques d'une débutante: Chevalières?" *Femina*, April 15, 1910.

22. Gury, *Les Académiciennes*, 90.

23. Lafitte had overextended himself with the high production cost of the photographic news daily *Excelsior* that he had launched in 1910.

24. See Mary Louise Roberts, *Civilization without Sexes: Reconstructing Gender in Postwar France, 1917–27* (Chicago: University of Chicago Press, 1994), 17–45.

25. In her study of mid-century femininity in the French mass press, Susan Weiner describes *Elle* as the first French magazine to portray a fantasy of work-life balance: "for the first time, a women's magazine displayed the fantasy of having both a fulfilling career and a traditional home life." Weiner, *Enfants Terribles: Youth and Femininity in the Mass Media in France, 1945–1968* (Baltimore: Johns Hopkins University Press, 2001), 21.

26. Kemp stops in the early 1900s only to note Colette and Anna de Noailles, with an allusion to Gabrielle Réval and Marcelle "Tinagre" (sic) as minor characters along the way.

27. Lafitte's *La Vie au Grand Air* has been studied for its contribution to the history of photography and the invention of the modern magazine, while *Femina*'s particular innovations have been largely ignored, despite their crucial role in Lafitte's own history and his development of *Je sais tout* and *Excelsior*. See for example, "L'invention du magazine," in Thierry Gervais and Gaëlle Morel's excellent history, *La photographie: Histoire, techniques, art, presse* (Paris: Larousse, 2008), 113–16. The more recent *La Civilisation du journal* addresses *Femina* in the essay on "La presse féminine," which is followed by an essay on "La presse féministe," which makes no mention of it; Gervais' essay on photography for that collection, which discusses the development of photographic interviews, makes no mention of either magazine, nor does his essay on the illustrated magazine, despite its emphasis on Pierre Lafitte. See Rosemonde Sanson, "La presse féminine," Michèle Riot-Sarcey, "La presse féministe: la politique des femmes ou la plume exclusive," Thierry Gervais, "Les premiers magazines illustrés" and "Poétique de l'image 2: La photographie au service de l'information visuelle (1843–1914)," in *La Civilisation du journal: Histoire culturelle et littéraire de la presse française au XIXe siècle*, ed. Dominique Kalifa et al. (Paris: Nouveau Monde éditions, 2011), 523–42; 543–55; 851–64; 453–63.

# SELECTED BIBLIOGRAPHY

The full run of *Femina* from 1901 to 1914 can be consulted at the Bibliothèque historique de la Ville de Paris and at the Bibliothèque Marguerite Durand, which also houses the full run of *La Vie Heureuse* to that date. Both magazines can be consulted on microfilm at the Bibliothèque nationale de France. *Femina* issues from January 1910 to December 1912 can be consulted on Gallica.

Accampo, Elinor, Rachel Fuchs, and Mary Lynn Stewart, eds. *Gender and the Politics of Social Reform in France, 1870–1914.* Baltimore: Johns Hopkins University Press, 1995.
Apter, Emily. *Continental Drift: From National Characters to Virtual Subjects.* Chicago: University of Chicago Press, 1999.
Armstrong, Nancy. *Desire and Domestic Fiction: A Political History of the Novel.* New York: Oxford University Press, 1987.
Arwas, Victor. *Art Nouveau: The French Aesthetic.* London: Andreas Papadakus, 2002.
Barthes, Roland. "Novels and Children." In *Mythologies.* Translated by Annette Lavers. New York: Noonday Press, 1972.
Baudorre, Philippe. *Barbusse: Le pourfendeur de la Grande Guerre.* Paris: Flammarion, 1995.
Beale, Marjorie. *The Modernist Enterprise: French Elites and the Threat of Modernity, 1900–1940.* Stanford: Stanford University Press, 1999.
Beaulieu, Jill, and Mary Roberts, eds. *Orientalism's Interlocutors: Painting, Architecture, Photography.* Durham, NC: Duke University Press, 2002.
Beetham, Margaret. *A Magazine of Her Own? Domesticity and Desire in the Woman's Magazine, 1800–1914.* New York: Routledge, 1996.
Behdad, Ali. "Orientalist Desire: Desire of the Orient." *French Forum* 15, no. 1 (January 1990): 37–51.
Beizer, Janet. *Thinking Through the Mothers: Reimagining Women's Biographies.* Ithaca, NY: Cornell University Press, 2009.
———. *Ventriloquized Bodies: Narratives of Hysteria in Nineteenth-Century France.* Ithaca, NY: Cornell University Press, 1994.
Belenky, Masha, and Rachel Mesch. "Introduction." In "State of the Union: Marriage in Nineteenth-Century France," edited by Masha Belenky and Rachel Mesch. Special issue, *Dix-Neuf: The Journal of the Société de dix-neuviémistes* 10, no.1 (November 2008).

Bellanger, Claude, Jacques Godechot, Pierre Guiral, and Fernand Terrou, eds. *L'Histoire générale de la presse française, Tome 3: De 1871 à 1940*. Paris: PUF, 1972.
Berenson, Edward. *The Trial of Madame Caillaux*. Berkeley: University of California Press, 1992.
Bergman-Colter, Janis. *The Woman of Ideas in French Art, 1830–1848*. New Haven: Yale University Press, 1995.
Berlanstein, Lenard. *Daughters of Eve: A Cultural History of French Theater Women from the Old Régime to the Fin de Siècle*. Cambridge: Harvard University Press, 2001.
———. "Historicizing and Gendering Celebrity Culture: Famous Women in Nineteenth-Century France." *Journal of Women's History* 16, no. 4 (2004): 65–91.
———. "Ready for Progress? Opinion Surveys on Women's Roles and Opportunities in Belle Epoque France." *French Politics, Culture & Society* 27, no. 1 (Spring 2009): 1–22.
———. Review of *Les dames de* Femina: *Un féminisme mystifié*, by Colette Cosnier. *H-France* 9, no. 134 (November 2009): 566–69.
———. "Selling Modern Femininity: *Femina*, a Forgotten Feminist Publishing Success in Belle Epoque France." *French Historical Studies* 30, no. 4 (Fall 2007): 623–49.
Bowlby, Rachel. *Just Looking: Consumer Culture in Dreising, Gissing and Zola*. New York: Methuen, 1985.
Braudy, Leo. *The Frenzy of Renown: Fame and Its History*. New York: Vintage Books, 1997.
Broche, François. *Anna de Noailles, un mystère en pleine lumière*. Paris: Laffont, 1989.
Carter, Cynthia, and Linda Steiner, eds. *Critical Readings: Media and Gender*. Maidenhead, UK: Open University Press, 2004.
Chartier, Roger, and Henri-Jean Martin, eds. *Histoire de l'édition française*. Vol. 3, *Le temps des éditeurs: Du Romantisme à la Belle Epoque (1830–1900)*. Paris: Cercle de la Librairie, 1983.
Chombard Gaudin, Cécile. *Une orientale à Paris: Voyages littéraires de Myriam Harry*. Paris: Maisonneuve et Larose, 2005.
Cohen, Margaret. *The Sentimental Education of the Novel*. Princeton: Princeton University Press, 1999.
Collado, Mélanie. *Colette, Lucie Delarue-Mardrus, Marcelle Tinayre: Emancipation et resignation*. Paris: l'Harmattan, 2003.
Cosnier, Colette. *Les Dames de* Femina: *Un féminisme mystifié*. Rennes: Presses Universitaires de Rennes, 2009.
Cross, Màire. "1890–1914: A 'Belle Epoque' for Feminism?" In *A Belle Epoque?* edited by Diana Holmes and Carrie Tarr, 23–36. New York: Berghahn Books, 2006.
Datta, Venita. "Superwomen or Slaves? Women Writers, Male Critics and the Reception of Nietzsche in Belle-Epoque France." *Historical Reflections/Réflexions Historiques* 33, no. 3 (Fall 2007): 421–47.
Delarue-Mardrus, Lucie. *Mes mémoires*. Paris: Gallimard, 1938.
Douthwaite, Julia. *Exotic Women: Literary Heroines and Cultural Strategies in Ancien Régime France*. Philadelphia: University of Pennsylvania Press, 1992.
Ducas, Sylvie. "Le Prix Femina: La consécration littéraire au féminin." *Recherches Feministes* 16, no. 1 (2009): 43–95.
DuPlessis, Rachel Blau. *Writing Beyond the Ending*. Bloomington: Indiana University Press, 1985.
Dyer, Richard. *Stars*. London: British Film Institute, 1979. 2nd ed. 1998.

Emery, Elizabeth. "Dornac's 'At Home' Photographs, Relics of French History." In *Proceedings of the Western Society for French History* 36 (2008), http://hdl.handle.net/2027/spo.0642292.0036.016 (accessed January 7, 2013).

———. *Photojournalism and the Origins of the French Writer House Museum (1881–1914): Privacy, Publicity and Personality.* Burlington, VT: Ashgate, 2012.

Ender, Evelyne. *Sexing the Mind: Nineteenth-Century Fictions of Hysteria.* Ithaca, NY: Cornell University Press, 1995.

Fassin, Eric. "The Purloined Gender: American Feminism in a French Mirror." *French Historical Studies* 22, no. 1 (1999): 113–38.

Ferguson, Marjorie. *Forever Feminine: Women's Magazines and the Cult of Femininity.* Aldershot, UK: Gower, 1985.

Feyel, Gilles. *La presse en France des origines à 1944.* Paris: Ellipses, 1999.

Foley, Susan K. *Women in France since 1789: The Meanings of Difference.* New York: Palgrave Macmillan, 2004.

Forth, Christopher E., and Elinor Accampo, eds. *Confronting Modernity in Fin-de-Siècle France: Bodies, Minds and Gender.* New York: Palgrave Macmillan, 2010.

Garber, Marjorie. "The Chic of Araby: Transvestism and the Erotics of Cultural Appropriation." Chap. 12 in *Vested Interests: Cross-Dressing and Cultural Anxiety.* New York: Routledge, 1992.

Garval, Michael. *Cléo de Mérode and the Rise of Celebrity Culture.* Surrey, UK: Ashgate, 2012.

Gernsheim, Helmut, and Alison Gernsheim. *A Concise History of Photography.* New York: Grosset & Dunlap, 1965.

Gervais, Thierry. "L'Illustration photographique: Naissance du spectacle de l'information, 1843–1914." PhD diss., École des hautes études en sciences sociales, 2007.

Gervais, Thierry, and Gaëlle Morel. *La photographie: Histoire, techniques, art, presse.* Paris: Larousse, 2008.

Geyh, Paula. *Cities, Citizens and Technologies: Urban Life and Postmodernity.* New York: Routledge, 2009.

Goldsmith, Elizabeth C., and Dena Goodman. *Going Public: Women and Publishing in Early Modern France.* Ithaca: Cornell University Press, 1995.

Gregory, Derek. "Emperors of the Gaze: Photographic Practices and Productions of Space in Egypt, 1839–1914." In *Picturing Place: Photography and the Geographical Imagination,* edited by Joan Schwartz and James Ryan, 195–225. London: I.B. Tauris, 2003.

Gruber Garvey, Ellen. *The Adman in the Parlor: Magazines and the Gendering of Consumer Culture, 1880s to 1910s.* New York: Oxford University Press, 1996.

Gury, Christian. *Les académiciennes.* Paris: Éditions Kimé, 1996.

Habermas, Jürgen. *The Structural Transformation of the Public Sphere: An Inquiry into a Category of Bourgeois Society.* Translated by Thomas Burger, with the assistance of Frederick Lawrence. Cambridge: MIT Press, 1989.

Hamilton, Peter, and Roger Hargreaves. *The Beautiful and the Damned: The Creation of Identity in Nineteenth-Century Photography.* London: Lund Humphries, 2001.

Harry, Myriam. *Mon amie Lucie Delarue-Mardrus.* Paris: Ariane, 1946.

Higonnet-Dugua, Elisabeth. *Anna de Noailles, cœur innombrable: Biographie, correspondence.* Paris: Michel de Maule, 1989.

Hiner, Susan. *Accessories to Modernity: Fashion and the Feminine in Nineteenth-Century France.* Philadelphia: University of Pennsylvania Press, 2010.

Holmes, Diana, and Carrie Tarr, eds. *A Belle Epoque? Women in French Society and Culture, 1890–1914.* New York: Berghahn Books, 2006.
Houbre, Gabrielle. "L'honneur perdu de Marcelle Tinayre: L'affaire de la Légion d'honneur ratée (1908)." In *Les ratés de la littérature*, edited by Jean-Jacques Lefrère, Michel Pierssens and Jean-Didier Wagneur, 89–101. Tusson, FR: Du Lérot, 1999.
Irvine, Margot. "Une Académie de femmes?" *@nalyses* 3, no. 2 (Spring–Summer 2008), http://www.revue-analyses.org/index.php?id=1134 (accessed November 29, 2012).
———. "Re-Reading Early Prize Winners: The 1904 Prix Goncourt and Prix Vie Heureuse." In *Re-Reading/La Relecture: Essays in Honour of Graham Falconer*, edited by Rachel Falconer and Andrew Oliver, 153–66. Newcastle: Cambridge Scholars Press, 2011.
———. "The Role of Women's Magazines in the Creation of the Prix Vie Heureuse." In *Francophone Women's Magazines: Inside and Outside France*, edited by Annabelle Cone and Dawn Marley, 23–31. New Orleans: University Press of the South, 2010.
Iskin, Ruth E. "Popularising New Women in Belle Epoque Advertising Posters." In *A Belle Epoque? Women in French Society and Culture, 1890–1914*, edited by Diana Holmes and Carrie Tarr, 95–112. New York: Berghahn Books, 2006.
Kale, Steven D. *French Salons: High Society and Sociability from the Old Regime to the Revolution of 1848.* Baltimore: Johns Hopkins University Press, 2004.
Kalifa, Dominique. "Enquête et culture de l'enquête au XIXe siècle." *Romantisme* 149 (September 2010): 3–23.
Kalifa, Dominique, Philippe Régnier, Marie-Eve Thérenty and Alain Vaillant, eds. *La Civilisation du journal: Histoire culturelle et littéraire de la presse française au XIXe siècle.* Paris: Nouveau Monde éditions, 2011.
Kessler, Marni Reva. *Sheer Presence: The Veil in Manet's Paris.* Minneapolis: University of Minnesota Press, 2006.
Kleinert, Annemarie. *Le journal des dames et des modes ou la conquête de l'Europe féminine (1797–1839).* Stuttgart: Jan Thorbecke Verlag, 2001.
Klejman, Laurence, and Florence Rochefort. *L'Egalité en marche: Le féminisme sous la Troisième République.* Paris: Presses de la Fondation nationale des sciences politiques/ E?ditions des Femmes Antoinette Fouque, 1989.
Lancaster, Clay. "Oriental Contributions to Art Nouveau." *The Art Bulletin* 34, no. 4 (December 1952): 297–310.
Landes, Joan B. *Women and the Public Sphere in the Age of the French Revolution.* Ithaca: Cornell University Press, 1988.
Leroy, Géraldi, and Julie Bertrand-Sabiani. *La vie littéraire à la Belle Epoque.* Paris: Presses Universitaires de France, 1998.
Lewis, Reina. *Gendering Orientalism: Race, Femininity, and Representation.* New York: Routledge, 1996.
Marchand, Roland. *Advertising the American Dream: Making Way for Modernity, 1920–1940.* Berkeley: University of California Press, 1985.
Martin, Marc. *Trois siècles de publicité en France.* Paris: E?ditions Odile Jacob, 1992.
Martin-Fugier, Anne. *Les salons de la IIIe République: Art, littérature, politique.* Paris: Perrin, 2003.
Mayeur, Françoise. *L'éducation des filles en France au XIXe siècle.* Paris: Hachette, 1979.

McMillan, James F. *France and Women, 1789–1914: Gender, Society and Politics.* 2nd ed. New York: Routledge, 2000.

Mesch, Rachel. "A Belle Epoque Media Storm: Gender, Celebrity and the Marcelle Tinayre Affair." *French Historical Studies* 35, no. 1 (Winter 2012): 93–121.

———. "Housewife or Harlot? Sex and the Married Woman in Nineteenth-Century France." *Journal of the History of Sexuality* 18, nos. 1–2 (January–May 2009): 65–83.

———. "Husbands, Wives and Doctors: Marriage and Medicine in Rachilde, Jane de la Vaudère and Camille Pert." In "State of the Union: Marriage in Nineteenth-Century France" (edited by Masha Belenky and Rachel Mesch), special issue of *Dix-Neuf: The Journal of the Société de dix-neuviémistes* 10, no.1 (November 2008), 90–104.

———. *The Hysteric's Revenge: French Women Writers at the Fin de Siècle.* Nashville: Vanderbilt University Press, 2006.

———. "Louise-Marie Compain." In *Dictionnaire des femmes créatrices*, edited by Antoinette Fouque, Mireille Calle-Gruber, and Béatrice Didier. Paris: Éditions des femmes, forthcoming.

———. "A New Man for the New Woman? Men, Marriage and Feminism in the Belle Epoque." *Historical Reflections/Réflexions Historiques* 38, no. 3 (Winter 2012): 85–106.

Miller, Michael B. *The Bon Marché: Bourgeois Culture and the Department Store, 1896–1920.* Princeton: Princeton University Press, 1981.

Mistler, Jean. *La Librairie Hachette de 1826 à nos jours.* Paris: Hachette, 1964.

Moore, Kevin. *Jacques Henri Lartigue: The Invention of an Artist.* Princeton: Princeton University Press, 2004.

Mutman, Mahmut, and Meyda Yegenoglu, eds. *Orientalism and Cultural Differences.* Santa Cruz: Center for Cultural Studies, University of California, 1992.

Nesci, Catherine. *Le flâneur et les flâneuses: Les femmes et la ville à l'époque romantique.* Grenoble: ELLUG, Bibliothèque stendhalienne et romantique, 2007.

Nochlin, Linda. "Foreword: Representing the New Woman—Complexity and Contradiction." In *The New Woman International: Representations in Photography and Film from the 1870s Through the 1960s*, edited by Elizabeth Otto and Vanessa Rocco, vii–xi. Ann Arbor: University of Michigan Press, 2011.

———. "The Imaginary Orient." Chap. 3 in *The Politics of Vision: Essays on Nineteenth-Century Art and Society.* New York: Harper and Row, 1989.

Offen, Karen. "Defining Feminism: A Comparative Historical Perspective." *Signs: Journal of Women in Culture and Society* 14, no.1 (1988): 119–57.

———. "Depopulation, Nationalism and Feminism in Fin-de-Siècle France." *American Historical Review* 89, no. 3 (June 1984): 648–76.

———. "Is the 'Woman Question' Really the 'Man Problem'?" In *Confronting Modernity in Fin-de-Siècle France: Bodies, Minds and Gender*, edited by Christopher E. Forth and Elinor Accampo, 40–62. New York: Palgrave Macmillan, 2010.

———. "On the French Origin of the Words *Feminism* and *Feminist*." *Feminist Issues* 8, no. 2 (Fall 1988): 45–51.

———. "Weighing Women's Words." *The European Legacy* 5, no. 5 (2000): 737–41.

———. "Women, Citizenship and Suffrage with a French Twist, 1789–1993." In *Suffrage and Beyond: International Feminist Perspectives*, edited by Melanie Nolan and Catherine Daley, 151–70. Auckland, NZ: Auckland University Press, 1994.

Olivier, Nora. "La visite au grand écrivain." In *Les lieux de mémoire*, edited by Pierre Nora. Vol. 2, 131–56. Paris: Gallimard, 1997.

Otto, Elizabeth, and Vanessa Rocco, eds. *The New Woman International: Representations in Photography and Film from the 1870s through the 1960s*. Ann Arbor: University of Michigan Press, 2011.

Ozouf, Mona. *Women's Words: Essay on French Singularity*. Translated by Jane Marie Todd. Chicago: University of Chicago Press, 1997.

Parinet, Elisabeth. "L'édition littéraire: 1890–1914." In *Histoire de l'édition française*, edited by Roger Chartier and Henri-Jean Martin. Vol. 4, *Le livre concurrencé, 1900–1940*, 148–87. Paris: Promodis, 1986.

Pedersen, Jean Elisabeth. *Legislating the French Family: Feminism, Theater, and Republican Politics, 1870–1920*. New Brunswick, NJ: Rutgers University Press, 2003.

Perrot, Michelle. "The New Eve and the Old Adam: Changes in French Women's Condition at the Turn of the Century." Translated by Helen Harden-Chenut. In *Behind the Lines: Gender and the Two World Wars*, edited by Margaret R. Higonnet, Jane Jenson, Sonya Michel, and Margaret Collins Weitz, 51–60. New Haven, CT: Yale University Press, 1987.

Perry, Catherine. *Persephone Unbound: Dionysian Aesthetics in the Work of Anna de Noailles*. Lewisburg, PA: Bucknell University Press, 2003.

Pinson, Guillaume. "La femme masculinisée dans la presse mondaine de la Belle Epoque." *CLIO: Histoire, femmes et societés* 30 (2009): 211–29.

Plat, Hélène. *Lucie Delarue-Mardrus: Une femme de lettres des années folles*. Paris: Grasset, 1994.

Plott, Michelle. "The Rules of the Game: Respectability, Sexuality and the *Femme Mondaine* in Late Nineteenth-Century Paris." *French Historical Studies* 25, no. 3 (2002): 531–36.

Pottier, Paul, and Vauxcelles, Louis, eds. "La presse d'aujourd'hui: *Femina*." *Gil Blas* (April 30, 1904).

Prévost, Marcel. *Lettres à Françoise mariée*. Paris: Librairie Félix Juvan, 1908.

Quella-Villéger, Alain. *Belles et rebelles: Le roman vrai des Chasteau-Tinayre*. Bordeaux: Aubéron, 2000.

Reynolds, Siân. "Albertine's Bicycle, or: Women and French Identity during the Belle Epoque." *Literature and History* 10 (Spring 2001): 28–41.

Roberts, Mary Louise. *Disruptive Acts: The New Woman in Fin-de-Siècle France*. Chicago: University of Chicago Press, 2002.

Rochefort, Florence. "The French Feminist Movement and Republicanism, 1868–1914." In *Women's Emancipation Movements in the Nineteenth Century: A European Perspective*, edited by Sylvia Paletschek and Bianka Pietrow-Ennker, 77–101. Stanford: Stanford University Press, 2004.

Rogers, Juliette. *Career Stories: Belle Époque Novels of Professional Development*. University Park: Penn State University Press, 2007.

———. "Educating the Heroine: Turn-of-the-Century Feminism and French Women's Educational Novels." *Women's Studies* 23 (1994): 321–34.

Rogers, Rebecca. *From the Salon to the Schoolroom: Educating Bourgeois Girls in Nineteenth-Century France*. University Park: Penn State University Press, 2005.

Rosny, J.-H. *Mémoires de la vie littéraire*. Paris: G. Crès et Cie, 1927.

Said, Edward. *Orientalism*. New York: Vintage Books, 1978.

Schwartz, Vanessa. *Spectacular Realities: Early Mass Culture in Fin-de-Siècle Paris.* Berkeley: University of California Press, 1999.
Scott, Joan W. *Only Paradoxes to Offer: French Feminists and the Rights of Man.* Cambridge: Harvard University Press, 1997.
Silverman, Debora L. *Art Nouveau in Fin-de-Siècle France: Politics, Psychology, Style.* Berkeley: University of California Press, 1989.
———. "Art of Darkness: African Lineages of Belgian Modernism, Part I." *West 86th* 18, no. 2 (Fall–Winter 2011): 139–81.
———. "The 'New Woman,' Feminism, and the Decorative Arts in Fin-de-Siècle France." In *Eroticism and the Body Politic*, edited by Lynn Hunt, 144–63. Baltimore: Johns Hopkins University Press, 1991.
Silverman, Willa. *The Notorious Life of Gyp: Right-Wing Anarchist in Fin-de-Siècle France.* New York: Oxford University Press, 1995.
Solomon-Godeau, Abigail. "The Legs of the Countess." *October* 39 (Winter 1986): 65–108.
Sowerwine, Charles. "Revising the Sexual Contract: Women's Citizenship and Republicanism in France, 1789–1944." In *Confronting Modernity in Fin-de-Siècle France*, edited by Christopher E. Forth and Elinor Accampo, 19–42. New York: Palgrave Macmillan, 2010.
Sullerot, Evelyne. *Histoire de la presse féminine en France, des origines à 1848.* Paris: A. Colin, 1966.
———. *La Presse féminine.* Paris: A. Colin, 1963.
Thompson, Christopher, and Fiona Ratkoff. "Un troisième sexe? Les bourgeoises et la bicyclette dans la France fin de siècle." *Le Mouvement Social* 192 (July–September 2000): 9–39.
Tiersten, Lisa. *Marianne in the Market: Envisioning Consumer Society in Fin-de-Siècle France.* Berkeley: University of California Press, 2001.
Turner, Graeme. *Understanding Celebrity.* London: Sage, 2004.
Waelti-Walters, Jennifer, and Steven Hause, eds. *Feminisms of the Belle: A Historical and Literary Anthology.* Lincoln: University of Nebraska Press, 1994.
Weiner, Susan. *Enfants Terribles: Youth and Femininity in the Mass Media in France, 1945–1968.* Baltimore: Johns Hopkins University Press, 2001.
Weisberg, Gabriel. *Art Nouveau Bing: Paris Style 1900.* New York: Harry Abrams, 1986.
Williams, Rosalind. *Dream Worlds: Mass Consumption in Late Nineteenth-Century France.* Berkeley: University of California Press, 1982.
Wolff, Janet. "Gender and the Haunting of Cities: Or, the Retirement of the *Flâneur.*" Chap. 3 in *AngloModern: Painting and Modernity in Britain and the United States.* Ithaca: Cornell University Press, 2003.
———. "The Invisible *Flâneuse*: Women and the Literature of Modernity." In *Feminine Sentences: Essays on Women and Culture*, 34–50. Berkeley: University of California Press, 1990.

# INDEX

Page numbers in italic type indicate illustrations.

Abbéma, Louise, 70, 210*n*28
Académie des sciences, 184
Académie féminine, 49, *50*, 51–52, 174, *176–77*, 182
Académie française, 7, 27, 48–49, 173–89, 191
Achievement: conventional roles compatible with, 1, 34, 81–82, 84, 156; images of, 22–23, *23–26*, 203*n*54; magazines' featuring of, 13, 15, 22, 41, 174, 188–89; motherhood as form of, 77; royals as examples of, 37; as threat, 148; women writers as examples of, 48, 52, 81–82, 84, 117, 119, 153
Adam, Juliette, 142
Adam, Paul, 5, 9, 197*n*4
Advertising, *12*, 12, 33–34, *34*, 43, 43–44, 146, 206*n*22
*Affaire Tinayre*, 155–71
Alexandra, Queen, *37*
American feminism, 27, 204*n*55
*Annales politiques et littéraires*, 174
Anti-Semitism, 69
Apter, Emily, 86
*Arabian Nights*, 85
Artemis, 13
Article 213, Civil Code, 126, 130, 134, 187, 222*n*18
Art nouveau, 13, 72–76, 84, 210*n*30, 210*n*33

"At Home" photography, 57–74, 208*n*7
Audience and readers: Belle Epoque literary feminism and, 35; of British women's magazines, 206*n*25, 207*n*30; characteristics of, 44; as community, 38, 41; contests and surveys involving, 44–47, 54, 206*n*25; of *Femina*, 10, 13, 38–41, 44, 51, 53–54, 112, 157; for feminism, 138; of *La Vie Heureuse*, 16–17, 35, 53–54, 157; of women's magazines, 5; writers' addressing of, 109
Audoux, Marguerite, 63
*Aurore, L'*, 163
Automobiles, 13
*Autorité, L'*, 160
Avryl, Hélène, 52, 179, 183, 186
Ax, Simone d', 174

Babies and children, 1, 76–78. *See also* Motherhood
Balzac, Honoré de, *La muse du département*, 150–51
Barbey d'Aurevilly, Jules, 7, 82, 199*n*19
Barbusse, Henri, 9, 200*n*22
Barney, Natalie, 118, 212*n*6, 215*n*16
Bartet, Julia, 162
Barthes, Roland, 81, 191
*Bas bleus* (bluestockings), 7, *8*, 46, 55, 60, 82, 84, 150–51, 159, 199*n*19, 208*n*2

Belle Epoque: celebrity culture in, 167; character of, 4; feminism and the New Woman in, 18–19, 29, 134; *femme moderne* in, 1, 4; gendered behavior in, 167; women's status in, 186–90

Belle Epoque literary feminism, 27; caricatures of, 7, *8*; characteristics of, 114, 152–53, 186; complexity of, 120, 168; defined, 6, 8; feminism vs., 9; limits of, 174; and marriage, 126, 138–43; relational feminism vs., 203*n*52; role and status of readers in, 35; subversive aspect of, 119; women's magazines and, 52, 188; work-life balance of, 55–84, 123–24. *See also* Women writers

Berlanstein, Lenard, 6, 36, 40, 46, 199*n*16

Bernhardt, Sarah, 86, 155, 160, 213*n*8

Berringer, Emile, 138

Bertaut, Jean, 153

Bertheroy, Jean, 51, 52

Berthon, Paul, 75; poster of Liane de Pougy, *75*

Bluestockings. See *Bas bleus*

Bonaparte, Roland, 11, 38, *39*

Books, 1, 52–53

Bovet, Marie-Anne, 20–21

Bréval, Mlle (opera singer), 11

Briand, Aristide, 156

Brieux, Eugène, 218*n*39

British women's magazines, 42, 200*n*23, 206*n*25, 207*n*30

Broutelles, Caroline de, 4, 10, 15, 48, 174

Caricatures and stereotypes: feminists, 132; New Woman, 19, *20*, 84, 133–34, 138; women, 152; women's magazines, 144–54; women writers, 7, *8*, 55, 80, 82, 119, 150–51, 153

Cassatt, Mary, "Mrs. Duffee Seated on a Striped Sofa, Reading," *71*, 71

Catulle-Mendès, Jane (formerly Jeanne Nette), 5, 127, *128–29*, 184, 197*n*4

Celebrity culture: in Belle Epoque France, 167; Delarue-Mardrus and, 118; and domestic settings, 57–74; femininity and, 166–68; and *femme moderne*, 6; marriage and, 127; media and, 157; and modesty, 163; power of, 118; public and privates spheres and, 157, 164, 166–68; satire on, 144–54; theatricality and, 86; Tinayre and, 157–68; women's magazines and, 6, 35–38; women writers and, 47

*Censeur politique et littéraire, Le,* 158–59

Chaignon, André, 22

*Charivari, Le,* 7

Chic *Parisienne,* 41–46, *46*

Children. *See* Babies and children

Cim, Albert, 199*n*19

Cinderella, 205*n*2

Cinderella powder, *33–34, 34*

Civil Code, 125–26, 130, 132, 134–36, *136*, 187, 216*n*13, 218*n*39, 222*n*18

Clarétie, Jules, 5, 197*n*4

Clinton, Hillary, 161

Clothing: for Académie française, 184, *185*, 186; advertisements for, *43*, 43; conventional bourgeois, 88; Delarue-Mardrus's, 100, 104, 106, 116–18; Legion of Honor decoration, 155–56, 161–62; masculine, 55, 59, 100, 104, 116–19, 197*n*4; Oriental, 86–88, 91–94; of women writers, 55

Colette (Mme Gauthier-Villars), 67–68, *68*, 72, 152, 191, 215*n*16, 219*n*11

Compain, Louise Marie, 130–31, 216*n*22; *L'un vers l'autre,* 130–31, 134–40, 142, 187–88, 216*n*20

Conseil de l'Ordre, 170

*Conseil des Femmes, Le,* 201*n*39, 208*n*51

Conservatism and tradition, 4, 13, 20–21, 60. *See also* Women's roles: traditional

Consumption: desire and, 147, 150; *Femina* and, 42, 44, *45*; femininity and, 6, 41–42; women's magazines and, 147

Contests, 44–46, 54, 146, *147*, 206*n*25. *See also* Literary prizes
Controversy, 13, 15
Coppée, François, 53
Corday, Michel, 45
Cosnier, Colette, 6, 40, 117, 199*n*16, 204*n*57, 214*n*15
Curie, Marie, 124, 140, 184

Dati, Rachida, 161
Daudet, Alphonse, 5, 65, *66*, 197*n*4
Daudet, Julia (Mme Alphonse), 5, 12, 47–48, 51, 66–67, *67*, 197*n*4
Daumier, Honoré, 7, 19, 80; "Les bas bleus," *8*
Delarue-Mardrus, Lucie, 5, 38, 52–54, 85–86, 107, 145, 152, 174, 182, 212*n*6, 214*n*15, 214*n*29, 215*n*17; contributions of, to women's magazines, 108, 112–15; images of, 96–106, *97–99, 101–5*, 115–19, *116*, 149; satire on, 149
Delaunay, Berthe, 162, 169
Democratization: of culture, 5, 33–46, 72; of intellect, 34; of literature, 46–47; mass culture and, 205*n*7
Department stores, 33, 43
Desire: advertising and, 146; consumerism and, 147, 150; conventional notions of, 145–46, 154; moral cautions about, 151
Desks, writers at their, 61–72, 82–84
D'Houville, Gérard (Mme de Régnier), 78, *79*, 80, 127, 184
Dieulafoy, Jane, 5, 59, *60*, 197*n*4, 209*n*14
Dieulafoy, Marcel, 5, 59, 197*n*4
Divorce, 125
Dorchain, Auguste, and wife, *128–29*
Dornac (pseudonym of Paul Cardon), 58, 61, 65, *66*, 80, 209*n*7, 209*n*14
Dorys, G., 92
D'Ourlac, Marie, 55, 208*n*4
Dreyfus, Alfred, 69
Driving, 12–13, *14*
Dufau, Mlle, 160
Duflot, Cécile, 161

DuPlessis, Rachel Blau, 141
Durand, Marguerite, 6, 58, 110, 199*n*16, 199*n*17
Duras, Claire de, *Ourika*, 139
Dutreuil, Nicole, 81
Duvernois, Henri, 120

*Écho de Paris, L'*, 163, 175, 179
*Éclair, L'*, 160
Elisabeth, Queen of Romania (pseudonym: Carmen Sylva), 47, *70*, 70–72, 149
Elite culture: access to, 33, 35–46; domestic settings of, 57–74; women's magazines and, 4–5. *See also* Royals
*Elle*, 81, 191
Ernest-Charles, Jean, 153, 158–59
*Excelsior*, 29
Exercise machine, 12, *12*
Exoticism, 85–88, 91, 95, 96, 99, 117
Exposition Universelle (1900), 74

Faguet, Emile, 161–62, 168, 189
Fashion magazines, 9–10
*Femina*: advertising in, 43–44; "at home" photography in, 57–72; audience of, 5, 10, 13, 38–41, 44, 51, 53–54, 112, 157; character of, 10; and consumption, 42, 44, 45; content of, 9–13, 15, 53; contests conducted by, 6, 44–52, 54, 146, *147*; cost of, 11–12; Delarue-Mardrus in, 96–99, 112–20, 152; early issues of, 9–15, *11, 12, 14*; editors of, 4–5, 6–7, 43, 120; elites portrayed in, 38–41; and feminism, 5–7, 19, 52–53, 113, 118–19, 152–53, 168–71, 174, 187–89, 199*n*16, 204*n*57; and *femme moderne*, 10, 20–23, *23–25*, 28–29, 33–35, 186; gender of staff of, 7, 14, 22; icon of, 10–11; impact of, 15; influences on, 200*n*23; innovations of, 6; intimacy of features in, 157; later history of, 29, 190; and Legion of Honor award, 162, 170–71; and

literary prizes, 46–52; and literature, 52–53; and marriage, 125–27, *128–29*, 135–36, 140–42; mission of, 9–10; offices of, 15, 51; and politics, 6, 9, 13, 28, 46, 52; publisher of, 7; satire on, 144–54; scholarship on, 223*n*27; significance of, 1, 4–9; surveys conducted by, 6, 45–46, 49–50, 107, 146, 174, 179, 182; *La Vie Heureuse* compared to, 16–17, 82; visual design and imagery of, 7–8, 10–12, 22, 72; and women's admission to Académie française, 173–89; women writers featured in, 55–85, 163–64, 210*n*21. *See also* Women's magazines

*Femina et La Vie Heureuse Réunis*, 190

Femina Prize. *See* Prix Femina

Femininity: art nouveau and, 74–76; and celebrity culture, 166–68; conflicting notions of, 156–57; and consumption, 6, 41–42; feminism and, 1, 27–28, 76, 81–82, 132–34, 156, 168–71, 199*n*17, 204*n*55; *femme moderne* and, 4; the Orient and, 95; performance of, 120; private sphere as locus of, 166–67; of women writers, 57–72

Feminism: American, 27, 204*n*55; Belle Epoque, 18–19, 29; caricatures of, 19, *20*, 132; complexity of, 120, 152–53; emergence of, 18; and femininity, 1, 27–28, 76, 81–82, 132–34, 156, 168–71, 199*n*17, 204*n*55; *femme moderne* and, 1, 5, 9, 18, 20–21, 28; French vs. American, 27, 204*n*55; issues addressed by, 18; and marriage, 130–43; men and, 112, 131–41, 189, 217*n*30; New Woman and, 19; reception of, 138; rejection of, 5–6, 18–21, 48, 52, 95, 117–19, 134, 186, 214*n*15, 215*n*16; women's magazines and, 5–7, 19, 52–53, 113, 118–19, 152–53, 168–71, 174, 187–89, 199*n*16, 204*n*57. *See also* Belle Epoque literary feminism

Feminist historiography, 208*n*4

*Femme moderne*, 17–26; achievements of, 4, 13, 15, 22–23, 23–26, 34, 203*n*54; appearance of, 161–62, 184; characteristics of, 1, 4, 8–9, 17, 17–21, 203*n*51; complexity of, 4, 13, 20–22, 28–30, 45–46, 57, 84, 112, 132–34, 143, 156, 169; *Femina* and, 10, 20–23, *23–25*, 28–29, 33–35, 186; feminism and, 1, 5, 9, 18, 20, 28; and freedom, 8; imagining, 4, 6, 8–9, 21–22, 29, 33–35, 162, 188–89; influence of, 29; and marriage, 124, 126–27, 132–43; New Woman and, 1, 20, 28, 132–34, 190–91; postwar, 190–91; *La Vie Heureuse* and, 17; woman writer as exemplar of, 7, 53, 84; women's magazines and, 20–22, *23–26*, 28–29, 162. *See also* Belle Epoque literary feminism

*Femme nouvelle*. *See* New Woman

Fey, Tina, 211*n*33

*Figaro, Le*, 163

Flat, Jules, 153

Flaubert, Gustave, *Madame Bovary*, 114, 138, 140, 145–47, 151, 154

*Française, La*, 131, 170

Franc-Nohain (pseudonym of Maurice Étienne Legrand), 160, 161, 175

Frapié, Léon, 49

Freedom: conservatism linked to, 13; *femme moderne* and, 8; in Western culture, 94–95

*Fronde, La*, 6–7, 58, 61, 199*n*17, 207*n*35

*Gaulois, Le*, 161

Gauthier-Villars, Henry "Willy," 67

Gautier, Judith, 197*n*4

Gender roles. *See* Women's roles

Geyh, Paula, 146

*Gil Blas*, 158–59, 166

Graffigny, Françoise de, 139; *Lettres d'une péruvienne*, 141

*Grelot, Le*, 19, *20*

Gréville, Mme Henry, *65*, 65–66

Gruber Garvey, Ellen, 42, 206*n*25, 207*n*30
Guitry, Sacha, 119
Gyp (Sibylle de Riquetti de Mirabeau), 68–70, *69*, 191, 199*n*18

Habermas, Jürgen, 198*n*13
Hachette publishing house, 10, 15, 29, 190
Haraucourt, Edmond, 53
Harry, Myriam, 49, 52, 85–95, *87*, *89*, *90*, *93*, 107, 118–19, 145, 174, 184, 191, 206*n*23, 212*n*2; *La conquête de Jérusalem*, 85, 106, 212*n*3
Henriot (pseudonym of Henri Maigrot), *136*, 136, 156, 163, 216*n*13
Heredia, J.-M. de, 80
Hervieu, Paul, 5, 126, 197*n*4, 199*n*19, 218*n*39
Huysmans, Joris-Karl, 174

*Illustration, L'*, 9, 10, 138
Intellect, female: democratization of, 34–35; encouragement of, 154; femininity in harmony with, 68, 77, 139–40; male vs., 189; as threat, 66, 145, 152; women's magazines and, 53–54, 57–58, 61
*Intransigeant, L'*, 163, 184
Irvine, Margot, 49
Iskin, Ruth E., 202*n*48

*Je sais tout*, 175, 179, 200*n*21, 200*n*22
*Journal des femmes*, 170, 174

Kemp, Robert, 191
Kessler, Marni, 95, 213n10

Lafitte, Pierre, 4–5, 9–10, 15, 29, 40, 107, 148, 175, 190, 200*n*21, 200*n*22, 223*n*27
Lafayette, Madame de (Marie-Madeleine Pioche de la Vergne), 182; *La Princesse de Clèves*, 139, 141
Lapauze, Jeanne. *See* Lesueur, Daniel
Laval, Maurice, 53, 54

Leblanc, Maurice, 9
Legion of Honor, 7, 9, 155–71, 173, 183, 184
Lesbianism, 67, 85, 117–18, 150, 152, 153, 212*n*6, 214*n*15
Lesueur, Daniel (pseudonym of Jeanne Lapauze), 9, 12, 51, 61, *62*, 63, 74–76, 95, 107, 126, 145, 149, 155, 160, 174, 184, *185*, 199*n*17, 199*n*18; *La force du passé*, 142
L'Heureux, Marcel, 9, 51, 200*n*22
*Liberté, La*, 155–57, 159, 164, 167, 175, 179
Literary prizes, 7, 46–52
Literary salons, 5
Literary *Tout Paris*, 4–6, 127, 174
Lorrain, Jean, 27, 183, 215*n*17; *Maison pour dames*, 144–54
Loti, Pierre, 91
Louvre, furniture museum, 74
Love: independence in relation to, 132, 137–38; marriage based on, 126, 215n4

Maizeroy, René, 9
Marbo, Camille, 123–24, 139–41, 154
Marchand, Roland, 206*n*22
Mardrus, Joseph-Charles, 85, 96, 99, 100, 115, 118
Marni, Jeanne, 51, 63–64, *64*, 142, 145
Marriage, 123–43; crisis in, 125–29; feminist, 130–43; the law and, 125–26, 130, 132, 134–36, *136*, 186–87, 216*n*13, 218*n*39, 222*n*18; love and, 126, 215*n*4; modern, 124–27, 130–43; reform of, 125–26, 136, 186–87, 218*n*39, 222*n*18; wife's role in, 127, 130–32, 137, 139–40, 141; in women's fiction, 130–43; women's magazines and, 125–27, *128–29*, 135–36, 140–42; working women and, 123–24, 140–41
Martel de Janville, Roger de, 69
Martial, Régine, 169–70
Marty, A. E., cover of *La Vie Heureuse*, 26

Mass culture: aspirations of, to elite status, 33, 35–46, 88; and democratization, 205n7; and *femme moderne*, 6; women's magazines and, 5
*Matin, Le*, 169
Maupassant, Guy de, "The Necklace," 151
Maurras, Charles, 153
Media: and celebrity culture, 157; femininity as portrayed in, 156–58; scandals in, 160; Tinayre scandal in, 155–71. See also Advertising; Women's magazines
Men, and feminism, 112, 131–41, 189, 217n30
Mendès, Catulle, 5, 53, 60, 127, *128–29*, 197n4
Mérode, Cléo de, 86, 213n8
Migeon, Gaston, 74
*Mode Pratique, La*, 10, 15, 40, 201n39
Modesty, 163–68
Morisot, Berthe, 70; *Girl Reading*, 67
Morny, Mathilde de, "Missy," 67
*Moroccan Beauty*, 92
Motherhood: ideal of, 77; women writers and, 1, 76–84, 159, 191
Mucha, Alphonse, 75
Musée Grévin, Paris, 74
*Musica*, 200n21

Nadar, Félix, 61; studio portrait of Zola, *63*
Napoleon, 155, 158, 160
Naquet laws (1884), 125
New Woman (*femme nouvelle*): caricatures and stereotypes of, 19, *20*, 84, 133–34, 138; characteristics of, 18–19; feminism and, 19; *femme moderne* and, 1, 20, 28, 132–34, 190–91, 203n48; satire on, 152; as threat, 7, 19, 57, 138, 210n30; threat of, 72; Tinayre and, 203n50; woman writer as, 55
Ney Sœurs, 45
Noailles, Anna Elisabeth de Brancovan, comtesse de, 1, *2–3*, 5, *26*, 37, 47, 49, 51, 61, 72–74, 76–78, *77*, 107, 142, 145, 174, 182–84, 191
Noailles, Mathieu Fernand Frédéric Pascal de, 73
Nochlin, Linda, 203n49
Nouvion, Jacques de, 49, 109

Offen, Karen, 18, 198n11, 217n30
Orient: defined, 212n1; femininity of, 95; otherness of, 91; taming of, in women's magazines, 86; unconventional characteristics associated with, 86; Western superiority to, 91–95; women writers associated with, 85–106
Otherness: Delarue-Mardrus and, 100; of the Orient, 91; photography and, 86
Ozouf, Mona, 204n55

Palin, Sarah, 161
Pants, women's wearing of, 59, 100, 104, 116–19
Parmelin, Hélène, 81
Pascal, Blaise, 169
*Patrie, La*, 155, 157, 164, 167
Performance and theatricality: Delarue-Mardrus, Harry, and, 86, 91, 96, 105–6; of femininity, 120; and the Orient, 86
Pert, Camille, *Leur égale*, 17–21, 111, 139, 188
*Petit Echo de la Mode, Le*, 40
*Petit Journal, Le*, 155
Peyrebrune, Georges de (Mathilde-Marie Georgina Elisabeth de), 51, 160
Photography: color, 87; *femme moderne* portrayed in, 21–22; and otherness, 86; satire on, 148–49; and women writers in domestic settings, 57–74, 163–64
"Poet Households," 127, *128–29*
Politics: in *Femina*, 6, 9, 13, 28, 46, 52; in *La Vie Heureuse*, 6, 9, 28
Pougy, Liane de, 75, *75*, 206n23, 215n16

*Presse, La*, 160
Prévost, Marcel, 5, 40–41, 112, 197*n*4, 205*n*12, 218*n*39; *Lettres à Françoise mariée*, 130
Pride, 167
Private vs. public spheres, 163–68
Prix Femina, 7, 49, 51, 106, 175, 191
Prix Goncourt, 9, 48–49, 85, 174
Prix Vie Heureuse, 49, 51–52, 85, 87, 106, 107, 124, 142, 174–75, 221*n*6
Progressivism, 1, 4, 21. *See also* Women's roles: expansion of
Prostitution, 148, 150–51
Proudhon, Pierre-Joseph, 199*n*19
Psichari, Michel, 166–67
Public vs. private spheres, 163–68

Rachilde, 152, 191, 215*n*16
Readers. *See* Audience and readers
Régnier, Henri de, 78, 127
Régnier, Mme de. *See* D'Houville, Gérard
Rothschild, A. de, 72, 78
Relational feminism, 203*n*52
Resurrection biography, 208*n*4
Reutlinger Photography Studio, 10
Réval, Gabrielle, 40, 78, 145, 149
*Revue Encyclopédique*, 20, 61, 203*n*51
Richard, Georges, 13
Roberts, Mary Louise, 58, 152
Rochefort, Florence, 29, 203*n*52
Roles. *See* Women's roles
Roosevelt, Alice, 91
Rosny, J.-H., 5
Rostand, Edmond, 5, 127, *128*–*29*, 148–49, 197*n*4
Rostand, Rosemonde, 5, 127, *128*–*29*, 148–49, 184, *185*, 197*n*4
Royals, 34, 36, 37, 38, 47, 70–72. *See also* Elite culture

Said, Edward, 212*n*1
Salons, 5
Sand, George, 55, *56*, 57, 151, 169, 182, 208*n*4; *Indiana*, 139
"Sapho 1900," 85, 152, 212*n*6

Schickel, Richard, 157
Schwartz, Vanessa, 36, 39, 205*n*7
Scott, Joan, 204*n*56, 221*n*29
Scudéry, Madeleine de, 182
Séverine (Caroline Rémy), 58–59, *59*, 145, 174, 199*n*18
Sévigné, Marie de Rabutin-Chantal, marquise de, 182
Sexuality, 150, 152
Shapira, William, 212*n*2
Silverman, Debora, 72, 210*n*33
Société des gens de lettres, 7, 153
Staël, Germaine de, *Corinne*, 139
Stereotypes. *See* Caricatures and stereotypes
Success. *See* Achievement
Suffrage, 186–87
Surveys, 6, 45–46, 49–50, 107, 124, 141, 146, 174, 179, 182, 184
Sylva, Carmen. *See* Elisabeth, Queen of Romania

*Temps, Le*, 7, 155–57, 164, 167, 175, 179
Theatricality. *See* Performance and theatricality
Thoren, Maurice de, 12–13
Ticho, Anna, 212*n*2
Tiersten, Lisa, 41
Tinayre, Marcelle, 5, 27, 61, 82, *83*, 84, 107–12, *109*, 126, 130–31, *165*, *170*, 174, 179, 182–84, *185*, 186, 191, 199*n*18, 203*n*50, 211*n*31, 221*n*26; Legion of Honor scandal involving, 155–71, 183, 189, 220*n*5; *La maison du péché*, 108–9, 131; *La rebelle*, 109–12, 130–40, 142–43, 168, 187–88, 203*n*50, 214*n*7
*Tout Paris. See* Literary *Tout Paris*
Tradition. *See* Conservatism and tradition

*Union française pour le suffrage des femmes, L'*, 131
Uzanne, Octave, 153

Vandérem, Fernand, 120, 182–84, 189

Vaudère, Jane de la, 152, 219n11
Vautel, Clément, 159–60
Veils, 91–95, 213n10
*Vie au grand air, La*, 9, 10, 200n21, 223n27
*Vie Heureuse, La*: and Académie française, 187; aesthetic concerns of women portrayed in, 42; "at home" photography in, 57–72; audience of, 5, 16–17, 53–54, 157; content of, 16–17, 53, 208n51; contests conducted by, 47, 51–52, 146; Delarue-Mardrus in, 99–106, 116, 152; early issues of, 15, *16*; editors of, 4–5, 15–16, 200n22, 201n39; elites portrayed in, 35–38; *Femina* compared to, 16–17, 82; and feminism, 19, 52–53, 152–53, 168–71, 187–89; and *femme moderne*, 17, 20–23, 25–26, 28–29, 33–35; inaugural issue of, 1, *2–3*; innovations of, 6; intimacy of features in, 157; later history of, 29, 190; and literary prizes, 48–49, 51–52; and marriage, 125–27, 135–36, 140–41; mission of, 35, 126, 139; and politics, 6, 9, 28; satire on, 144–54; significance of, 1, 4–9; surveys conducted by, 124, 141, 146; visual design and imagery of, 7–8, 16–17, 72; women writers featured in, 57–59, 67–68, 72–84, 163–64. *See also* Women's magazines

Vie Heureuse Prize. *See* Prix Vie Heureuse

Vivien, Renée, 118, 152, 212n6

Wilhelmine, Queen, 11–12, 38
Wolff, Janet, 198n14
Women: in Belle Epoque France, 186–90; caricatures and stereotypes of, 152; characteristics of, 114; as Legion of Honor recipients, 160; modesty as virtue of, 163–68; morality tales concerning, 144–54. *See also* Intellect, female

Women's fiction: marriage in, 130–43; women's magazines in relation to, 21, 53, 107–9, 113–14, 124, 135–36; women's magazines portrayed in, 110–12, 144–54. *See also* Women writers

Women's magazines: advertising in, 206n22; British, 42, 200n23, 206n25, 207n30; and consumerism, 147; content of, 9–12; elites portrayed in, 35–46; impact of, 1, 4–9, 29; scholarship on, 223n27; in women's fiction, 110–12, 144–54; women's fiction in relation to, 21, 53, 107–9, 113–14, 124, 135–36. *See also magazines by name*

Women's roles: changing social expectations concerning, 159–61, 189–90; expansion of, 4, 6, 17, 19–22, 28, 57, 81–82; in marriage, 127, 130–32, 137, 139–40, 141; Tinayre scandal and, 158; traditional, 4, 7, 13, 19–22, 28, 57, 81–82, 199n19; and work-life balance, 55–84. *See also Femme moderne*: complexity of

Women writers: and Académie française, 7, 27, 49, 173–89, 191; as accomplished/successful, 48, 52, 81–82, 84, 117, 119, 153, *180–81*; caricatures and stereotypes of, 7, 8, 55, 80, 82, 119, 150–51, 153; as celebrities, 47; complex (modern/traditional) role of, 57, 72–78; featured in women's magazines, 38; and femininity, 168–71; as *femmes moderne*, 7, 53, 84; growing numbers of, 53, 153–54, 158, 175, 178, *178*; as Legion of Honor recipients, 155; literary prizes for, 7, 46–52; mid-twentieth century, 191, *192–93*; and motherhood, 1, 76–85, 159, 191; as New Women, 55; photographs of, in domestic settings, 57–72; and public vs. private roles, 164, 166–68; readers of women's magazines as, 113–15; status of, 48–

49; as threat, 153, 158–61, 175, 179; women's magazines and, 7, 46–85, 163–64, 166–67; work-life balance of, 55–84. *See also* Belle Epoque literary feminism; Women's fiction
Working women, 123–24, 140–41
Work-life balance, 55–84, 123–24
World War I, 190

Yacca, Sada, 91
Yourcenar, Marguerite, 81, 187, 191
Yver, Colette, 182; *Princesses de science*, 123–24, 139–42, 154

Zola, Emile, 33, 61, *63*, 130; *Nana*, 138, 151